SHIPMASTER'S HANDBOOK ON SHIP'S BUSINESS

SHIPMASTER'S HANDBOOK

ON

SHIP'S BUSINESS

SECOND EDITION

Based on the original edition by Ben Martin

BY JAMES R. ARAGON

CORNELL MARITIME PRESS

Centreville, Maryland

Library of Congress Cataloging-in-Publication Data

Shipmaster's handbook on ship's business.

    Includes index.
    1. Shipmasters—Handbooks, manuals, etc.
2. Ship's papers. I. Martin, Ben, 1897–
Shipmaster's handbook on ship's business. II. Aragon,
James R., 1951–
VK211.S52   1988   387.5′068   87-47998
ISBN 0-87033-378-X

Manufactured in the United States of America

First edition, 1969. Second edition, 1988; second printing, 1992

To my wife, Barbara

CONTENTS

PREFACE TO THE SECOND EDITION

Since publication of the original *Shipmaster's Handbook on Ship's Business* almost two decades ago, there have been many changes in law and practice affecting ship's business, thus necessitating this revision. Shipping commissioners have been abolished and Congress has enacted a partial revision of Title 46, U.S. Code *(Shipping)*, to name two of the more significant changes.

Because merchant shipping is more closely regulated by government these days, the various certificates that prove compliance with the many applicable laws, conventions, and regulations are increasingly important. A new chapter, "Documents and Certificates," has been added to give an overview of the more important papers necessary to the operation of a seagoing merchant vessel.

The ubiquitous hand-held calculator, once almost unheard of aboard ship, is now commonplace at sea. For this reason, the conversion tables found in the first edition have been omitted from this revision. Instead, a single table of conversion factors has been retained. With these factors and an electronic calculator, the reader can readily make any desired conversion.

My thanks to the following for their assistance in preparing the second edition: The faculty and staff of the California Maritime Academy for permission to use the academy facilities; Capt. William B. Hayler, California Maritime Academy, for his advice on the publishing business; Mr. Paul O'Bannon, California Maritime Academy librarian, for help with legal research; Mr. Jay Zercher, CPA, for assistance with the chapter on accounting; Mr. Rod Miller, for legwork and assistance with government forms; Lt.(jg) Sean Connaughton, Capt. F. J. Grady, and Mr. F. J. Flyntz, all of the U.S. Coast Guard, for answering questions regarding shipping articles; and Capt. E. Norman George for the hours spent reviewing the manuscript and for the many suggestions for improvement.

James Aragon

1987

PREFACE TO THE
FIRST EDITION

There has, for some time, been a real need for an up-to-date, practical guide book to assist the new shipmaster in the preparation and completion of the large amount of complicated paper work which is required in the operation of the present-day merchant vessel. The primary object of *Shipmaster's Handbook on Ship's Business* is to provide a useful source of information and ready reference regarding the many phases of ship's business and paper work with which the master must be concerned.

The paper work necessary for the efficient operation of the modern cargo vessel may appear onerous at first, but it will be noted, after a voyage or two, that the work will be less troublesome and difficult if it is started as early as possible on the voyage and as much is done towards completion as available information and details permit. This is especially true of making up the payrolls and other accounting items. There will be occasions, however, when some paper work, involving reports and official documents, must be done on short notice. The details of such reports and documents may not be known in advance so to attempt their preparation early could lead to serious errors.

This book is principally for the newly appointed master of a merchant vessel but it may also be of assistance to more experienced masters as a check in completing the paper work required; and much of the information herein will be found useful by masters of foreign flag vessels calling at U.S. ports.

Of necessity there is some duplication due to various subjects coming under several headings. However, all subjects are covered by the index, which has been made as comprehensive as possible.

Much of the paper work throughout the voyage is for the home office or charterer and many special forms are issued by both. These differ in various companies but the information required is essentially the same.

An attempt has been made to cover all phases of paper work connected with the duties of the master. Many of the forms used are shown in facsimile. It must be kept in mind that forms issued by federal agencies are occasionally changed in size or text, or the form number may be changed, usually with the idea that the new form will save work. The master should endeavor to learn of these changes from the customhouse broker or from his home office. Too often the altered form comes as a total and not particularly welcome surprise, especially if the old form has already been completed with no small effort. However, the completed old form is usually accepted up to a definite date. Obsolete forms should be disposed of as soon as new ones are received.

Most companies issue "Instructions to Masters," which are written by men who have a thorough knowledge of the shipmaster's business and problems. Generally, such instructions allow much latitude to the master's prudence, discretion and common sense, taking it for granted that he will at all times endeavor to protect his company's interests.

In some foreign ports it is necessary to use metric figures in making out certain reports. Included in the appendix are U.S. and metric conversion tables as well as other tables and information of interest to shipmasters.

Ben Martin

1969

SHIPMASTER'S HANDBOOK ON SHIP'S BUSINESS

ONE

THE MASTER

GENERAL RESPONSIBILITIES

The office of master is one of great personal responsibility. Although you are in supreme command of the vessel and have authority over all on board, you should exercise that authority without undue arrogance or harshness. You are directly responsible for all actions and procedures on board which may affect the interests of your company, for violations of regulations of the U.S. Coast Guard or other federal agencies, and for breach of the laws of foreign countries when your vessel is in their ports.

On accepting command of a vessel you tacitly attest that you will act honestly and to the best of your ability to protect the interests of your company, to look after the safety of your vessel, cargo, passengers, and crew at all times, and to do whatever is required to keep your vessel in a seaworthy condition.

As master you are the direct representative of your company and, in some chartered vessels, the representative of the charterer as well. You are responsible for all damage and accidents which happen on board, not only through your own personal fault or neglect, but also in many cases for those that are caused by the fault or negligence of your crew. You are responsible for all persons legally on board and, in some cases, even those illegally on board.

It is taken for granted that you will exercise care, prudence, discretion, and your best ability in all business transactions with the various government officials and others with whom you may deal in the many ports you make.

The Vessel

You alone are responsible for the safe navigation of your vessel. If you request advice from your home office, agent, or others, including surveyors, and act on that advice, the responsibility for

3

any occurrence resulting from such action is still entirely your own. You may find that you are in the unhappy position where you are damned if you do and damned if you don't.

Load Line Regulations.   Safety must at all times be your first consideration and this also applies to compliance with the load line regulations. Under no circumstances permit your vessel to be loaded beyond the draft for the season and area. Do not allow coaxing, threats, or blandishments of the agent, company, charterer, or others to influence you. If your vessel's draft is excessive, don't sail before discharging cargo, fuel oil, or fresh water to bring her back to the proper draft.

Remember that it is you, the master, who will be fined for load line offenses and it is very doubtful that your company will reimburse you. Well-managed companies issue instructions from time to time that their vessels are not to be loaded beyond the applicable draft. Make certain that any action you take is entered in the logbook and be prepared to do some explaining as to why the vessel was over her proper draft in the first place.

The Cargo

The proper loading and stowage of the cargo is your responsibility, even though in most trades the loading, stowage, and discharging of cargo is in charge of the chief officer. In many ports the cargo is loaded under the directions of cargo supervisors employed for this purpose by the company or charterer. Generally these supervisors, many of them former seagoing officers, are highly competent and experienced. They will listen to you and will abide by your orders if the cargo operations do not meet with your approval, though perhaps not without some heated discussion or persuasive argument. A new master, or even a seasoned one, will do well to cooperate as much as possible with all concerned and to refrain from making changes or issuing orders just to exercise his authority. Bear in mind, however, that if the vessel is overloaded, or if loading has been done in such a way as to make the vessel unseaworthy, you are the one who will be held responsible.

Officers and Crew

As master you should work in close harmony and cooperation with your deck and engine officers, at the same time maintaining discipline. A prudent shipmaster will not hesitate to listen to suggestions made by his chief mate or chief engineer but he will always bear in mind that he alone is responsible for whatever action is taken.

As master you are responsible, through the heads of the various departments, for the maintenance of discipline and good order on your vessel. You may be held to account for any disorder, irregularity, or violation of the law committed by a member of your crew, such as smuggling, oil spills, throwing refuse or garbage overboard in port, or any other illegitimate acts which might have been prevented by proper supervision.

Gratuities.   In the interest of your company you should see that no gratuities, presents, rebates, commissions, or kickbacks are offered to any of the crew by persons doing business with your vessel and that none are accepted by any of the vessel's personnel. No member of the crew should be permitted to influence the purchase of supplies, stores, equipment, or repair.

Cleanliness of Crew's Quarters.   As master you are responsible for the cleanliness, sanitation, and good conditions of the living quarters on your vessel. Inspections should be made, daily when possible, of the messrooms, washrooms and toilets, galley, storerooms, iceboxes, hospital, and other such areas.

ON TAKING COMMAND

The master you are replacing will probably have prepared an inventory of items for which he will want a receipt. The inventory will, as a minimum, list the cash on hand and may also include the controlled drugs, any firearms on board, the more important ship's documents, and various valuable items of equipment such as sextants, binoculars, etc. Signing a duplicate copy of the list is usually sufficient. If you are taking command of a new or laid-up vessel where there is no former master or he is not on board, the documents and certificates may be found in the vessel's safe or files, or in the company's office.

Be sure to get the safe combination as early as possible. If not available from the former master it should be obtained from the home office. Also consider having the combination changed if circumstances warrant.

As soon as possible after taking command ascertain the operating details of your vessel. Confer with the chief engineer on fuel consumption, speed, and ballasting. Much information can be obtained from the logbooks. When time permits, make a complete inspection of the vessel.

List of Items to Check When Taking Command

1. Any D-1 aliens in the crew (see Chapter 6, "Immigration").

2. Any crew changes to be made before sailing.
3. Any outstanding deficiencies or unfulfilled requirements of the Coast Guard, Customs, or other federal agency. Clearance may be denied if certain deficiencies are not corrected (see Chapter 5, "Customs").
4. Status of shipping articles.
5. Amount and type of ballast and where stowed.
6. Bonded stores on board.
7. Cargo on board and cargo orders for the current voyage and, if known, for the next voyage.
8. Cash on hand and whether any cash has been ordered.
9. Charts and publications for the voyage.
10. Fresh water on board.
11. Fuel on board, where stowed, and fuel ordered.
12. Logbooks, both deck log and official log.
13. Light lists, tide tables, almanacs, etc., ordered for the next year if the voyage is to extend into the next year.
14. Narcotics on board. All narcotics should be kept in your safe. Check the amount on board when taking over to see that it agrees with that shown on the stores list.
15. Slop chest sufficiently stocked.
16. Combination to safe.
17. Repairs needed or ordered.

Your Notebook. This is an important item which, if properly kept, will save you many headaches. Regardless of how good your memory is, always make notes of what you require or what you should check. List information you must have for entering and clearing and for the office, such as draft, fuel, and water on arrival, crew replacements, stores required, etc.

Standing Orders

Standing orders should be made up for the guidance of your watch officers. You should ensure that your standing orders are strictly complied with; many officers read and sign the standing orders but later become careless about following them. These orders should be supplemented with night orders whenever circumstances require.

THE PAPERWORK

As master taking your first command you may be dismayed with what appears to be a vast amount of paperwork and greatly concerned about having the necessary papers properly made out and in order when required. If you start the paperwork early on the voyage, rather than allowing it to accumulate, you will find that it can all be done in ample time.

It is important that you read carefully all instructions or information on any forms which you may be required to fill out or sign at different ports. If such forms are in a foreign language have your local agent translate them for you. Many foreign countries print the text in English as well as in their own language. Make it a rule not to sign any papers until you have read them and understand what you are signing. Do not sign anything that will needlessly obligate your company or cause it unnecessary expense. When possible get a copy of any form or paper you sign, especially bills. Keep on file copies of all papers made up on the voyage, including manifests, stores lists, bills of lading, crew lists, passenger lists, crew effects lists, and so forth, as well as copies of all letters and radio messages sent out. You may have occasion to refer to some of these a voyage or two later. Put the date, name of the vessel, voyage number, and port on every letter you write and every form you make up.

Ship's Documents

Many of the permanent documents and certificates on the vessel will be checked by government officials from time to time. Keep them where you can put your hands on them at a moment's notice. It can be very embarrassing and irritating to be unable to find the papers and documents asked for by the boarding officers.

One of the first things you should do after taking command is to check that you have all the required documents. Make a note of any that will expire soon and see that they are renewed promptly. See Chapter 3, "Documents and Certificates," for an explanation of the more important documents.

Reports issued by ABS or other classification societies when repairs are made to the vessel should be kept in a separate file, as they may be called for when the vessel goes through inspection or survey. Be sure to file them as soon as they are received.

Other Papers to Have on Board

Special forms are issued by shipping companies and these will vary in accordance with each company's requirements. The following will cover many of them although some may be known by different titles. Check with your company for complete lists.

1.Blank Customs and Immigration forms.
2. Spare logbooks.
3. Master's cash statement or other form of settlement.
4. Cash receipt book or similar record.
5. Company operations manual.
6. Company safety manual.
7. Cable addresses and telephone numbers of agents, domestic and foreign.
8. Telephone numbers, office and home, of company officials to be contacted in case of emergency.
9. Slop chest account forms.
10. Bill of lading forms.
11. Wage and overtime scales.
12. Overtime support sheets.
13. Payroll sheets.
14. Stevedore damage report forms.
15. W-4 forms.
16. Wage vouchers.
17. Stores list forms.
18. Union agreements with supplements and clarifications issued by your company.
19. Illness and injury report forms.
20. Medical attention forms.
21. Crew information forms.

General Checklist of Items to Complete during the Voyage

These should be ready on arrival at the first U.S. port. They are explained in detail in the appropriate chapters. When forms or papers are completed, file them in a safe place.

1. A day after sailing from the last foreign port distribute Customs Form 5129, Crew Member's Declaration, for the crew to fill out. These forms should be signed and returned within a definite time, usually twenty-four to forty-eight hours. If a crew member has nothing to declare he should write "None" across the form and sign it.
2. From the above forms type the crew effects declaration. If a man has nothing to declare, his name is not listed on the declaration, but all curios to remain on board (termed "ROB") must be listed.
3. Make up the inward foreign manifest (see Chapter 5, "Customs").
4. If you have passengers, draw up an alphabetized passenger list (if this was not supplied by the agent) on Form I-418. If passengers

were taken at several ports and a passenger list supplied at each port, the names should all be put on one list in alphabetical order.

5. If any alien passengers are on board, make up a set of Form I-94, Arrival/Departure Record, for each such passenger.

6. If there are any nonresident aliens among the crew, fill out Form I-95A, Crewman's Landing Permit, for each such nonresident alien crew member. Do not fill out the form for registered aliens.

7. Make up and sign crew discharges and have the crew sign them. Do not fill in the date and place of discharge until that information is definitely known.

8. Make up wage vouchers as far as possible. Names, ratings, and other known data can be inserted on the outward voyage.

9. Start rough payroll.

10. Check that all entries in the official log are properly signed.

11. Check and tally overtime sheets to date. This should be done weekly.

12. Check and sign stores requisitions.

13. Start the voyage letter, if your company requires one. You should keep notes throughout the voyage of things to include in your letter.

14. Make up, total, and balance the list of miscellaneous vouchers.

15. Inventory the slop chest and complete the slop chest account forms.

16. Start making up your expense account from your notes. You should keep expenses to a minimum.

TWO

SHIPPING ARTICLES

Probably no other area of ship's business is currently so confusing to masters as the procedures for shipment and discharge of seamen. In 1983, Congress enacted a partial revision of Title 46 of the U.S. Code (laws pertaining to shipping). Almost all of the statutes applicable to merchant seamen were repealed and then re-enacted in revised form. The new laws governing shipping articles can be found in Title 46 beginning at Section 10101.

Shipping articles are a written agreement between the master and the crew covering the conditions and terms the crew will conform to, and particulars regarding the crew—their ratings, wages, document numbers, Social Security numbers, dates of birth, and so forth. The articles give a description of the intended voyage and the ports and areas the vessel will make. They constitute a legal and binding document. Shipping articles—foreign or intercoastal, and coastwise—are required by law, and are divided by law into the above two classes, with different rules for each. The more stringent requirements apply to articles for foreign and intercoastal voyages; the rules are somewhat relaxed for coastwise voyages.

In the case of foreign or intercoastal articles, 46 USC 10304 provides that "the form of the agreement . . . shall be in substance as follows . . ." and then goes on to show the preferred format and wording of the articles (see Appendix A). Coastwise articles are not subject to this section; they may be in any format and may use any wording desired, provided they clearly set out the nature of the agreement and they contain at least the minimum information specified by law.

The Coast Guard has said that officers in charge, marine inspection, will, on request, supply masters with Coast Guard Form CG 705A, Shipping Articles, which will be considered as complying with the requirements of law; any other form of shipping articles that meets the statutory requirements may also be used.

Shipping articles must, as a minimum, contain the following:

1. The nature, and, as far as practicable, the duration of the intended voyage, and the port or country in which the voyage is to end.
2. The number and description of the crew and the capacity in which each seaman is to be engaged.
3. The time at which each seaman is to be on board to begin work.
4. The wages each seaman is to receive.
5. Regulations about conduct on board, and information on fines, short allowance of provisions, and other punishment for misconduct provided by law.
6. A scale of the provisions that are to be provided each seaman (does not apply to coastwise articles).
7. Any stipulation in reference to advances and allotments of wages (foreign or intercoastal only; coastwise articles may not contain a provision on the allotment of wages).
8. Other matters not contrary to law.

Foreign or intercoastal articles must also include the text of the following section of federal law (46 USC 10303(a)):

A seaman shall be served at least 3 meals a day that total at least 3,100 calories, including adequate water and adequate protein, vitamins, and minerals in accordance with the United States Recommended Daily Allowances.

In addition, a copy of the text must be posted in a conspicuous place in the galley and the forecastle of the vessel.

FOREIGN OR INTERCOASTAL ARTICLES

Foreign or intercoastal articles are mandatory for a U.S. vessel:

(1) on a voyage between a port in the United States and a port in a foreign country (except a port in Canada, Mexico, or the West Indies); or (2) of at least 75 gross tons on a voyage between a port of the United States on the Atlantic Ocean and a port of the United States on the Pacific Ocean.

Voyages to Canada, Mexico, or the West Indies are referred to as "nearby foreign" and, because of their nearness to the United States, come under the rules for coastwise voyages.

The principal difference between foreign or intercoastal articles and coastwise articles is that when any crew are engaged or discharged in a foreign port, they must be signed on or off before a U.S. consular officer whenever one is available. All engagements and discharges, whether or not before the consul, must be entered in the official log as well as on the articles.

The articles for a foreign or intercoastal voyage should be prepared in duplicate and the original retained on board as part of the vessel's permanent record. The duplicate may be sent to the Coast Guard in lieu of the Master's Report of Seamen Shipped or Discharged (see "Reporting Shipment and Discharge of Seamen," below).

Engaging a Seaman in a Foreign Port

When a seaman is engaged outside the United States on foreign articles, he must be signed on before the U.S. consul. Both the master and the seaman appear before the consul. If there is no consul at the port of engagement, you may engage the seaman, but do not have him sign the articles. You must have the consul verify his signature at the next port that has a consul. The date of engagement shown on the articles should be the actual date that the man was engaged, and not the date that the man's signature is witnessed by the consul.

Discharging a Seaman in a Foreign Port

When a man is to be discharged in a foreign port, both the seaman and the master must appear before the U.S. consul if one is available. The release on the shipping articles is to be executed by both the master and the seaman in the presence of the consul. If no consul is available, then the release may be executed by the master and the seaman alone.

Regulations allow the consul to excuse the master from personally appearing in the following circumstance: when the seaman to be discharged has been incapacitated by injury or illness; his condition is such that prompt medical attention is necessary and cannot be furnished on shipboard; and the master cannot go with the seaman to the consul's office without risk to the crew, the vessel, or the cargo.

In such a case you must send a written statement to the consul giving all the facts, including the reasons why it is necessary to discharge the seaman and the reasons why you are unable to appear before the consul. The statement should include an account of the wages due the seaman and should be accompanied by the cash to pay him his wages or, if the cash is not available, by an order to the owner for the amount due.

If the consul considers the statement satisfactory he may discharge the seaman just as though the master were present. If he does not consider the statement satisfactory he may refuse to discharge the seaman and may order him returned to the vessel at the vessel's expense.

Failing to Join in U.S. Port after Clearing Foreign

If any of the crew fail to join when the vessel sails from the last U.S. port after signing foreign or intercoastal articles, do not remove the man from the articles at sea. Log the complete facts in the official log and have the man removed from the articles by the U.S. consul at the first port or, if there is no consul at the first port, note that fact in the log and then remove the man from the articles yourself as in the case of any foreign discharge where there is no consul. His discharge should be dated as of the date that he failed to join. Enter full details in the official log.

Failing to Join in Foreign Port

If a man fails to join on sailing from a foreign port, you may have him removed from the articles by the consul at the next port or, if you think it likely that the man will rejoin the vessel and you are willing to accept him back, you may leave him on the articles for the time being. In any case, you should stop his pay for the time he is off the ship. Radio full details to your company and enter all the facts in the official log.

Allotments

When on a foreign or intercoastal voyage, a seaman may designate that any part of his wages be paid by the shipping company directly to any of the following:

1. The seaman's grandparents, parents, spouse, sister, brother, or children;
2. An agency authorized by the Department of the Treasury for the purchase of U.S. savings bonds for his account; and

3. A savings or investment account maintained by the seaman in a federally insured bank or savings and loan association.

An allotment to any other person or agency is invalid; however, it is likely that future legislation will eliminate these restrictions governing to whom a seaman may allot his pay.

To be valid, an allotment note must be in writing and must be signed by and approved by a shipping commissioner. This includes the U.S. consul when he performs the duties of shipping commissioner in a foreign port, and the master when he is required to perform the duties of shipping commissioner in a U.S. port.

COASTWISE ARTICLES

Coastwise articles are required for a voyage ". . . from a port in one state to a port in any other than an adjoining state."

Shipping articles are not mandatory on a vessel that is making voyages solely between ports in the same state or between ports in two adjoining states. Shipping articles are required at all other times, and it is probably best to have the crew on articles even when it is not strictly required, in case the vessel is diverted while at sea.

Unlike foreign or intercoastal articles, coastwise articles may not contain a scale of provisions or any provision on the allotment of wages. All signing on and off is done solely by the master. Only a single copy of the coastwise articles need be made out.

When running coastwise, many of the men may remain on the vessel to make several voyages. In such cases, continuous coastwise articles can be used, the new men being signed on as they are engaged.

SIGNING ON

Technically, the crew must be signed on and off foreign or intercoastal shipping articles in the presence of a shipping commissioner; however, in 1980 Congress abolished the shipping commissioners, for all practical purposes, by passing an appropriations bill that prohibited the expenditure of any public funds for pay or administrative expenses in connection with shipping commissioners in the United States.

In U.S. ports the duties of shipping commissioner now fall, by default, upon the master. In foreign ports the U.S. consul continues to supervise the shipment and discharge of seamen.

In order to guide masters in the shipment and discharge of

seamen, the Coast Guard has prepared regulations to supplement the statutes. These regulations can be found in Part 14 of Title 46 of the *Code of Federal Regulations.*

They have also issued a *Navigation and Vessel Inspection Circular* (NVIC) outlining the proper procedures. NVICs may be updated from time to time, in which case the existing NVIC is cancelled and a new one issued. You should have the latest version on board.

When the articles are opened, you as master should sign and date the articles first, then the crew should sign. After any of the men have signed on, no changes may be made to the agreement unless the written consent of each seaman who has already signed the articles is obtained.

A rider is an attachment to the shipping articles that modifies or amplifies the printed form. If a rider is attached to the articles before the men sign on, it forms part of the original agreement, in which case it should be referred to in the main agreement form and also called to the attention of each man before he signs the articles.

The law requires that you have an agreement with each seaman, but it is not necessary that you have the same agreement with each man. It sometimes happens, in unusual circumstances, that you will sign on a seaman after the voyage has begun and use a rider to modify the agreement as to that seaman only. For example, if a crew member is hospitalized during the voyage and there is not enough time before sailing to obtain a regular company employee as a replacement, you might sign on a temporary relief seaman but have him sign a rider stating that he is engaged to serve only to the next port rather than for the duration of the voyage.

Many shipping companies are now printing and using shipping articles whereby each seaman signs an individual agreement form rather than having the entire crew sign one agreement. This allows you to customize the agreement for special circumstances, as above, without using riders and therefore with no confusion as to which terms of the agreement apply to a particular crew member.

As with any contract, each man signing the articles must do so freely and voluntarily and he must have knowledge of what he is agreeing to. It is therefore unlawful to sign on a seaman who is so intoxicated as to be unable to clearly understand what he is signing. If any seaman is unable to read the articles they must be read to him.

Before each man signs on, you must ensure that he presents to you a U.S. merchant mariner's document properly endorsed for the rating in which he is to serve. This includes a food handler's endorsement for each member of the steward's department who is in any way engaged in the preparation or serving of meals. Each officer must also present a valid license in the proper grade. Each watch-standing deck officer must have a current radar observer's endorsement and each radio officer must have both a Coast Guard license and a current radio license issued by the Federal Communications Commission.

Even if a man has been on the ship before and you remember that he had the proper documents, you should still insist that he present his papers to you. It sometimes happens that a seaman or officer will lose his documents and will try to sign on anyway, hoping that you won't check. If he doesn't have the proper papers in his possession, he cannot sign on. If time permits, you can send him to the local Coast Guard office to apply for a duplicate or temporary document.

Forecastle Card

Before sailing on the voyage, you must post a copy of the agreement, omitting signatures, in a place accessible to the crew. This is known as a "forecastle card" and is usually posted in the messrooms. If there are any riders attached to the articles then copies of the riders must also be posted as part of the forecastle card. The Coast Guard will supply Form CG-704 on request for use as a forecastle card.

VOYAGE DESCRIPTION

The voyage description is perhaps the most important part of the articles. It must set out the nature and probable duration of the voyage in clear and unambiguous terms. The voyage description is a binding part of the contract between the master and the crew. A seaman cannot legally be carried to sea against his will or compelled to serve on a voyage other than the one that was described in the agreement that he signed.

The nature and duration of the voyage are whatever the shipping articles define them as being. Any language that clearly describes the contemplated voyage may be used; however, the courts have held that shipping articles which are so ambiguous or vague that they are not informative are invalid. For the guidance of masters, the U.S. Coast Guard has prepared the following examples of voyage descriptions:

(1) VOYAGE DESCRIPTION FOR A VESSEL ABOUT TO EMBARK ON A FOREIGN VOYAGE:

From the port of New York, N.Y., to Antwerp, Belgium, and Rotterdam, Holland, and such other ports and places in any part of the world as the master may direct, and back to a final port of discharge in the United States, excluding Alaska and Hawaii, for a term of time not exceeding six (6) calendar months.

(2) VOYAGE DESCRIPTION FOR A VESSEL ABOUT TO EMBARK ON AN INTERCOASTAL VOYAGE:

From the port of Philadelphia, Pa., to one or more ports on the Pacific Coast via one or more ports on the Atlantic and/or Gulf Coast and back to a final port of discharge on the Atlantic Coast for a term of time not exceeding six (6) calendar months.

(3) VOYAGE DESCRIPTION FOR A VESSEL ABOUT TO EMBARK ON A TRAMP VOYAGE:

From the port of Galveston, TX., on a tramp freighter (or tanker, as appropriate) voyage to ports in the U.S. Gulf and/or Caribbean Sea and/or South American and/or European ports and/or African ports and/or ports in the Far and Near East and/or Australia and such ports and places in any part of the world as the master may direct and back to a final port of discharge in the United States, excluding Alaska and Hawaii, not exceeding twelve (12) calendar months.

(4) VOYAGE DESCRIPTION FOR A VESSEL WHOSE DESTINATION SHOULD NOT BE DISCLOSED FOR SECURITY REASONS:

From the port of New York to a point in the Atlantic Ocean to the eastward of New York and thence to such ports and places in any part of the world as the master may direct or as may be ordered or directed by the United States Government or any department, commission, or agency thereof and back to a final port of discharge in the United States, excluding Alaska and Hawaii, for a term of time not exceeding twelve (12) calendar months.

(5) VOYAGE DESCRIPTION FOR A VESSEL EMPLOYED OVERSEAS FOR LONG PERIODS:

(a) From the port of Hong Kong, R.C.C., to Singapore, and such ports and places in any part of the world as the master may direct and back to a final port or place of discharge for a term not exceeding six (6) calendar months.

(b) From latitude _____ and longitude _____ to remain at offshore mineral and oil exploration sites or to proceed to, and remain at, offshore mineral and oil exploration sites off the Pacific

Ocean coast of New Zealand and/or Australia for a term not exceeding twelve (12) calendar months.

(6) VOYAGE DESCRIPTION FOR A VESSEL EMBARKING ON A SINGLE COASTWISE VOYAGE:

From the port of Boston, MA., to one or more U.S. Gulf ports or places and such other coastwise ports or places as the master may direct and back to a final port or place of discharge in the United States on the Atlantic Coast north of Cape Hatteras, for a term of time not exceeding three (3) calendar months.

(7) VOYAGE DESCRIPTION FOR A VESSEL EMBARKING ON A SERIES OF COASTWISE VOYAGES:

From the port of Boston, MA., to one or more U.S. Gulf ports or places and such other coastwise port or place as the master may direct, for one or more voyages and back to a final port of discharge in the United States on the Atlantic Coast, north of Cape Hatteras, for a term of time not exceeding six (6) calendar months.

REPORTING SHIPMENT AND DISCHARGE OF SEAMEN

All engagements and discharges of merchant seamen must be reported to the U.S. Coast Guard. These reports are normally made on Form CG-735(T), Master's Report of Seamen Shipped or Discharged (Fig. 3). The completed forms should be mailed to: Commandant (G-MVP-1/TP12), U.S. Coast Guard, Washington, DC 20593.

On a foreign or intercoastal voyage, a Form CG-735(T) must be sent in prior to sailing from the port where the articles are opened and again upon completion of the voyage. On a coastwise voyage, a report must be sent in prior to sailing from the port where the articles are opened and then a supplementary report at the end of each calendar month during which men are shipped or discharged. A final report is made when the voyage is completed. Vessels on foreign or intercoastal voyages may submit a copy of their shipping articles in lieu of the CG-735(T).

Form CG-735(T) calls for the following information:

1. Name of the vessel;
2. Official number of vessel;
3. Name and address of the owner or operator;
4. Description of the voyage (Great Lakes, coastwise, nearby foreign, or foreign);
5. Full name of each seaman;

6. Number of his merchant mariner's document or continuous discharge book;
7. Number of each officer's license or certificate of registry;
8. The capacity each man is engaged in;
9. Date and port of engagement;
10. Date and port of discharge;
11. The year of each man's birth;
12. Percentage of U.S. citizens in the crew;
13. Name of each alien in the crew;
14. Master's name;
15. Master's merchant mariner's document number; and
16. Master's license number.

In order for the Coast Guard to keep a proper record of his sea service, the master should be listed on Form CG-735(T) the same as any other member of the crew.

The 735(T) form also includes a statement for the master to sign attesting that:

1. He has entered into an agreement with each of the crew as required by law.
2. At least 65 percent of the deck crew (excluding licensed officers) are rated not less than able seamen.
3. At least 75 percent of the crew in each department are able to understand orders given by the officers.
4. The vessel has in her service the number of lifeboatmen required by her certificate of inspection and every lifeboatman possesses a document endorsed as such.
5. Every member of the crew possesses the appropriate license, certificate of registry, or U.S. merchant mariner's document for the rating in which he is engaged.

This master's report of seaman shipped or discharged does not take the place of shipping articles. It is not an agreement; its purpose is to inform the Coast Guard as to the number of men shipped and discharged by the master and to enable the Merchant Vessel Personnel Division of the Coast Guard to keep proper records of the service of all U.S. merchant seamen. Such records can be vitally important to a seaman if, for instance, he has lost his discharges and must establish proof of service on U.S. merchant vessels in order to upgrade his document or license or in order for him to prove eligibility for benefits that may be provided by his company or union.

Dates of service on the vessel should not overlap. If a seaman has been discharged and re-engaged, he should be shown as a new man and subsequent reports on Form CG-735(T) should show the date he commenced after the discharge, not the date of his original engagement.

If a seaman's rating is changed, he should be listed on the form as if he were discharged on the last date he served in his old rating and engaged again on the date he started in his new rating. Two discharges should be made out for the seaman in this case, one for each rating. He cannot serve in two ratings on the same date.

From time to time you may have additional persons on board, such as riding gangs, repair technicians, owner's representatives, supercargoes, etc. These people are not members of the crew for the purpose of shipping articles. They are not required to have seamen's papers and they do not go on the articles. They do, however, go on the crew list, usually as "extra." Such people, who are not members of the crew but who are connected with the operation of the vessel, are not considered passengers; they are "persons in addition to the crew." Your vessel's certificate of inspection specifies how many such persons you may carry.

DISCHARGES

When a seaman who holds a merchant mariner's document is discharged and paid his wages, he shall be issued a Certificate of Discharge to Merchant Seaman, Coast Guard Form CG-718A. The discharge must be signed by both the master and the seaman. The original goes to the seaman, the yellow copy is for the ship or company records, and the white copy goes to the Coast Guard when the CG-735(T) is submitted.

If the seaman holds a continuous discharge book instead of a merchant mariner's document, then an entry is made in his book and Form CG-718E, Record of Entry in Continuous Discharge Book, made out in duplicate and signed by both the master and the seaman. The seaman does not sign the continuous discharge book. The original record of entry is sent to the Coast Guard when the 735(T) is submitted and the duplicate is for the ship's files. The seaman does not get a copy of the record of entry; the entry in his book serves as his copy.

The newer discharges have a check-off box printed on them labeled "Check if entry made in continuous discharge book." This is not in use at the present time. In accordance with current law, a book holder does not get a discharge. The check-off box is for future use when the Coast Guard's supply of Form CG-718E is exhausted. The Coast Guard will issue appropriate instructions if and when procedures are implemented for giving discharges to book holders.

Continuous discharge books are seldom issued anymore and you will very rarely encounter a seaman who holds one.

The discharges should be made up early on the voyage. Many masters have the men sign their discharges when they sign on. Then, if a seaman is not on board when the vessel pays off, his wages are sent to the office as unclaimed and his copy of the discharge is either sent to the office along with his wage voucher or else mailed to his address of record. This commonly occurs when a man misses the ship or when one of the crew must be hospitalized. The master will then have all the white copies of the discharges, signed by the crew members and himself, to send in with the 735(T). Of course, if a man objects to signing a discharge that has not yet been completed, he cannot be required to do so.

While the above procedure is common practice and is in widespread use, it is contrary to current law and regulation. Discharges are properly supposed to be signed when a seaman signs off the articles and signs the mutual release. U.S. Coast Guard *Navigation and Vessel Inspection Circular 1-86* states that when a seaman is incapable of completing the release at the time of discharge in a foreign port, the certificate of discharge should be kept by the master until the end of the voyage and then delivered to the vessel's owner or agent along with the shipping articles. The seaman is to sign the discharge when he completes a mutual release and presents it to the company for payment of his wages.

The discharge sent in to the Coast Guard with the 735(T) should be arranged in the same order as the names appear on the form, and not in a haphazard batch.

As previously mentioned, when a seaman is discharged in a foreign port, he must be signed off in the presence of the U.S. consul, if there is one. If there is no consul at the port, the master may sign the man off.

For each man who is signed off, your official logbook entry as well as the articles should show the reason for the discharge. The usual reasons shown in the logbook and on the articles for discharging a man are:

1. Mutual consent (sometimes abbreviated "MC"). A seaman may be discharged at any time, in any port, regardless of whether or not he has completed his agreement, if both the seaman and the master agree to the discharge.
2. Medical—not fit for duty ("NFFD"). When a man is treated by a doctor and is declared not fit for duty you may want to discharge him unless he is expected to be fit for duty again within a short time. This will depend upon how soon he is expected to be fit for duty and how difficult or expensive it will be to obtain a relief. When a man is hospitalized and cannot rejoin the vessel before sailing then he is unable to complete his agreement and you will certainly sign him off.
3. Failed to join. When a man fails to sail with the ship and he knew, or should have known, when the ship was departing, then he has broken his agreement and may be discharged. To avoid argument, see that the sailing board is properly posted sufficiently in advance so that all hands are aware of the sailing time. The board should be posted in strict accordance with the provisions of any applicable union agreements.
4. Discharged for cause. A seaman may be discharged for cause in any port, but in a foreign port it is best avoided if possible. It will probably cost your company considerable expense to repatriate the man to the United States and to send a replacement; in addition, you may not be able to get a replacement before the ship sails. Unless the man's conduct actually represents a danger to his ship or shipmates, it is usually better to log him for each offense and then fire him at the first U.S. port.
5. End of voyage. The voyage described in the shipping articles has been completed and the agreement between the master and the seamen is therefore ended.

It is important in making up the articles, the discharges, Form CG-735(T), or other such forms that the seaman's name and document number be correctly entered. His name should appear in full—not just his initials and surname. For example: John J. Jones, not J. J. Jones. His document number should include the issue number, if any. If the number is 999-99-9999 D3, write it as such, not 999-99-9999. His name and document number should be shown exactly as they appear on his mariner's document.

All of the above forms should be checked carefully to see that the data entered on the various records all agree. Names of the ports of engagement and discharge should be written in full and not abbreviated. For example: New Orleans, not N.O. or NOLA. Keep several spare pads of discharges on hand.

REPORTING CREW SHORTAGE TO COAST GUARD

The required manning of U.S. merchant vessels is provided for by 46 USC 8101. Under this statute a vessel for which a complement has been established, as shown on the vessel's certificate of inspection, is prohibited from being operated unless fully manned. If the vessel is deprived of the services of any of the required crew, the vacancies must be filled with replacements of the same or higher ratings, if available. These vacancies are usually filled by day workers if the ratings can be covered.

The owner, charterer, or managing operator can be fined if the ship is operated with less than the required crew except that the vessel may proceed on her voyage without all the ratings called for if:

1. Their services were lost without the consent, fault, or collusion of the owner, charterer, managing operator, agent, master, or person in charge;
2. The master finds that the vessel is sufficiently manned for the voyage; and
3. Replacements are not available to fill all the vacancies.

If the vessel sails shorthanded as permitted above, the master must report the cause of the shortage, in writing, to the nearest officer in charge, marine inspection, within twelve hours of the vessel's arrival at her destination. Coast Guard Form CG-729, Report of Crew Shortage, may be used to make this report but its use is optional and any format that properly sets out the required information may be used. This written report should contain the following information:

1. The name and merchant mariner's document number of each missing crew member;
2. A statement of the cause of the shortage;
3. The port and the date on which the shortage occurred;
4. A certification that no replacements of the same or higher rating were obtainable and that, in the master's judgment, the vessel was sufficiently manned to proceed safely.

Be sure to keep a copy for the vessel's file.

THREE

DOCUMENTS AND CERTIFICATES

Many documents and certificates of varying degrees of importance are necessary in the operation of a modern merchant vessel. One of your first duties on taking command should be to see that all the necessary documents are on board and current.

The more important documents, except those required to be posted, should be carefully indexed and filed in a place where you can lay your hands on them instantly should they be called for. It is a good idea to put all these more important papers in a single large binder with each certificate in its own clear plastic cover. This will make it easy to find individual documents or to carry the papers ashore should that be necessary. The less important documents that are seldom asked for can be filed in a single file, suitably indexed.

You should have a list showing the expiration dates of all the various certificates. Your company's head office should keep track of the expiration dates and should arrange for renewals, but you may have to remind them if an expiration date is near and no action is being taken.

CERTIFICATE OF DOCUMENTATION

Every merchant vessel, no matter what flag it flies, has a document that attests to the nationality and ownership of the vessel. This document is known as the register in most countries. Formerly, U.S. oceangoing vessels had to have one of two documents: a Certificate of Registry when in foreign trade, or a Consolidated Certificate of Enrollment and License when in coastwise trade. The two documents have now been combined into a single one called the Certificate of Documentation, but still referred to informally as the register. It is issued by the U.S. Coast Guard documentation office at the vessel's port of registry.

The certificate of documentation shows the vessel's name, official number, dimensions, owner's name and address, nationality, and details of the mortgages, if any. It shows the trades for which the vessel is documented. Your vessel may not engage in a trade for which she is not documented. A vessel may be documented for more than one trade and, if so, she may change between those trades at will. U.S. vessels may be documented as follows:

1. Registry. A vessel under registry may be employed in foreign trade, trade with Guam, American Samoa, Wake, Midway, or Kingman Reef; and other employments for which a coastwise license, Great Lakes license, or fishery license is not required.
2. Coastwise license. A vessel with a coastwise license endorsement may engage in the coastwise trade, the fisheries, and any other employment for which a registry or Great Lakes license is not required.
3. Great Lakes license. A Great Lakes license endorsement entitles the vessel to engage in the coastwise trade and the fisheries on the Great Lakes and their tributary and connecting waters, in trade with Canada, and in any other employment for which a registry, coastwise license, or fishery license is not required.
4. Fishery license. This entitles the vessel to fish within the fishery conservation zone and to landward of the conservation zone, and to land her catch, regardless of where caught, in the United States.
5. Pleasure license. A pleasure license entitles the vessel to pleasure use only.

There is no expiration date shown on the certificate of documentation itself, but there should be a sticker attached to the face of the certificate showing the month and year of expiration. The certificate of documentation is good for one year only and must be renewed annually by the end of the month shown on the sticker. When it is renewed, the Coast Guard will send you a new sticker to be attached to the face of the certificate. If any changes have to be made to the certificate of documentation, it must be sent to the Coast Guard documentation office which issued it.

There are very heavy fines for operating an undocumented vessel or one with an expired document, so be sure your company is aware of the expiration date well in advance. Each day that the vessel is operated without a proper certificate is considered a separate offense.

When you are in the foreign trade, the local authorities in almost all ports will want to see your register. Many countries require you to deposit your register with the government authorities while you are in port. When you are in the foreign trade and calling at U.S. ports, your agent will pick up your register and surrender it to U.S. Customs when he enters the vessel and they will keep it until the ship clears outward. If the ship is not clearing foreign, but is going into the coastwise trade, they will return the register when all the foreign cargo has been discharged or, in some ports, they may not even collect it.

TONNAGE TAX RECEIPTS

Each time the vessel enters the United States from foreign she will have to pay tonnage tax. The "tonnage year" begins on the date of her first such entry. The vessel may be liable for a maximum of five payments at six cents per net registered ton and five payments at two cents per ton, depending upon where the vessel has come from. After those ten entries and ten payments of tonnage tax, the vessel does not owe any more tax for the remainder of the tonnage year, regardless of how many times she enters from foreign. See Chapter 5, "Customs," for further details.

Tonnage tax receipts should be kept with the certificate of documentation as the Customs boarding officer will want to see both on arrival. The Customs officers will number each receipt, as "Second payment at 6-cent rate," "Fifth payment at 2-cent rate," etc. When the vessel receives her first receipt of a new tonnage year the receipts from the previous tonnage year may be disposed of.

CERTIFICATE OF INSPECTION

This document certifies that the vessel has been inspected by the Coast Guard and that she is in conformance with the applicable vessel inspection laws and regulations; it also sets forth the conditions under which she may operate. The vessel may not be navigated without a valid certificate of inspection except under two circumstances:

1. A vessel whose certificate of inspection expires at sea or in a foreign port may complete her voyage without a valid certificate if her certificate did not expire within the first fifteen days after she left the last U.S. port and if the voyage will be completed within thirty days after the expiration date.

2. The officer in charge, marine inspection, may issue a Permit to Proceed to Another Port for Repairs, Form CG-948.

The certificate of inspection is issued by the U.S. Coast Guard and is good for two years (one year for nuclear vessels). Each time the certificate of inspection is renewed the vessel will undergo an inspection for certification. After the inspection for certification is complete, the marine inspector will issue a temporary certificate of inspection, valid for a limited time. The permanent certificate will usually be sent to the vessel within a few weeks. The certificate of inspection must be posted under glass in a conspicuous place.

A midterm inspection must be made between the tenth and fourteenth months after the certificate is issued. Both the inspection for certification and the midterm must be requested and scheduled in advance.

Sometimes the shipping company will request that changes be made to the certificate. In this case, amendment pages may be issued. These pages then become part of the certificate.

BRIDGE RECORD CARD

Every vessel must have a bridge record card posted in the wheelhouse or chartroom. This card is for the use of Coast Guard inspectors and will most likely be checked whenever the Coast Guard comes aboard for any sort of inspection. Anytime your vessel is issued a requirement to correct deficiencies, usually on Coast Guard Form CG-835, the inspectors will note that fact on the bridge record card. When the deficiency is cleared, that also should be noted on the card.

INTERNATIONAL LOAD LINE CERTIFICATE

The load line certificate is issued by the American Bureau of Shipping on behalf of the U.S. Coast Guard under the provisions of the International Convention on Load Lines, 1966. It shows the maximum draft (stated in terms of minimum freeboard) to which the vessel may load in each load line zone and season of the world.

The load line certificate is normally good for four years, but is subject to annual surveys, which must be endorsed on the back of the certificate. The annual surveys must be made within three months either way of the anniversary date of the original certificate issuance.

SHIP RADIO STATION LICENSE

The ship radio station license is issued by the Federal Communications Commission (FCC) and is generally good for five years. It lists the allowable frequencies for all the vessel's transmitting equipment including the radiotelegraph, emergency lifeboat transceiver, VHF radiotelephone, radars, and on-board communications (walkie-talkies). No transmitting equipment may be operated without a ship radio station license.

INMARSAT ACCESS AUTHORIZATION CERTIFICATE

This certificate is required aboard vessels with satellite communications systems that utilize the Inmarsat satellite system. Frequency allocations for satellite access are not shown on the ship radio station license; however, FCC regulations require the Inmarsat access authorization certificate to be displayed in the radio room along with the ship radio station license.

The access authorization certificate will be granted only after installation of the satellite system is complete and the system has been through its commissioning tests. These are a series of test transmissions and receptions made under the supervision of an authorized technician to verify that the equipment is operating correctly and is not causing any interference which would adversely affect the satellite communications system.

This certificate has no stated expiration date and is good as long as the satellite communications equipment is operating properly, unless revoked by Inmarsat.

CARGO SHIP SAFETY RADIOTELEGRAPHY CERTIFICATE

This certificate is issued by the FCC under the provisions of the International Convention for the Safety of Life at Sea, 1974. It is valid for one year. It certifies that the radio direction finder, main and emergency transmitters, auto alarm, and operator's watch hours all comply with international regulations. It should be posted in a conspicuous place.

BRIDGE-TO-BRIDGE RADIOTELEPHONY CERTIFICATE

Issued by the FCC, this certificate verifies that the vessel complies with the Bridge-to-Bridge Radiotelephone Act. It must be renewed every year. This is strictly a U.S. requirement and it applies only to vessels within the navigable waters of the United States. If the certificate expires on a foreign voyage you will be unable, and it will be unnecessary, to renew it in a foreign port; you must renew it at the first U.S. port.

CARGO SHIP SAFETY CONSTRUCTION CERTIFICATE

This certificate is issued by the American Bureau of Shipping on behalf of the U.S. Coast Guard. It is issued under the provisions of the International Convention for the Safety of Life at Sea, 1974, and it certifies that the vessel is constructed in accordance with international standards for subdivision and stability; machinery and electrical installations; and fire protection, detection, and extinction. A supplement to the cargo ship safety construction certificate is required for all tankers and all cargo ships engaged in carrying oil. An attachment to the cargo ship safety construction certificate is required for all vessels and is endorsed on completion of the mandatory annual surveys.

All three certificates are combined into one multipage form. The basic certificate and the supplement are good for a maximum of five years, provided the mandatory annual surveys are made and endorsed as required.

CARGO SHIP SAFETY EQUIPMENT CERTIFICATE

Issued by the U.S. Coast Guard under the provisions of the International Convention for the Safety of Life at Sea, 1974, it attests that the ship is properly equipped with lifeboats, life rafts, life buoys, life jackets, fire extinguishers, fathometer, gyro compass, navigation lights and shapes, pilot ladder, whistle, and bell.

Any tanker or cargo ship engaged in the carriage of oil must also have a supplement to the cargo ship safety equipment certificate. Both the basic certificate and the supplement are valid for two years.

NUCLEAR CARGO SHIP SAFETY CERTIFICATE

This certificate is good for one year only and is required on all nuclear-powered cargo vessels. It is issued by the Coast Guard under the provisions of the International Convention for the Safety of Life at Sea, 1974.

PASSENGER SHIP SAFETY CERTIFICATE

This certificate is issued to passenger ships under the International Convention for the Safety of Life at Sea, 1974. It is the passenger ship equivalent of the cargo ship safety construction certificate, cargo ship safety equipment certificate, and cargo ship safety radio-telegraphy certificate.

STABILITY LETTER

Every U.S. vessel must have a letter from the Coast Guard certifying that calculations have been made showing that the vessel can be maintained in a satisfactory condition of stability. The letter must be posted under glass in the pilothouse. Any operating restrictions contained in the letter must be strictly complied with.

CERTIFICATE OF FINANCIAL RESPONSIBILITY (WATER POLLUTION)

This is issued to the vessel operator by the Federal Maritime Commission. It shows that the operator has posted a bond or otherwise demonstrated, to the satisfaction of the Federal Maritime Commission, that he is financially able to meet future obligations that may result because of pollution from his vessel.

If the operator is not the owner as shown on the certificate of documentation then there should be a letter signed by both the operator and the owner acknowledging that the operator is responsible for the operation of the ship including any pollution control and cleanup. In the absence of such a letter, Customs will want to know why the owner of the vessel and the person to whom the certificate of financial responsibility is issued are not the same.

CERTIFICATE OF INSURANCE OR OTHER FINANCIAL SECURITY IN RESPECT OF CIVIL LIABILITY FOR OIL POLLUTION DAMAGE

This is very similar in purpose to the U.S. Federal Maritime Commission's certificate of financial responsibility but it is an international certificate issued under the provisions of Article VII of the International Convention on Civil Liability for Oil Pollution Damage, 1969. All ships carrying more than 2,000 tons of oil in bulk must have insurance or other acceptable security.

TOVALOP

The International Tanker Owners Pollution Federation Ltd. is an association of tanker owners and bareboat charterers. The members of the federation, who are parties to the TOVALOP agreement (Tanker Owners Voluntary Agreement concerning Liability for Oil Pollution), have provided an agreement by which persons (including governments) who have suffered damages as a result of oil pollution may be compensated. The TOVALOP certificate expires annually on February 20.

The International Tanker Owners Pollution Federation was formed before the International Convention on Civil Liability for Oil Pollution Damage, 1969, as a means of convincing governments and port and terminal operators that the federation members were responsible tanker owners and operators who could and would meet their financial obligations in case of pollution damage. Since the convention now provides an international legal means of accomplishing the same end, the TOVALOP agreement now applies only to parts of the world where the convention does not apply. In accordance with its bylaws, the federation will probably disband when the convention has come into force worldwide.

INTERNATIONAL OIL POLLUTION PREVENTION CERTIFICATE (IOPP)

This certificate is issued by the U.S. Coast Guard under the provisions of the International Convention for the Prevention of Pollution from Ships, 1973, as modified by the Protocol of 1978. It certifies that the vessel is equipped with pollution prevention equipment as required by international agreement. The IOPP is valid for four years, subject to annual surveys.

DERAT

This is a combination form which functions either as a deratting certificate or as a certificate of deratting exemption, as appropriate. The authorities will want to see the derat in most foreign ports. It is good for six months and can be renewed in almost any port in the world. It is not needed in the U.S. coastwise trade but it should be kept current if there is any chance the vessel might sail foreign on short notice. This certificate is issued by the Public Health Service in the United States and by the port health officer in most foreign ports.

If the inspector does not find any traces of rodent infestation he will issue a certificate of deratting exemption. If he does find traces of rats, such as droppings, he will take measures to eliminate the rats, such as setting out rat poison or traps, and will then issue a deratting certificate. In some ports the inspector will not do the actual deratting and you will have to hire a pest exterminator.

TONNAGE CERTIFICATES

Most taxes and fees which are levied against vessels by the various governments are assessed on the basis of so much per net registered ton. The vessel's international tonnages, so-called because they are internationally accepted—except by the Panama and Suez canals—are the gross tonnage and net tonnage shown on her certificate of documentation. Tolls for transit of the Panama Canal and the Suez Canal are also based on tonnage, but the authorities at the two canals each have their own methods of measuring tonnages which are different from each other and from the international tonnages.

The vessel should have a Panama Canal tonnage certificate and a Suez Canal tonnage certificate if she has ever transited the canals, otherwise she will have to obtain such a certificate before her first transit. The appropriate canal tonnage certificate must be presented to the boarding officer on each transit of either of the canals.

Originally the Suez Canal tonnage certificate was kept on board the vessel, like most other certificates. Each time the ship transited the canal, the agent took the tonnage certificate ashore, showed it to the authorities, and returned it to the vessel.

For a while, the canal officials decided to keep all tonnage certificates ashore in their files. If a ship transited during this time, her certificate was taken ashore but was not returned to the vessel. If your vessel does not have a Suez Canal tonnage certificate, it could be that the canal officials still have it in their files. In such a case, it would be prudent to request your agent to return the certificate on your next Suez Canal transit; the authorities are once again allowing the certificates to be kept on board ship.

DEADWEIGHT CERTIFICATE

This is usually in the form of a letter from a naval architect at the time of the vessel's construction. It certifies the vessel's full load summer draft, the displacement at that draft, the light ship weight, and the resulting deadweight capacity.

CERTIFICATES OF CLASSIFICATION

When a vessel is first classed by the American Bureau of Shipping, she will receive two certificates showing her ABS classification: a Certificate of Classification for Hull, and a Certificate of Classification for Machinery. The vessel must go through periodic surveys in order to maintain her class, but the certificates have no expiration date and are good indefinitely unless ABS revokes or modifies the vessel's classification.

CANADA COMPLIANCE CERTIFICATE

In the United States this certificate is issued by the American Bureau of Shipping. It is valid for two years and is required on all ships calling at Canadian ports. It is required by the Canada Shipping Act and it certifies that the vessel meets standards imposed by that act.

CERTIFICATE OF SANITARY CONSTRUCTION

This certificate is issued by the U.S. Public Health Service at the time a vessel is built. It certifies that the vessel was constructed in accordance with Public Health Service regulations. This certificate is rarely, if ever, called for.

MASTER CARPENTER'S CERTIFICATE

Also known as the builder's certificate, it is signed by an official of the shipyard that constructed the vessel and certifies the name, year of completion, principal dimensions, international tonnages, and person or company for whom the vessel was built.

EQUIPMENT CERTIFICATES

Your vessel should have equipment certificates issued by the American Bureau of Shipping for all her ground tackle: anchors, chain, connecting shackles, etc. The certificates show the manufacturer, markings, and the proof load that was applied during testing. You may also find equipment certificates for other pieces of gear, such as deck winches or hose-handling booms.

FREEBOARD ASSIGNMENT

This is issued by the American Bureau of Shipping when the vessel is first surveyed to determine her allowable load lines. It shows the required freeboard for each of the seasonal load lines she is assigned. This document is seldom asked for after the international load line certificate is issued, as officials prefer to see the latter.

NOTICE OF PREFERRED FLEET MORTGAGE

When a preferred fleet mortgage is taken out on a vessel, a notice must be prominently posted in a conspicuous place. It is usually in language similar to the following:

This vessel is covered by a Preferred Fleet Mortgage dated _____ to
[name of bank] . Under the terms of said mortgage, neither the
owner, charterer, master, or any other person has any right, power,
or authority to create, incur, or permit to be placed or imposed upon
this vessel any lien whatsoever other than liens for crew's wages or
salvage.

GRAIN LOADING CERTIFICATE

Every vessel that carries grain in bulk must have a certificate of
authorization prior to loading and a certificate of loading prior to
sailing. These certificates are evidence that she has complied with
the grain stability regulations. The National Cargo Bureau is recognized by the U.S. Coast Guard for the purpose of issuing these
certificates. A tanker that has a grain stability letter does not need a
certificate of authorization.

GRAIN STABILITY LETTER

When tankers load grain they generally are exempted from complying with certain of the stability requirements of international
and Coast Guard grain regulations. This is because the high com-
partmentalization of most tankers makes them inherently more
stable and safer for carrying grain than dry cargo vessels.

If the arrangement and structure of the vessel are such that the
angle of list due to a twelve-degree shift of grain, with all cargo
spaces slack, and under the most unfavorable condition of loading,
is less than five degrees, then the National Cargo Bureau will issue a
letter so certifying. If your vessel has such a letter, keep it in a safe
place, as it will save the time and expense of having to repeat the
calculations if she should ever load grain again.

FIRE EXTINGUISHER TEST AND INSPECTION
CERTIFICATE

At the vessel's midterm inspection or inspection for certification, a
private contractor is usually hired to perform the required annual
test and inspection of all portable fire extinguishers and to replace
or recharge the extinguishers as necessary. At the completion of the
work he will issue a certificate on his company's form showing the
condition of all portable fire extinguishers on board the vessel; this
certificate is then shown to the Coast Guard inspectors. The same is
usually done, on the same or a separate certificate, for the fixed
carbon dioxide or halon fire-extinguishing systems.

INFLATABLE LIFE RAFT TEST AND INSPECTION CERTIFICATE

The vessel's inflatable life rafts must be sent ashore annually for servicing by a company approved by the Coast Guard. The company will issue a certificate on its own form when the inflatable life rafts are returned to the vessel.

REGISTER OF CARGO GEAR

Every vessel equipped with masts, stays, booms, winches, cranes, elevators, conveyors, standing and running rigging, etc., for loading and unloading the vessel, must keep records of the following:

1. An initial proof load test, disassembly, and examination of the cargo gear before it is placed into service.
2. A proof load test, disassembly, and examination of the cargo gear every four years.
3. Loose gear certificates, showing compliance with proof load test requirements for all chains, rings, hooks, links, shackles, swivels, blocks, or other loose gear used as cargo gear.
4. Test certificates for wire rope.
5. Annealing certificates for all wrought iron gear required to be annealed.
6. Alterations, renewals, or repairs of cargo gear.
7. Annual visual examination of cargo gear.
8. Monthly inspection of cargo gear by ship's officer.

See the *Code of Federal Regulations,* Title 46, Part 91, for Coast Guard regulations pertaining to cargo gear. If the records required by the regulations are in the form of cargo gear certificates and registers issued by the American Bureau of Shipping or other classification society recognized by the Coast Guard, the marine inspectors will accept such records as prima facie evidence of compliance with the regulations.

FOUR

CREW LISTS

You should have up-to-date crew lists available at all times. The officials in all foreign ports will require crew lists; U.S. Customs and the Immigration and Naturalization Service will require crew lists when arriving or departing the United States on a foreign voyage; and many cargo terminals will want a crew list in order to check crew members in and out at the gate. This is especially true at military terminals; sometimes they will want more than one. Some shipping companies will want you to send the office a crew list from each port, either on Customs and Immigration Form I-418 (Fig. 16) or on their own company form, or they may have a form for reporting only the changes in personnel without listing the entire crew. If there is much turnover among the crew, your department heads would probably appreciate receiving an updated crew list from time to time.

Crew lists in almost all ports and countries should list the men in order of rank: deck officers (including the radio officer) first, then the unlicensed deck crew, the licensed engineers, the unlicensed engine crew, and finally the steward's department. Supercargoes, riding gangs, and other persons in addition to the crew can go at the end. The only exception to this is upon arrival in the United States, when you should have an alphabetically arranged crew list for the Immigration inspector (see "Returning to the United States," below).

THE MASTER COPY

The master copy should usually be typed on the vessel rather than in the agent's or broker's office. If it is done ashore you are more likely to find misspelled names, errors in the document numbers, or other inaccuracies.

THE CERTIFIED CREW LIST

When clearing for foreign from the United States, two copies of the crew list, on Form I-418, must be delivered to U.S. Customs. They may check the crew list against the shipping articles and possibly the certificate of inspection (to verify that you have all of the required ratings) after which they will keep one copy and certify the other, which will be returned to you. This, the certified crew list, is an important document and must not be misplaced or lost. If possible, lock it up.

Once this list has been certified by Customs, you may not make any changes to it. You must submit the original certified crew list to the Customs boarding officer at the first port of arrival in the United States when the vessel returns from foreign. Failure to produce it will make you liable to a fine. If your arrival crew list is not the same as your departure certified crew list, the Customs officer may ask you to account for the differences. This can be done by showing him your official logbook entries for the crew changes, or he may want to see the yellow copies of the discharges for the men no longer aboard, or the U.S. consul's notations on the shipping articles.

The serial numbers and grades of all the officers' licenses should appear on the certified crew list. Place this information in the same block as the surname for each officer.

PIERHEAD JUMP

If, after clearing for foreign in the last U.S. port of call, a member of the crew fails to rejoin, or is hospitalized, and it is necessary to get a replacement, you should sign on the new man just before sailing, making certain that he reads the details of the articles and any riders (see Chapter 2, "Shipping Articles"). Enter all the facts in the official log. The name of the man who did not join remains on the certified crew list and the new man's name is not entered on the certified crew list.

The new man's name and other data should then be added to your regular crew list and the name of the man who failed to join deleted. As noted earlier, always send copies of the altered crew list to your home office.

CREW LISTS REQUIRED IN FOREIGN PORTS

Crew lists will be demanded by port officials in all foreign ports of call and the agent in each such port will want a copy. In many foreign ports the officials will want the crew lists to bear the ship's stamp, in addition to being signed by the master. The number of crew lists required at foreign ports varies greatly. You will usually need at least a half-dozen to a dozen crew lists, occasionally more.

Many countries are more liberal about forms than the United States is and will accept crew lists prepared on the U.S. Form I-418, or on your company forms, or even on plain paper, as long as all the pertinent information is given. A few foreign countries require that the crew lists be on their own forms. Your agent at the preceding port should be able to advise you if this is necessary and to obtain the blank forms for you. If you do not have any forms and the crew lists are required immediately on arrival, you can radio the particulars to your agent at the port so that he can make up the crew lists in advance.

VISAED CREW LIST

Do not confuse this with the visaed alien crew list required by the United States. Some countries require that you have a crew list, on their own form, that must be visaed by their consul at the last port prior to arrival in their country. If you do not have the visaed crew list in a port where it is required, the vessel is liable to a fine, and you may be sure that if the officials in a foreign port can think of any reason to fine the vessel, they will do so.

THE VISAED ALIEN CREW LIST

This is a crew list made up in duplicate on the regular Form I-418, showing only those members of the crew who are nonresident aliens. Registered aliens, for this purpose, are not considered nonresident aliens, and need not be listed. The names must be alphabetically arranged regardless of rating or department. The lists are taken to the U.S. consul's office at the last foreign port of call having one, where the consul will visa the original and keep the other copy. The visaed alien crew list is given to the Immigration boarding officer on arrival at the first U.S. port.

When making up the alien crew list you must show, in column 4, the date, city, and country of birth of each alien. If the alien has a passport, show the number, place of issue, and the issuing authority in column 5; if he does not have a passport, write "None" in that column.

If you are unable to have the alien crew list visaed, for example if there is no U.S. consul at the last port and the alien crew list has not been visaed in a previous port, that fact should be noted in the official log. The same applies if you are diverted to a U.S. port while at sea. If your logbook properly documents the reason you were unable to have the alien crew list visaed you can apply for a waiver of visa upon arrival in the United States. Otherwise, there is a fine for each nonresident alien you bring to the United States who is not visaed on the alien crew list, unless such an alien has had an individual visa issued and stamped in his passport.

RETURNING TO THE UNITED STATES

Before arriving at the first U.S. port from foreign, make up a crew list with the names alphabetically arranged. The Immigration officer will use this list to check the names of the crew. The vessel will not be cleared by Immigration until this check is made. If the Immigration officer uses the regular crew list, checking the crew may take considerable time, whereas if he uses the alphabetically arranged crew list the work will be greatly expedited.

Follow the instructions on the reverse of Form I-418 exactly. This crew list, for the Immigration officer, does not need to have the next-of-kin data filled in; only the name, rating, document number, nationality, date and place of birth, and passport number are required. Do not list the passport number for U.S. citizens and resident aliens. Instead, list the state of birth for U.S. citizens and the alien registration number for resident aliens.

If any crew member was born in a foreign country but is a naturalized U.S. citizen, list his citizenship thus: "U.S. (Nat.)."

You should also have two arrival crew lists arranged by rating for Customs, and extras for the agent and others as mentioned above. The Customs officer will also want the certified crew list.

U.S. Customs and Immigration officials in some ports will not accept photocopies, so you may have to type the required number of crew lists using carbon paper. Do not try to type too many at once or the bottom copies will be illegible.

In ports where the officials do accept photocopies, your copy machine must be capable of reproducing both the front and back of Form I-418 onto the front and back of a single sheet of copy paper so that the I-418 can be signed on the back as required by regulation. Also remember that Form I-418 is slightly wider than standard size 8½-inch paper; be sure your copy machine does not cut off any required information at the edges.

Keep at least fifty sheets of blank crew list forms (I-418) on board. These are supplied through your office or agent.

FIVE

CUSTOMS

Every vessel entering a U.S. port from a foreign port or place and subject to Customs treatment must report arrival, make preliminary and formal entry, and on departure must clear. There are some exceptions to this procedure. U.S. vessels departing for a coastwise port with no foreign cargo, passengers, or baggage on board need not clear. For Customs purposes, a U.S. vessel sailing between two U.S. ports but with foreign cargo on board is in the foreign trade and must enter and clear.

ENTERING THE UNITED STATES FROM FOREIGN

The papers required for entering from foreign should be started as early as possible on the homeward voyage so as to be completed before arrival; bear in mind that neatness and legibility are important. Make up a few extra copies of all required papers in case additional copies are called for.

Papers which will be required for Customs and other boarding officers when entering should be readily available. These include your certificate of documentation, load line certificate, inward foreign manifest, clearance from the last port, SOLAS certificates, etc.

Reporting Arrival

Within twenty-four hours after arrival of any vessel from a foreign port or of a foreign vessel from either a domestic port or the high seas, or of a U.S. vessel carrying bonded merchandise or foreign merchandise for which entry has not been made, such arrival shall be reported by any means of communication to the district director of Customs or to the Customs boarding officer assigned to the vessel.

For Customs purposes the time of arrival is considered to be the time when the vessel first comes to rest, whether at anchor or at a dock, in any harbor within the Customs territory of the United

40

States. The time of departure is the time when the vessel gets underway and proceeds on her voyage without thereafter coming to rest in the harbor from which she is departing.

Boarding Officers

Upon arrival at the first U.S. port from a foreign port of call, the Customs officer will board at the first dock, usually accompanied by the Immigration officer. At subsequent ports only the Customs officer will board, and then only if the vessel is carrying inward foreign cargo or inward-bound passengers for landing. The Department of Agriculture no longer routinely boards every vessel arriving from foreign, so you may or may not see an Agriculture boarding officer, either at the first port or at subsequent ports.

Under federal law, the master of any vessel who obstructs or hinders any officer who is lawfully boarding the vessel for the purpose of enforcing any of the revenue or navigation laws of the United States is liable to a penalty of not less than $500 nor more than $2,000.

Going on or Leaving Vessel

Customs regulations state that prior to clearance by the Customs boarding officer, no person may go on a vessel arriving directly from a place outside the U.S. Customs territory without permission from the Customs boarding officer or the district director of Customs; however, the pilot, Coast Guard officers, Immigration officer, health officer, an inspector of the Animal and Plant Health Inspection Service of the U.S. Department of Agriculture, the vessel's agent, or a consular officer may go on board. No one may go ashore except the above-listed officials and the master or other authorized officer, who may go ashore to report arrival or to make formal entry.

At the first port of entry from a foreign port and at subsequent U.S. ports where inward foreign cargo is on board, either for discharge or in transit, the crew and passengers should be informed that no one is permitted to go ashore until the vessel has been cleared by Customs. The vessel must also be cleared by Immigration at the first port (see Chapter 6, "Immigration"). Permission for the crew and passengers to go ashore may be given soon after the Customs officer boards but no one should be allowed ashore until that permission is given. You should post a watch at the gangway to see that these rules are enforced.

Preliminary Entry

If the vessel has on board any inward foreign cargo, passengers, or baggage and you desire to load or discharge any cargo, passengers, or baggage before making formal entry, you must make preliminary entry. This is done by delivering to the Customs boarding officer the same manifest and other documents that are required for formal entry and certifying the truth and accuracy of the manifest by executing the Master's Certificate on Preliminary Entry on Customs Form 1300 (Fig. 6).

Merchant ships always make preliminary entry immediately upon docking in order to obtain Customs clearance to start working cargo. Making preliminary entry does not excuse you from also making formal entry at the customhouse.

Formal Entry

Formal entry must be made at the customhouse within forty-eight hours after arrival from a foreign port or place, Sunday and holidays excepted. The master, the purser, or a licensed deck officer may enter the vessel by appearing in person at the customhouse; or the required documents, properly executed by the master or authorized officer, may be delivered to the customhouse by the vessel's agent or other personal representative of the master. The latter procedure is almost always followed; it is very rare for a master to personally enter his vessel at the customhouse. Regardless of who enters or clears a vessel, the master is still personally responsible for any statutory penalties that may apply.

Failure to report arrival or to enter as required by law carries a fine of up to $1,000. If the vessel has on board any merchandise (sea stores excepted) which is prohibited from importation into the United States or any alcoholic liquors, there is an additional penalty of a fine not exceeding $2,000 and/or imprisonment for up to one year.

The papers which will be required for entering are an original and one copy of all of the documents that make up the manifest (see "Inward Foreign Manifests," below), the certified crew list, tonnage tax receipts from previous entries, clearance from the last port, the certificate of documentation, and any other vessel certificates that the Customs officers want to verify. Usually they ask for the load line certificate and the SOLAS certificates; these will be sighted and returned to you; however, Customs will probably keep your certificate of documentation on deposit at the customhouse until you clear.

You will have to send the original documents ashore, as Customs generally will not accept photocopies. Be sure to get a receipt from your agent when he takes any of your vessel's permanent documents ashore to enter or clear at the customhouse, or for any other reason for that matter. You should, however, have photocopies of all these documents in your files for use in having the original replaced should any document be lost. If any of these documents are lost you will have much trouble explaining to the issuing agencies why they were not properly safeguarded.

Some foreign ports no longer issue clearances. If that is the case at your last foreign port, ask your agent for a letter stating that the officials at that port do not issue clearances. You may need to present this letter to Customs in the United States in lieu of a clearance. If you arrived via the Panama Canal you should have the canal clearance along with the clearance from the previous foreign port.

Any master who presents any forged, altered, or false document or paper on making entry, knowing the document to be false and not so revealing to the Customs officer accepting entry, is subject to a fine of $50 to $5,000 and/or imprisonment for not more than two years. This is in addition to any forfeiture to which the vessel may be subject.

Mail. Federal law requires that a vessel arriving at a U.S. port with mail on board cannot make formal entry or break bulk until all mail has been delivered to the nearest post office. Generally, however, the agent makes arrangements with Customs to permit passengers to land and work to start. Merchant vessels very rarely carry mail these days and it is unlikely you will encounter this situation.

Inward Foreign Manifests

Every vessel arriving from foreign must present an original and one copy of her manifest to the boarding officer. Failure to produce this manifest on demand can carry a $500 penalty. If the vessel will proceed to another U.S. port with inward foreign cargo or passengers remaining on board then an additional copy of the manifest will be required to be certified as the traveling manifest. The manifest consists of the following documents:

1. Master's Oath of Vessel in Foreign Trade, Customs Form 1300 (Fig. 6);

2. General Declaration, Customs Form 1301 (Fig. 7);
3. Cargo Declaration, Customs Form 1302 (Fig. 8);
4. Ship's Stores Declaration, Customs Form 1303 (Fig. 10);
5. Crew's Effects Declaration, Customs Form 1304 (Fig. 11);
6. Crew List, Customs and Immigration Form I-418 (Fig. 16);
7. Passenger List, Customs and Immigration Form I-418 (Fig. 16).

Any document which is not required may be omitted from the manifest if the word "None" is inserted in the appropriate block of items 17 through 22 of the general declaration. For example, a tanker would not have a passenger list since tankers are prohibited by law from carrying passengers.

Besides the two copies of the manifest required by law (three if a traveling manifest will be required), the district director of Customs may require additional copies for local use. Customs regulations state that a "reasonable" amount of time is to be allowed vessel personnel for the preparation of these additional manifests. In actual practice, it is much better to make up extra manifests before arrival so that you will already have them ready if they are called for.

Master's Oath of Vessel in Foreign Trade.   Customs Form 1300, Master's Oath of Vessel in Foreign Trade, is the form on which you make oath, as required by law, that the vessel's ownership and nationality are as set forth in her certificate of documentation and that the manifest is complete and accurate. Form 1300 also contains the Master's Certificate on Preliminary Entry.

General Declaration.   Customs Form 1301, General Declaration, calls for a brief description of the voyage, particulars of the other documents that make up the manifest, and details of the vessel's agent, nationality, documentation, and tonnage.

Cargo Declaration.   Customs Form 1302, Cargo Declaration, is a list of all inward foreign cargo on board, regardless of the intended port of discharge.

Merchandise should be described on the cargo declaration in order of discharging and loading ports. For example: a vessel loads cargo at Cebu, Kobe, Nagoya, and Yokohama for discharge at Honolulu, New Orleans, Savannah, and New York. All Honolulu cargo is listed in order of ports of loading: Cebu for Honolulu, Kobe for Honolulu, etc. The same is then done for New Orleans cargo, then Savannah cargo, and finally New York cargo. These sheets are then made up into complete sets in order of ports of discharge with the cargo for discharge at Honolulu on top. These complete sets should be checked against each other to make certain the sheets are in the same order in all the sets. After checking, number the sheets consecutively.

Each sheet of the cargo declaration must show the port of loading and the port of discharge in the appropriate blanks. These are sometimes omitted when the sheets are made up (see "Optional Cargo," below).

When inward foreign cargo is containerized, each bill of lading is to be listed in the column headed "B/L Nr." in numerical order according to bill of lading number. The number of the container which contains the cargo covered by that bill of lading and the number of the container seal will be listed in column 6 opposite the bill of lading number. The number of any other bill of lading for other cargo in that same container must appear in column 6 immediately under the container and seal numbers. Only the cargo covered by the bill of lading listed in the column headed "B/L Nr." is to be described in column 7.

The quantity of each shipment of cargo shall be stated either in column 8 or column 9 of the cargo declaration, as appropriate. Column 8 is the gross weight in either pounds or kilograms. Column 9 is the quantity expressed according to the unit of measure specified in the Tariff Schedules of the United States (19 USC 1202). Do not use both columns.

For containerized or palletized cargo, Customs officers will accept a cargo declaration that has been prepared on the basis of information furnished by the shipper. If the cargo declaration covers containerized or palletized cargo only, the following statement may be placed on the declaration:

> The information appearing on the declaration relating to the quantity and description of the cargo is in each instance based on the shipper's load and count. I have no knowledge or information which would lead me to believe or to suspect that the information furnished by the shipper is incomplete, inaccurate, or false in any way.

If the cargo declaration covers both conventional cargo and also containerized or palletized cargo, the abbreviation "SLAC" (shipper's load and count) may be placed next to each containerized or palletized shipment on the declaration and the following statement placed on the declaration:

The information appearing on this declaration relating to the quantity and description of cargo preceded by the abbreviation "SLAC" is in each instance based on the shipper's load and count. I have no information which would lead me to believe or to suspect that the information furnished by the shipper is incomplete, inaccurate, or false in any way.

The appropriate statement, if one is used, should be placed on the last page of the cargo declaration. Words similar to "shipper's load and count" may be substituted but Customs will not accept vague expressions such as "said to contain" or "accepted as containing."

Each shipment listed on the cargo declaration must show the name of the person or company to whom it is consigned. If the shipment is consigned "to order," state so on the declaration.

If the vessel loads cargo for the United States at foreign ports, the agent, customs broker, or steamship company representative at the loading ports will put the bills of lading on board. In the case of general cargo, they may also make up the cargo declaration, omitting the date of arrival. If this is not done, then the cargo declaration will have to be made up on the vessel, getting the required particulars from the bills of lading. Cargo declarations are usually made up on board in the case of tankers, ore carriers, or other bulk cargo vessels.

When a bundle of completed cargo declaration sheets is placed on board in a foreign port, check to see that they are for your vessel and double-check the data in the upper part, as agent's clerks are apt to be careless when typing the required information. It is not uncommon for them to insert the wrong name of the vessel or master. A good practice is to type this information on a blank declaration for the clerk to copy.

When the cargo declaration is typed, be sure that it is neat and legible, and leave at least one blank line between each entry so that the form will be easily readable. Customs officers may refuse to accept sloppy or illegible declarations.

If the cargo declaration has been omitted from the manifest because the vessel arrived in ballast with no cargo on board insert the word "None" in block 17 of the general declaration and the statement "No merchandise on board" in block 13. However, should the vessel have solid ballast, it must be shown on the manifest, stating the type and quantity and where stowed. For example: "350 tons iron ballast (ingots), in No. 3 hold"; or "250 tons sand ballast on deck, to be discharged at sea."

Ship's Stores Declaration.   Federal law requires that goods which are to remain on board the vessel as ship's stores or sea stores must be listed separately from merchandise which is to be landed. Such items must be listed on Customs Form 1303, Ship's Stores Declaration. Customs regulations allow less than whole packages of sea or ship's stores to be described as "sundry small and broken stores."

Ship's stores are goods that become part of the ship's equipment for use on board in the running of the vessel; sea stores are goods for consumption by the crew or passengers. Bunker fuel, paint, mooring lines, etc., are ship's stores. Cigarettes, soft drinks, liquor, and other slop chest items are sea stores.

If more ship's stores or sea stores are found on board than are listed in the manifest, or if any ship's stores or sea stores are landed without a permit, the goods are subject to forfeiture. If any sea stores or ship's stores are landed, with the appropriate Customs permit, they will be treated as imported merchandise.

Crew's Effects Declaration.   The Crew's Effects Declaration, Customs Form 1304, is a list of all articles acquired abroad by ship's officers and crew members (known as crew curios). Before a U.S. vessel arrives from foreign, each crew member must fill out Customs Form 5129, Crew Member's Declaration (Fig. 12). This declaration must list all items procured abroad by the crew member, regardless of how they were acquired, and the cost, or if the item was not acquired by purchase, the fair market value. As master, it is your responsibility to see that crew curios are manifested and that each crew member lists his curios. All costs or values are to be stated in U.S. dollars. If a man has no goods to declare, he must still submit a Form 5129 with the notation "None" or "Nothing to declare" on the face.

Articles exclusively for use on the voyage which will not be landed in the United States and items which have previously been entered and cleared through Customs need not be declared. If there is any doubt whether an item should be declared or not, the crew member should be told to declare the item and to clarify the matter with the Customs boarding officer on arrival. If a crewman has declared an item that he intends to keep on board the vessel and that will not be landed in the United States, he should note "ROB" ("remain on board") after the item on his declaration. Any undeclared or undervalued items that are found are subject to forfeiture and the master and the owner of the goods are each liable to a penalty equal to the value of such goods. If the value exceeds $500, the vessel is also subject to forfeiture.

Notices should be posted in the crew's and officers' messrooms informing all hands of the importance of declaring everything. If you or the vessel are fined because a crew member fails to declare a curio, you are entitled to collect the amount of the fine from the crew member at fault.

After each man has submitted a signed declaration, the master uses the crew member's declarations to make up Customs Form 1304, Crew's Effects Declaration. The crew should be listed on the crew effects declaration in order by rating. In column 7 insert the serial number from each man's crewmember's declaration. If a man has nothing to declare state "None" in place of his serial number.

In lieu of describing the articles on Customs Form 1304, the master may instead furnish a crew list on Form I-418 endorsed as follows:

> I certify that this list, with its supporting Crew Member's Declarations, is a true and accurate manifest of all articles on board the vessel acquired abroad by myself and the officers and crew members of this vessel, other than articles exclusively for use on the voyage or which have been duly cleared through Customs in the United States.

On this crew list show each man's shipping article number opposite his name and, in column 5, the serial number of his crew member's declaration or the word "None."

Any seaman or passenger who has a foreign made article that has already been cleared, or that was purchased in the United States, such as a camera, sextant, binoculars, etc., may register the article with Customs before leaving the United States. This is done by taking the article to any customhouse and filling out a registration slip, Customs Form 4457, which will then be signed and stamped by a Customs officer.

Upon returning to the United States, the registration form is proof that the article has already been properly entered into the United States and is entitled to be brought ashore free of duty. Registered articles need not be declared on Customs Form 5129. For the article to be eligible for registration, Customs officers usually require that it have a serial number or similar unique identification.

If you or the vessel have been fined because of misconduct of a crew member, such as smuggling contraband or failing to declare crew curios, and the crewman is no longer available for you to recover the fine from him, your agent may apply to Customs to have the fine remitted. They will want to see logbook entries or other proof that you posted notices advising the crew to declare all curios, that you searched the vessel for contraband before arrival, and that you took all reasonable precautions to prevent smuggling.

Crew List. Crew lists are to be prepared on Form I-418 in accordance with regulations of the Immigration and Naturalization Service. Instructions for completing crew lists are printed on Form I-418. Complete regulations can be found in Title 8, *Code of Federal Regulations,* Part 231 (see Chapter 6, "Immigration").

Passenger List. Passenger lists are also to be completed in accordance with Immigration regulations. On the last page of the passenger list you must sign the certification that is on the back of Form I-418. If the vessel is carrying any baggage which is not accompanying a passenger, that baggage and the marks or addresses on the packages must be manifested on the last page of the passenger list under the heading "Unaccompanied baggage."

The Traveling Manifest

If the vessel is to proceed to any other U.S. ports after the first port of arrival with inward foreign passengers or cargo remaining on board (residue cargo), an additional copy of the manifest will be required for use as a traveling manifest. The manifest is assembled and taken to the customhouse when making formal entry, at which time the Customs officer will certify the complete set as the traveling manifest, called the traveler for short. The traveler will be returned to you when you clear. You must show it to the Customs boarding officer at each port when making preliminary entry and your agent will take it to the customhouse when making formal entry. You pick it up again when clearing. This is repeated at each port until all the inward foreign cargo has been discharged and all inward passengers have been landed. At that port the traveler is surrendered to Customs. You may not make any changes on the traveler once it has been certified.

Post Entry

If, after the cargo declaration and crew effects declaration are submitted and formal entry has been made, a discrepancy is discovered between the merchandise manifested on the declarations and the merchandise actually found on board the vessel, the error must be corrected by submitting Customs Form 5931, Discrepancy Report and Declaration (Fig. 14). Report the shortage or overage to the agent, customs broker, or company representative, who will prepare the post entry.

Customs charges a small fee for a post entry but there are no penalties provided that the discrepancy was the result of non-negligent clerical error or typographical mistake and there has been no loss of Customs revenue to the United States. Failure to submit a post entry may subject you to a $500 fine. If the same vessel or agent repeatedly has similar manifest discrepancies, the Customs officer may attribute it to negligence and refuse to allow it as clerical error.

You do not need to submit a post entry if the only discrepancy is an error in the marks or numbers listed for packages and the marks or numbers actually on the packages, provided that the quantity and description of the contents of the packages is correct.

Discrepancies in the manifested quantity of bulk petroleum products must be reported on Form 5931 if the difference exceeds 1 percent.

Foreign Repairs or Equipment

If any equipment, repair parts, or material are purchased, or if any repairs are made to a U.S. vessel outside the United States, the vessel is liable to a duty of 50 percent of the cost of the equipment or repairs. Labor cost is included in the cost of foreign repairs, but not the cost of any repair work done by regular members of the ship's crew.

For purposes of assessing duty on foreign repairs or purchases, the following places are not considered to be outside the United States: American Samoa, Guantanamo Bay Naval Station, Guam, Puerto Rico, or the U.S. Virgin Islands.

If the vessel remains outside the United States for two years or more, then only foreign repairs or purchases made during the first six months after leaving the last U.S. port are dutiable.

If the vessel is compelled to have foreign repairs made or to purchase foreign equipment due to stress of weather or other casualty, and if the repairs or equipment are necessary to secure the safety and seaworthiness of the vessel to enable her to reach her port of destination in the United States, then the duty may be remitted. "Casualty" does not include repairs or purchases necessary due to ordinary wear and tear; however, if any part is serviced or repaired immediately before leaving the United States and the part then fails within six months of the servicing or repair the failure will be deemed to be a casualty.

If the equipment, parts, or materials were produced in the United States, purchased by the vessel owner in the United States, and installed by residents of the United States or by regular members of the crew, the duty may be remitted, even though the work is done in a foreign port.

Duty will be remitted if the equipment, parts, materials, or labor were used as dunnage for cargo, for packing or shoring of cargo, for building temporary bulkheads or similar devices to control bulk cargo, or to prepare tanks to carry liquid cargo. Preparing tanks for carriage of liquid cargo does not include permanent repair or alteration.

The owner or master of every U.S. vessel arriving from foreign must declare all equipment, parts, or materials purchased and all repairs made outside the United States. This declaration is made on Customs Form 226 (Fig. 15) and is required regardless of whether the expenditures are dutiable or not. The declaration must be shown to the Customs boarding officer on demand and must be presented as part of the original manifest when making formal entry.

If no foreign repairs or purchases were made on the voyage, submit a Form 226 with "None" typed on the face. If any foreign repairs or purchases were made, then the declaration will probably be made up by a customs broker or other person who specializes in Customs regulations. This is because of the detailed paperwork that will be required to document the cost of the repairs or purchases and to support any claims for remission of duties.

If the repairs are for damage caused by heavy weather, you may need to prepare abstracts of the deck log covering the periods of heavy weather. The damage will, of course, have been entered in the logbook and protest noted at the first port of call after the heavy weather. Copies of these abstracts and protests may be necessary in having the duty remitted. A copy of such protest should always be sent to your insurance department from the port where the note of protest was made.

Tonnage Tax

Every merchant vessel entering a U.S. port from foreign is liable to U.S. Customs for payment of tonnage tax as follows: If the vessel is coming from any foreign port in North America, Central America, the West Indies, the Bahama Islands, the Bermuda Islands, Newfoundland, the coast of South America bordering on the

Caribbean Sea (considered to include the mouth of the Orinoco River), or the high seas adjacent to the United States or to any of the above locations, a tonnage tax of two cents per net ton will be payable on each entry up to a maximum of ten cents per net ton in any one year. If the vessel is coming from any other foreign port, the tonnage tax is six cents per net ton on each entry, up to a maximum of thirty cents per net ton per year.

There can be up to five payments at the two-cent rate and five payments at the six-cent rate so that the maximum possible tonnage tax for any vessel is forty cents per net ton per year.

If the vessel arrives with cargo or passengers loaded at different ports to which different tax rates apply, tonnage tax will be collected at the higher rate. The tonnage year is computed from the date of the vessel's first such entry, regardless of the rate payable.

Tonnage tax does not apply to a vessel that arrives in distress; or to a vessel that comes into port for bunkers, sea stores, or ship's stores only, and that transacts no other business (including receiving orders) and departs within twenty-four hours; or to a passenger vessel making three trips or more per week between a U.S. port and a foreign port. A vessel that calls at a U.S. port for orders only must pay tonnage tax.

Tonnage tax also does not apply to a vessel entering directly from the U.S. Virgin Islands, American Samoa, Guam, Wake Island, Midway Island, Canton Island, Kingman Reef, or Guantanamo Bay Naval Station, or to a vessel engaged exclusively in laying or repairing cables.

Tonnage tax receipts for the current tonnage year should be kept with the certificate of documentation. The Customs boarding officer will usually want to see the receipts at the same time he examines the certificate of documentation.

A U.S. vessel entering from foreign is liable for an additional fifty cents per ton special tax and fifty cents per ton light money if any of the vessel's officers is not a U.S. citizen. This does not apply if the vessel is making her first arrival in the United States from a foreign or intercoastal voyage and all the officers who are not citizens are below the grade of master and are filling vacancies that occurred on the voyage. The master must be a U.S. citizen in any case.

Overcarried Cargo That Has Been Foreign

Outward foreign cargo which has been foreign but was overcarried and brought back to the United States must be manifested, even though it is of U.S. origin. If the cargo was overcarried by mistake and will be returned to the intended foreign port of discharge, note on the cargo declaration: "Undelivered—to be returned to original foreign destination."

Residue Cargo for Foreign Ports

If a vessel calls at a U.S. port with inward foreign cargo on board which will be retained on board for discharge at a foreign port, that cargo must still be manifested on the cargo declaration. If the vessel clears directly foreign from the first U.S. port of arrival, the cargo retained on board may be declared by inserting the following statement on the outward cargo declaration: "All cargo declared on entry in this port as cargo for discharge at foreign ports and so shown on the cargo declaration filed upon entry has been and is retained on board."

If any of the cargo originally manifested to remain on board has subsequently been landed, then the outward cargo declaration must list each item that has been retained on board.

If the vessel will proceed to any other U.S. ports, then the vessel must follow the same requirements previously mentioned for sailing coastwise with inward foreign cargo.

Sealing Sea Stores and Curios

When a vessel arrives from a foreign port or when a vessel in foreign trade arrives from a domestic port, the Customs boarding officer may, if he thinks it necessary, seal the storeroom where sea stores or ship's stores which are not necessary for immediate use are located. He may also require all crew curios which are to remain on board, and for which duty has not been paid and no permit to land has been issued, to be placed in one locker or storeroom, which he will seal.

In practice, U.S. Customs officers do not usually bother to collect and seal the curios or to seal the storerooms, particularly if the vessel is not carrying passengers and therefore has only a modest inventory of slop chest goods. If the Customs officer does require the curios to be collected and sealed, each crew member should securely tie, wrap, or box his curios and should print his name on the package.

Once a storeroom has been sealed by Customs, the seal may not be broken without permission from Customs until the vessel has departed port and dropped the pilot. If you break a seal at sea while proceeding coastwise, notify the Customs boarding officer at the next port so that he can reseal the storeroom.

Each crew member will be permitted to keep out 50 cigars, 300 cigarettes, or 2 kilograms of smoking tobacco, or a proportionate amount of each, and 1 liter of alcoholic beverages for use in port.

Lightering Offshore

A ship which enters the United States after visiting a vessel on the high seas has come from "a foreign port or place" if any export cargo from the United States is transshipped to the vessel on the high seas or if any cargo received from the vessel on the high seas is brought into the United States. Therefore, if your vessel lighters to or from another vessel in international waters, you will have to enter and clear the same as if you had called at a foreign country.

Arriving Intercoastal via the Panama Canal

The Canal Zone of the Panama Canal is "a foreign port or place" and vessels that call at the Canal Zone will have to enter and clear. Merchandise imported from the Canal Zone is treated the same as merchandise imported from any other foreign country. However, a U.S. vessel sailing between two U.S. ports that merely transits the Canal without transacting any business in the Canal Zone will not be required to enter and clear. She will, however, be required to report arrival to Customs because of such transit.

If the vessel did no business in the canal but the crew or passengers purchased curios from the line handlers on the vessel during the transit, then each crew member or passenger will have to submit a Crew Member's Declaration, Customs Form 5129, or passenger Customs Declaration, Customs Form 6059B, as appropriate, and you will have to make up a Crew's Effects Declaration, Customs Form 1304. You will have to telex your agent before arrival to request the services of a Customs officer to clear these curios.

Harbor of Refuge

Vessels arriving in distress or to take on bunkers, sea stores, or ship's stores only, and that will depart within twenty-four hours without having landed or taken on any passengers or merchandise except such bunkers or stores, need not enter and clear. However, the master, owner, or agent must report the dates and times of arrival and departure and the quantity of bunkers, sea stores, or ship's stores taken on board.

If any ship's business is transacted, other than as excepted above, you will have to enter and clear. This includes signing seamen off and on. If the vessel is in port over twenty-four hours, you must surrender your last clearance and enter and clear again.

CLEARING FOREIGN

Every vessel departing a U.S. port bound for a foreign port must clear. U.S. vessels sailing intercoastal that merely transit the Panama Canal without otherwise transacting any business at the canal will not be required to clear solely because of such transit.

Application for clearance is made by filing a Master's Oath of Vessel in Foreign Trade, Customs Form 1300, and a General Declaration, Customs Form 1301, at the customhouse along with other required documents listed below. As with entry, this can be done by the master, purser, or licensed deck officer, or by the agent or other personal representative of the master. If the vessel will be in port less than twenty-four hours, it is usual to enter and clear at the same time.

A vessel clearing outward must clear for a particular named port; no vessel may clear for the high seas except a vessel which will visit another vessel on the high seas for the purpose of transshipping export or import merchandise bound from or to the United States. If after departure your vessel is diverted to a port other than the one named in your clearance, telex your agent at the departure port and have him notify Customs of the diversion.

A vessel whose final destination is not known may clear for a named port "for orders" if the vessel is in ballast or if any cargo on board is to be discharged at a port in the same country as the port for which the vessel is clearing.

Clearance may be denied under various circumstances if the vessel is not in compliance with applicable navigation laws. A U.S. vessel will not be issued a clearance to a foreign port unless it is properly documented and has a valid certificate of inspection or, in lieu of a certificate of inspection, a Permit to Proceed to Another Port for Repairs on Coast Guard Form CG-948. See the Customs regulations for complete details of circumstances under which a clearance may be denied.

The clearance is valid until midnight of the second day after issuance; if the vessel does not depart before that time, you will have to get your clearance extended. The agent can do this for you. If the voyage is cancelled after clearance is granted, the reason for cancellation must be reported in writing and the certificate of clearance and any related papers returned to Customs within twenty-four hours after the cancellation. File the certificate of clearance in a safe place; the officials at the first foreign port will very likely want to see it.

No vessel, American or foreign flag, may sail directly foreign without a foreign clearance. This includes vessels in the foreign trade sailing coastwise on a permit to proceed. Sailing foreign without clearance will result in a heavy fine being imposed on the vessel the next time she calls at any U.S. port. If your vessel is sailing coastwise and the owners desire to divert to a foreign port, you will have to put into a U.S. port to clear. As expensive as this may be, there is no alternative to this procedure.

Outward Cargo Declaration

All outward-bound cargo must be manifested on Customs Form 1302-A (Fig. 9), Cargo Declaration Outward with Commercial Forms. Copies of bills of lading or equivalent commercial documents must be attached to the cargo declaration, along with any export declarations that may be required by regulations of the Department of Commerce. If any such export declarations are required, they should be provided by the customs broker or the shipper.

At a minimum, the outward cargo declaration must show the following:

1. Name and address of the shipper;
2. Description of the cargo, the number of packages, and their gross weight;
3. Name of the vessel;
4. Port of loading; and
5. Intended foreign port of discharge.

If the bills of lading or equivalent documents that are attached to the cargo declaration describe the cargo by showing on their face the information required by columns 6, 7, and either 8 or 9 of the cargo declaration, the information does not have to be repeated on the cargo declaration provided the cargo declaration makes reference to the bills of lading with a statement such as "Cargo as per attached commercial documents."

Cargo declarations for containerized or palletized cargo may be prepared using the shipper's load and count under the same rules already described for preparing Form 1302.

If, when the vessel is ready to depart, a complete outward cargo declaration is not ready, or not all the required export declarations are ready for filing, Customs may accept an incomplete manifest on Form 1301, General Declaration, if a bond is on file in accordance with Customs regulations and if the following statement is placed in block 16 of the general declaration: "This incomplete Cargo Declaration is filed in accordance with section 4.75, Customs Regulations."

The master or agent must deliver a complete outward cargo declaration, duplicate copies of all export declarations, a general declaration, and a master's oath on entry of vessel in foreign trade no later than the fourth business day after clearance.

Certified Crew List

The master of a U.S. vessel clearing foreign must deliver to Customs two crew lists on Customs and Immigration Form I-418. One will be retained by Customs and the other will be stamped as the certified crew list and returned to the master. The certified crew list must be given to the Customs boarding officer when the vessel returns to the United States.

Customs will match the arrival crew list against the certified crew list and, if there have been any changes in the crew during the voyage, they may want documentation of the differences. They may want to see your official log entries for the changes, or the U.S. consul's notations on the shipping articles.

Stores List

You will need to submit a stores list showing ship's stores and sea stores, the same as for arrival.

Certificate of Documentation

Customs will want to see the certificate of documentation to verify that the vessel is documented for registry (foreign trade) or, if bound for the Great Lakes, has a Great Lakes license endorsement. They will also verify the tonnage, nationality, and ownership of the vessel.

Certificate of Inspection

No U.S. vessel required to be inspected may be granted a clearance unless it has a valid U.S. Coast Guard certificate of inspection or, in lieu of a certificate of inspection, a Permit to Proceed to Another Port for Repairs on Coast Guard Form CG-948.

Shipping Articles

The Customs officers in some ports will want to see the shipping articles before granting clearance in order to ascertain that the vessel has a full complement as required by her certificate of inspection and that the laws respecting shipment of seamen have been complied with.

REPORTING ARRIVAL, ENTERING, AND CLEARING ON BOARD

A passenger vessel operating on a regular schedule which arrives in port at night between 5 P.M. and 8 A.M. the next morning, or on a Sunday or federal holiday and which will sail that same night, Sunday, or holiday, may report arrival, make entry, and clear on board the vessel. This avoids the necessity to make entry at the customhouse and is done to expedite the sailing of passenger vessels which have short in-port stays.

In order for the Customs boarding officer to receive the report of arrival, accept entry, and issue clearance on board the vessel, the owner, master, or agent of the vessel must have made advance application for this service and filed a bond in accordance with Customs regulations.

SAILING COASTWISE WITH RESIDUE FOREIGN CARGO OR PASSENGERS ON BOARD

If a vessel will discharge any of her inward foreign cargo or passengers at any U.S. port other than the first port of arrival, then one copy of the manifest must be certified as the traveling manifest at the first port of arrival. Before a vessel can proceed from one U.S. port to another with residue foreign cargo or passengers on board, the master must obtain a permit to proceed from the district director of Customs. The permit to proceed is applied for by submitting Customs Form 1301, General Declaration, in triplicate and making oath on Customs Form 1300. If no inward foreign cargo or passengers will be discharged at the next port, note that fact on Form 1301 by inserting the words "to load only" in parentheses after the name of the port to which the vessel is to proceed.

When Customs grants the permit, they will endorse the Form 1301 with the legend "Permission is granted to proceed to the port named in item 6." One copy of the permit to proceed will be attached to the traveling manifest and the other will be given to the master. The original will be retained by Customs. The traveling manifest, with the duplicate permit attached, will be returned to the master. If the vessel's certificate of documentation is on deposit with Customs, it will also be returned at this time.

Customs regulations call for a traveling crew effects declaration, along with the unused crew member's declarations for items that still remain on board, to be placed in a sealed envelope and given to the master for delivery to the Customs boarding officer at the next port. You may find, however, that the Customs officers may not follow this procedure in all ports. In any case, it is easier for all concerned if you try to clear all the crew curios at the first port of arrival, even if the items will not be landed until a subsequent port.

Upon arrival at the next port you must report arrival and make entry within twenty-four hours. You make entry by delivering to the district director of Customs the vessel's certificate of documentation, the endorsed permit to proceed, the traveling manifest, the traveling crew effects declaration and remaining crew member's declarations, and an abstract manifest for that port consisting of the following:

1. A new general declaration;
2. A cargo declaration of all cargo for discharge at that port;
3. A passenger list of all passengers to be landed at that port;
4. A crew effects declaration in duplicate of all unentered articles acquired abroad by officers and crew which are still on board; and
5. A ship's stores declaration in duplicate.

If no inward foreign cargo or passengers are to be discharged at that port you may omit the cargo declaration and the passenger list from the abstract manifest if you insert the following statement in block 12 of the general declaration: "Vessel on an inward foreign voyage with residue cargo/passengers for _____. No cargo or passengers for discharge at this port."

You must also execute a Master's Oath of Vessel in Foreign Trade, Customs Form 1300.

Preliminary entry may be made in the same way as for the first port of arrival.

This procedure is followed for each subsequent U.S. port. The traveling manifest is surrendered to Customs at the final port of discharge, except that if inward foreign cargo remains on board for discharge at a foreign port, the traveling manifest will be surrendered at the final port of departure from the United States, if it is different from the final port of discharge. If the vessel proceeds from one U.S. port to another via an intermediate foreign port, the traveling manifest is not surrendered when clearing for the foreign port if the vessel still has foreign cargo on board for discharge at a subsequent U.S. port.

The traveling crew effects declaration is surrendered at any port from which the vessel will depart directly for a foreign port.

Diversion between U.S. Ports with Inward Foreign Cargo

If, while you are enroute between two U.S. ports on a permit to proceed, you receive orders to divert to a U.S. port other than the one named in the permit to proceed, the papers must not be changed in any way. In such a case your agent should request the office of the district director of Customs where the permit was issued to telephone the district director at the new port in advance of the vessel's arrival. If the phone call is made after the vessel arrives in the new port she may be subject to a penalty; therefore, it is important that the first district director be requested to make the call in ample time before the vessel's arrival.

Optional Cargo

Inward foreign cargo is sometimes shipped without a U.S. discharge port being designated in the charter party or bill of lading, or the documents may show several optional ports, one or more of which will be designated as the discharge port or ports. There is usually a clause in the bill of lading or the charter party calling for the discharge ports to be designated before the vessel reaches a certain position or by a certain date. As soon as the port is known it should be entered on the manifest. When the vessel arrives at her first U.S. port, the discharge ports for all cargo to be discharged on that coast must be designated.

If a vessel arrives on either the Atlantic or Pacific coast with cargo for the opposite coast or the Great Lakes, or a vessel arrives on the Great Lakes with cargo for the Atlantic or Pacific coast, and the discharge ports are not yet known, Customs will accept a cargo declaration that shows such cargo as destined for "optional ports, Atlantic coast," or "optional ports, Pacific coast," or "optional ports, Great Lakes coast," as appropriate. At the first port on the next coast, all discharge ports for the optional cargo must be designated.

SAILING COASTWISE WITH OUTWARD FOREIGN CARGO

A vessel which has loaded cargo or passengers at a U.S. port for discharge at a foreign port must clear on a permit to proceed in order to depart for another U.S. port. This is done by filing a general declaration in duplicate, the same as when applying for a permit to proceed coastwise with inward foreign cargo. The general declaration must show all previous loading ports if the port to be cleared from is not the first port where outward foreign cargo was loaded.

An outward cargo declaration must also be filed in accordance with the same rules as when clearing foreign.

VESSEL IN COASTWISE TRADE TOUCHING AT FOREIGN PORT

A U.S. vessel which is on a voyage between two U.S. ports may also call at intermediate foreign ports to load or discharge merchandise or passengers. A permit to proceed or clearance must be obtained at each U.S. loading port for the foreign ports at which it is intended to touch.

An outward cargo declaration must be submitted, but it need only show the cargo for a foreign destination. The master must also submit a complete coastwise cargo declaration describing all merchandise which is to be transported to U.S. destinations via the foreign ports.

TRADE WITH NONCONTIGUOUS PORT

"Noncontiguous territory" means all of the island territories and possessions of the United States excluding the Canal Zone of the Panama Canal.

A vessel which is not required to clear but which is transporting merchandise from the District of Columbia or any state of the United States to any noncontiguous territory, including Puerto Rico, or from Puerto Rico to any other noncontiguous territory must, if required by Department of Commerce regulations, submit a complete manifest along with shippers' export declarations before departing. Alternatively, a bond may be posted if the documents are not ready before departure. See Title 15, *Code of Federal Regulations*, Section 30.24, for regulations of the Department of Commerce.

Requests for permission to depart in such a case may be oral or written and permission to depart will be granted orally by Customs. The Master's Oath of Vessel in Foreign Trade, Customs Form 1300, will not be required for a U.S. vessel departing with cargo for a port in noncontiguous territory.

A U.S. vessel which arrives at a port in any state of the United States, the District of Columbia, or Puerto Rico, from a port in noncontiguous territory other than Puerto Rico, will not be required to make entry, but the master must report arrival within twenty-four hours and must submit a cargo declaration to the Customs boarding officer on arrival, and to the district director of Customs at the customhouse within forty-eight hours. If the vessel proceeds to another port in any state, the District of Columbia, or Puerto Rico, the master must submit a cargo declaration the same as for a vessel proceeding to another port with inward foreign cargo on board, but no permit to proceed will be required.

FINES AND PENALTIES

When a vessel owner, master, or person in charge has become subject to any penalty for violation of the Customs or revenue laws of the United States, the vessel may be held for payment and may be seized and libeled to pay the penalty.

Complete regulations of the U.S. Customs Service may be found in Title 19 of the *Code of Federal Regulations* and the principal federal laws pertaining to Customs matters may be found in Title 19 of the U.S. Code.

SIX

IMMIGRATION

The Immigration boarding officer boards at the first U.S. port of entry. He will require a crew list in alphabetical order; the visaed alien crew list if there are any nonresident aliens in the crew; and one set of completed Crewman's Landing Permits, Form I-95A (Fig. 17), for each nonresident alien. If the vessel is carrying passengers the Immigration officer will require an Aircraft/Vessel Report, Form I-92 (Fig. 18); an Arrival/Departure Record, Form I-94, for each alien passenger except resident aliens and lawfully admitted immigrants; and a passenger list.

The Immigration officer will check each crew member and passenger against the crew list and the passenger list. This process will be considerably expedited if the lists are prepared, in accordance with the printed instructions, with the names alphabetically arranged, surnames first. This is different from the practice at most foreign ports, where crew lists are prepared in order of rank. The Immigration officer should be given a comfortable place to work and a ship's officer should be detailed to assist in getting the crew assembled as quickly as possible. The crew should bring their seaman's cards and passports with them. Resident alien crewmen will also have to show their Alien Registration Receipt Cards, Form I-551 (known as a "green card").

By Immigration and Customs rules neither passengers nor crew are permitted to go ashore until they are checked off by the Immigration boarding officer and the vessel is cleared by Customs. The vessel is subject to a fine if these rules are not strictly observed. It is therefore advisable to post a notice warning the crew and passengers that any person causing the vessel to be fined by going ashore prematurely will have the fine charged against him.

ALIEN CREW MEMBERS

Signing on Aliens in Foreign Ports

You may save your company great expense and yourself much trouble if you avoid signing on any nonresident aliens in foreign ports. The fact that many such an alien has a merchant mariner's document, a Social Security number, and can show discharges from American vessels means nothing to the Immigration officer, who may still refuse to admit him or may give him a D-1 permit, with all the red tape that it involves. Sailing shorthanded is definitely preferable to signing on a nonresident alien in a foreign port. If, despite all efforts to avoid it, you must sign on a nonresident alien to fill a vacancy as called for in the certificate of inspection, make certain that he is a bona fide seaman and has papers to prove it. Even so, there is a possibility that he will be detained on arrival in the United States. If he is not a bona fide seaman, the Immigration officer may order him detained on the vessel and deported. It may then be necessary to employ a guard to watch him all the time the vessel is in a U.S. port.

The Visaed Alien Crew List

If there are any nonresident aliens in the crew, it will be necessary to make up an alien crew list in duplicate on Form I-418 (Fig. 16). This crew list must be visaed by the U.S. consul at the last foreign port of call before sailing for the United States. If you are unable to do this, for example if there is no U.S. consul at the last foreign port or if the vessel has sailed for a foreign port and receives orders at sea to divert to a U.S. port, make an entry in the official log explaining the circumstances. The duplicate copy is kept by the consul. Registered (resident) aliens do not go on this list; they go on the regular crew list. The alien crew list, visaed or unvisaed, is given to the Immigration boarding officer on arrival at the first U.S. port. If it is not visaed the Immigration officer may ask to see the entry in the official log explaining why.

Crewman's Landing Permit

Before arriving at the first port in the United States, prepare a set of Form I-95A, Crewman's Landing Permit, for each nonresident alien crew member. These are the aliens appearing on the visaed alien crew list. The completed forms are given to the Immigration officer when he boards the vessel. The Immigration officer will classify each such nonresident alien in one of the following categories:

1. The Immigration officer may issue a conditional landing permit designated D-1. A D-1 permit is good for a maximum of twenty-nine days, the same as a D-2, but it limits the alien and the master as follows:

   a. The crewman's passport must be surrendered to the master for safekeeping.
   b. The crewman must sail with the vessel from every port in the United States unless he has advance permission in writing from the master or agent to join the vessel in another U.S. port.
   c. He must sail with the vessel when it leaves the United States.
   d. He may be re-examined by Immigration at any time during the period of his admission and for certain causes may be returned to the vessel under an order of detention as though he had been detained on arrival.
   e. He may not be discharged or paid off without written permission in advance from Immigration. For each violation of this requirement, the vessel will be liable to the district director of Customs for a penalty of $1,000.

2. The D-2 permit grants the alien crew member a conditional permit to land temporarily for a period not to exceed twenty-nine days if the Immigration officer is satisfied that the alien crew member intends to depart within twenty-nine days as a crewman on another vessel or as a passenger by any means of transportation. Aliens in this category may be paid off. If the vessel remains in the United States for more than twenty-nine days, the crewman's landing permit will have to be extended.

The Immigration officer will stamp each nonresident alien's crewman's landing permit "D-1" or "D-2" on the front according to the category assigned.

Request for D-2 Status. The Immigration officer should be requested to grant D-2 status to all alien crew members in order that the payoff may be completed without having a backlog of wages due. Should your request be refused, have your agent make written application to the Immigration officer in charge of the district for a D-2 type of admission. If this application is refused in the port of arrival, additional written requests may be made at subsequent ports. If these are also denied you should, to avoid keeping a backlog of wages, request permission to pay the alien his wages even though he may not be discharged. This is seldom granted, but it is worth a try. If it is granted, make certain that the alien sails with the vessel, otherwise the vessel will be fined.

Advances and Wages. Since the holder of a D-1 permit cannot be paid off, he will most likely ask for an advance and will probably want as much as he can get. This is a difficult question and discretion should be used in granting such advances. Consider the possibility that if the alien receives an advance close to the total amount he has coming to him he may leave the ship and not return. The Immigration and Naturalization Service may take a dim view of a large advance to an alien holding a D-1 permit.

There is, however, at least one federal court decision in which the court held that the term "pay off," as used in the shipping industry and in the federal law prohibiting the "pay off or discharge" of a D-1 alien, is synonymous with "discharge." In *U.S. v. Seaboard Sur. Co.* the court ruled that the law does not prohibit paying an alien seaman his full wages provided that the employer-employee relationship is not terminated.

Consult your company's attorneys or payroll department if you find yourself in such a situation and need advice as to the procedure to follow.

Holding back an alien's pay presents a small problem in accounting, as the amount represents unclaimed wages which you may have to pay a voyage or two later. Follow your company's instructions for dealing with this situation. If your company has no special instructions, give the seaman a voucher showing the wages due. Make a note in the official log of the reason why the seaman's wages are being withheld. You may also want to type a brief note on the face of the voucher.

Desertion

Federal law requires that the owner, agent, or master of a vessel immediately report to Immigration, in writing, any case of an alien crewman illegally landing or deserting in a U.S. port. This report should include the alien's name, nationality, passport number, personal description, time and circumstances of the landing or desertion, and any information or documents that might aid in apprehending the alien, specifically including any passport that the alien surrendered to the master.

You or your agent should notify Immigration by telephone as soon as the alien is discovered missing. This telephone notification should be followed by a written report as soon as possible, but in any case within twenty-four hours. Even though you immediately notify Immigration by telephone, you must still make the written report required by law.

Detainees

The Immigration officer may, instead of issuing a D-1 or D-2 permit, prohibit shore leave of any kind and may issue a detention order requiring you to detain the alien on board the vessel. If the Immigration officer prohibits shore leave he will stamp "Permission to land temporarily at all U.S. ports is refused" on the crewman's landing permit, which he will return to the master.

Alien passengers as well as crew members may be detained. You may need to employ a special guard to see that the detainee does not go ashore. The vessel is liable to a fine if the detainee goes ashore, even if he returns to the vessel.

Reporting Changes in Crew

Immigration regulations require that every vessel departing from the United States submit a Form I-418 showing all changes in the nonresident alien crew. The first line of the form should have the caption "Arrival Crew List, Form I-418 filed at _____." Insert the U.S. port of arrival in the blank.

Under the heading "Added Crewmen" list the names of all nonresident aliens who were not members of the crew when the vessel last arrived in the United States. For each such crewman, attach the Form I-94 or I-95A that was given to the crewman on his last arrival in the United States or, if he has no such form, a newly executed Form I-95A.

Under the heading "Separated Crewmen" list all nonresident aliens who were members of the crew when the vessel arrived in the United States but who are not departing with the vessel. For each such crewman you must show his nationality, passport number, port and date of separation, and the reason for his failing to depart. If an application to pay off or discharge an alien crewman was granted subsequent to arrival, attach the triplicate copy of Form I-408.

If there have been no changes, endorse the I-418 "No changes in nonresident alien crew upon departure." Immigration officers usually do not require this form from U.S. vessels that had no nonresident aliens on board on arrival and that do not have any nonresident aliens on board upon departure.

Medical Treatment of Nonresident Alien

If a nonresident alien who was refused a conditional landing permit or who was issued a D-1 landing permit requires medical treatment you will have to apply to Immigration for permission to land him. The Immigration Service will not give the alien a D-2 landing permit in such a case; instead, the crewman will be paroled into the custody of the agent or a company official. The crewman must have a Form I-94, which the Immigration officials will endorse to reflect the terms of parole.

The master, agent, or an official of the company will have to sign a guarantee for the seaman's medical expenses and other related expenses. When medical treatment or hospitalization is completed, the steamship company is responsible for departure of the alien from the country.

INWARD PASSENGERS

Some cargo vessels are equipped to carry up to twelve passengers. For Immigration and Customs purposes, a passenger is any person carried on board a vessel who is not connected with her operation, navigation, ownership, or business, and as such must be shown on the Passenger List, Form I-418.

The passengers' names must be listed in alphabetical order, family names first. If stowaways are discovered their names should be put on a separate list marked "Stowaways" with the name of the port where each one stowed away. The Immigration officer will require two copies of the passenger list at the first port of arrival. It is advisable to have some extra lists and to keep one for the vessel's file.

The death of a passenger must be noted on the passenger list with the cause of death. Of course your home office and the agent at the port of arrival should be notified immediately.

Before sailing from a foreign port it is advisable, if any of the passengers are aliens, that either you or the agent check their passports and visas. An alien passenger lacking a proper visa on his passport may be refused permission to land by the Immigration officer. This means that your company may have to return him to the port where he embarked and the vessel may be subject to a fine.

An alien passenger may be detained for other reasons than lack of a proper visa (see "Detainees" above). If the Immigration officer issues a detention order on the passenger, notify the company office or agent immediately. It may be necessary to employ a guard to see that the detained passenger remains on board.

STOWAWAYS

Stowaways are a nuisance, a source of much trouble when found, and a source of danger to the vessel when not found. Stowaways in various parts of vessels have been the cause of fires due to careless smoking. Some, with every intention of enjoying the trip, have been found equipped with cooking gear and a supply of candles, matches, and several decks of playing cards. Stowaways hiding in the holds have been injured in various ways and have had to be hospitalized on arrival in port, at the expense of the shipowner. If aliens, they must be sent back to the country they came from, also at the company's expense. All of this points up the importance of thoroughly searching the vessel for stowaways.

Every possible precaution should be taken to prevent stowaways from taking passage on the vessel. If you are sailing from a port where you think stowaways are likely, you should have the vessel searched thoroughly before she leaves the dock and again right afterward. If a stowaway is found soon after leaving the dock he can be sent back with the pilot. If the vessel is only a few hours from the pilot station when the stowaway is found it may be worthwhile to return to the port where he boarded.

If, after all precautions have been taken, one or more stowaways are found—they often travel in pairs—treat them humanely but do not pamper them. Unfortunately, it is sometimes necessary in dealing with stowaways to use force either in self-defense or to subdue a recalcitrant one, especially when they are first discovered. However, the searchers should exercise great care to see that no unnecessary force is used on a stowaway. They will too often seize the chance to sue your company for injuries received.

Sometimes when a stowaway is found or makes his presence known after the vessel is at sea, the passengers and crew will take up a collection for him. You should not permit this—regardless of how harmless it may seem—it only encourages the person to try it again.

Notify your company as soon as possible if a stowaway is found. If you do not return the stowaway to the port at which he stowed away, notify your agent at the port of destination.

When bringing a stowaway into the United States, assemble all the details possible concerning him: name, nationality, and physical description. If possible, take a photograph of him. All his papers and other belongings should be taken and inventoried before a witness and given to the Immigration officer on arrival. Also attempt to learn if any help was given to the stowaway by crew, passengers, or longshoremen.

Upon approaching the U.S. coast and before picking up the pilot the stowaway should be locked up and precautions taken to make it impossible for him to get out through a porthole, kickout panel, or other means. This usually means posting a crewman on guard outside the room where the stowaway is held. Stowaways have been known to jump over the side and swim ashore when the vessel was near a coast or proceeding upriver. If a stowaway escapes from the vessel your company will still be held responsible and it will mean much paperwork for you. In all such instances you should immediately notify your office or agent in the port bound for, and on arrival give all papers you took from the stowaway to the Immigration boarding officer. In addition, prepare a statement for your company and for the Immigration officer, in case he should ask for it, explaining the precautions you took to prevent the stowaway from getting away.

When sending your arrival message, if not before, mention that you have a stowaway on board and on arrival the boarding officers should be told about any stowaways. Some forms you must fill out will require information about stowaways. In some ports the stowaway may be put in jail or may be held in detention by Immigration, all at the expense of your company. The Immigration officer may order the stowaway kept on board the vessel, in which case it is necessary to employ a guard all the time the vessel is in port. Stowaways have been known to escape from a vessel even with a guard on board. The vessel may be fined if a stowaway gets ashore.

If the stowaway is a U.S. citizen the Immigration officer will probably pass him but your company may want to file criminal charges. If he is a seaman the Coast Guard may be interested. At any rate, keep him locked up and under guard until you get instructions from your office as to what is to be done with him.

It is poor policy to let outside pressure from passengers, crew, or do-gooders on shore have any influence on your treatment of stowaways. Many persons, having no responsibility in the matter, may plead for the stowaway's release while the vessel is in port, especially if the room in which he is confined is close and the weather warm. All suggestions from outsiders should be referred to your company office or agent or to Immigration.

Federal law states that any person who stows away on board a vessel in a U.S. port, or any person who stows away on board a vessel in a foreign port and is found on board in a U.S. port, is subject to a fine of $1,000 or imprisonment for up to one year, or both.

Regulations of the Immigration and Naturalization Service are found in Title 8, *Code of Federal Regulations*. Federal laws pertaining to immigration are contained in Title 8, U.S. Code.

SEVEN

ACCOUNTING

Very few merchant vessels carry pursers these days. It is therefore necessary that the master, or an officer directed by the master, prepare the vessel's accounts—payrolls, wage vouchers, portage, etc. Regardless of who handles the accounts the master is responsible for their accuracy.

After the shipping articles have been opened, the names of the crew should be entered in the official logbook, the slop chest account book, and the payroll. It will make your job easier if the names are entered in the same sequence on each of these forms. Most masters enter the names on all forms in the same order as they appear on the shipping articles and the crew list.

ACCOUNTING FORMS

Various forms of payrolls and wage vouchers are used by different companies. All are substantially the same although some may have additional items, such as company insurance, union benefits, etc., which are to be deducted from the seaman's wages.

For accounting purposes you should have on board the following forms, books, and information:

1. Cash receipt book or similar form.
2. The port and date where each seaman was engaged and, if different, the port and date where he joined. This is necessary in case transportation must be paid.
3. W-4 forms showing Social Security numbers and tax exemptions claimed. Each crew member should fill out this form the day he joins. Be sure to have an ample supply of blank forms.
4. A sufficient stock of blank wage vouchers.
5. An ample supply of blank payrolls.
6. Pay scales showing wages, overtime rates, and any special payments that may be called for under union agreements.

7. Copies of union agreements and working rules with the latest amendments and clarifications.
8. Accounting instructions and a supply of any special forms required by your company.
9. Treasury Department Form 1078, Certificate of Alien Claiming Residence in the United States (Fig. 4).
10. An ample supply of overtime sheets for each department.
11. Several blank official logbooks.
12. If on foreign or intercoastal articles, the amount of any allotment for each man and when payable.
13. The current rate for Social Security (FICA) and the amount of income that is taxable.
14. The current tax rate for state unemployment insurance. This varies by state and is often changed. It is generally a small amount, payable to the state in which the vessel is registered.
15. Current tax withholding tables.
16. An ample supply of earnings statements or similar forms. This shows the total earnings, taxes and other deductions, and the balance due for each member of the crew. It is copied from the payroll and a copy is given to each man on payoff.
17. Subsistence and room allowance rates (board and lodging). These rates are usually on the pay scales and are always in the union agreements.
18. Amount of deductions for company insurance and other benefits.
19. Master's cash statement (portage) forms.
20. Slop chest statement and inventory forms.

Always make a copy of all completed accounting forms—papers, vouchers, letters written regarding any payment of wages, etc.—for the vessel's file. Include the name of the vessel, date, voyage number, and port on all forms and papers you make up.

ORDERING CASH

In order to give advances and to pay the crew off at the end of the voyage, you will need to have sufficient cash on hand. Your company will probably specify how cash is to be ordered, and possibly how much you are to carry. The maximum cash you are allowed may be limited by the company's insurance policy. Aboard the vessel, the combination to the safe should be known only to you. Some steamship companies keep the combination on file in the office; in that case you should instruct the chief officer that he can obtain the combination from the office by radio if you should become incapacitated.

When you order cash be sure to specify the breakdown, that is, how the total amount is to be apportioned among the various denominations of currency. At payoff time, when the crew members have a lot of money to carry home with them, they will want mostly large bills, fifties and hundreds. When you give an advance during the voyage they will want smaller bills, mostly twenties. A seaman going ashore after banking hours may find that no one will accept or change a hundred-dollar bill.

Money is generally delivered in a sealed bag. The usual procedure is for the master to break the seal, count the money, and sign the receipt in the presence of the delivery guard. The guard will want your signature on several copies of the receipt and will undoubtedly want each copy to be stamped with the ship's stamp. Get two copies of the receipt, one for your file and one to be sent to the company along with the master's cash statement.

It sometimes happens that the guard will not allow you to break the seal until after you sign the receipt. In this case you should insert the words "One bag said to contain" in front of the dollar amount on the receipt and make a note to the effect that you were not allowed to count the money. Count the money as soon as you have signed the receipt and the guard has turned the bag over to you, and report any discrepancies immediately.

ADVANCES (DRAWS)

By law each crew member is entitled to an advance once on every entry into port, but only when the vessel is there to load or discharge cargo, and not more than once in every five days. However, union agreements may call for an advance every so many days regardless of why or how long the vessel is in port.

In practice there is no reason to restrict the crew to only one draw during an extended stay in port or to limit draws only to ports where cargo is to be worked; such a policy would certainly result in hard feelings between the master and the crew. Most masters will give an advance every five days or every week during a long port stay.

The seaman is entitled by law to draw half of the balance of his earned wages that remains unpaid. Most companies allow the seaman to draw the entire balance of his earned wages, less deductions. For obvious reasons it is poor policy to allow a seaman to draw all of his gross wages before deductions or to overdraw. In fact, technically it is illegal to advance a seaman wages that he has not yet earned (Title 46, U.S. Code, Sections 10314 and 10505).

Violating the law governing advances is punishable by a $500 civil fine. In addition, federal law states that "A payment made in violation of this subsection does not relieve the vessel or the master from the duty to pay all wages after they have been earned." In other words, in theory at least, a seaman who was allowed to draw wages that he had not yet earned could claim payment of the same wages again after they had been earned. Nevertheless, seamen will sometimes ask to overdraw and it is common practice with some masters to allow a man to overdraw in special circumstances.

Bear in mind that before a seaman is entitled to an advance he should have earned at least the amount necessary for paying the next allotment, if any, and previous advances, slops, taxes, and other deductions. If you allow a seaman to overdraw and he misses the sailing, you may find yourself in the hole for the amount overdrawn. It is, however, entirely your responsibility if, under special circumstances, you see fit to permit a seaman to overdraw.

If you make an error entering an advance in the official logbook, do not erase it or change it in any way; draw a line through the entire entry, make a new entry on the next line, and initial the correction. Always insert the date when the advance is made.

Union agreements usually call for the advance to be made in U.S. money. If foreign money is used and the agent does not supply you with a conversion table, make one up and post copies on the bulletin boards. The rate of exchange used should also be entered in the official log. Even though an advance may be made in foreign money, the crew should sign for the equivalent in U.S. dollars. In order to simplify the accounting as much as possible, it is much better to deal in U.S. money only.

PAYROLL

Wages in most shipping companies are now paid based on a 30-day month: a seaman's monthly salary divided by 30 is his daily pay. Under this most agreeable system there are actually 12 months and 5 days in each year. At least one company uses a 365-day year: the monthly salary multiplied by 12 and divided by 365 is the daily pay. The union agreements or company instructions will specify how daily pay is to be calculated.

On the voyage homeward, total up the advances for each man as shown in the official logbook. These should be double-checked and then entered in the proper column of the payroll. When the slop chest has been closed for the voyage, check and total the slop chest account book, if one was used. Do not destroy this book— keep it with the voyage file. Enter the totals in the proper column of the payroll and in the official log.

The crew are usually anxious to know how much is to be deducted for advances and slops at the end of the voyage. They will appreciate it if you issue the totals to them as soon as you have calculated them. Technically, when on a foreign or intercoastal voyage, federal law requires you to give each seaman an account of his wages and deductions forty-eight hours before he is paid off or discharged.

Start the payroll in ample time so that it can be completed before arriving at the payoff port. Early on the return voyage, or even on the outward voyage if time permits, the data that will not change should be entered: names, ratings, Social Security numbers, starting dates, wages per month, tax exemptions, and, when completed, advance, allotment, and slop chest amounts. These figures can be entered on a rough or pencil copy of the payroll, from which the required number of smooth copies are typed. The rough pencil copy, or one of the typed copies, is completed in pencil as soon as it is known when to close the payroll. This is generally midnight on the day of arrival.

It is preferable to complete a rough copy in pencil—there will probably be some erasures—and to transfer the figures to the original typed sheet after it is checked and balanced. Take care not to transpose any of the figures; this is a common error, easily made. Some companies may require several extra copies showing only the base wages earned by each man. These are for the unions in connection with welfare, pension, and vacation benefits. The extra copies may be carbon copies but they must be legible.

If the port of payoff is definitely known, you can estimate the day of arrival and, if time permits, make a payroll for that day, and for a day later, in case weather delays the vessel. These may be rough copies but both should be balanced; then, when you are sure of the arrival day, the figures from whichever copy is to be used can be entered on the original typed payroll. Again, care should be taken to avoid transposing any of the figures. This method, although it involves some extra work, will save time eventually and avoids the rush of making up a new payroll if the vessel is delayed.

Before balancing the payroll all the figures should be checked and rechecked. The Social Security numbers and tax exemptions should be checked against the W-4 forms. The overtime should be carefully checked and, if there are several sheets per man, the sheets for each man should be stapled or clipped together.

Some companies require that the payrolls be entirely typed—a lengthy job. Others, more practical, require that only a few items be typed, such as names and ratings, Social Security numbers, starting dates, and base pay. Needless to say, the payroll, if typed, should be checked before typing and checked against the rough copy after typing. Some companies do not use a master payroll at all. Instead, only individual wage vouchers are submitted.

The Change List

It may be necessary to make up a change list after the payroll is completed. A commonly used change list, for the deck department, is shown in Fig. 20. Other forms may be used. The total for each man is broken down to the highest denomination of bills and change, as shown. When completed, the lists should be balanced.

Some masters adjust the amount of taxes withheld so that the balance due each man comes out to an even dollar amount so that there is no need to worry about small change. (There is no objection to this procedure, since it can be accomplished by an adjustment of fifty cents or less.) On a large payoff, these masters may even adjust the amount to the nearest twenty or fifty dollars.

Port Payroll

The port payroll, if used, covers the period between paying off for the voyage just completed and opening articles for the next voyage. Discharges should be made up each time there is a payoff in port. Most masters sign on the men who will remain for the next voyage at the same time they sign off the crew for the completed voyage. This eliminates the necessity for a port payroll.

OVERTIME

Overtime Sheets

Overtime support sheets issued by the different companies vary in form but all require essentially the same data. The department heads should check and correct the overtime sheets for their departments every week or so. Be sure there is no overlapping of hours except as permitted by the union agreement, that times and total hours are correct, that work performed is clearly described, and that the overtime claimed is according to the agreement.

Many of the crew will have several overtime sheets. When a sheet is full it should be totaled and double-checked. If the total on one sheet is carried forward to the next sheet, that fact should be noted on both sheets. When a man has more than one sheet, his sheets should be numbered and stapled or clipped together.

Disputed Overtime

If a man turns in overtime that you do not believe is payable you should dispute it by drawing a single line through the disputed entry and writing a brief note explaining why it is disputed. Do not obliterate the entry or make it unreadable. Do not include the disputed overtime in the total hours and do not pay it. The seaman's copy of the overtime sheet is his proof that he submitted a claim for the overtime in case he later wants to file a grievance against the company.

Keep in mind that just because a seaman has written in overtime does not mean that it should automatically be paid. Some seamen do not know their agreement very well and will claim overtime when it is not payable, and occasionally you may even encounter a seaman who is actually trying to cheat.

Extra Earnings on Overtime Sheets

Extra earnings, such as division of wages, extra meals, passenger money, etc., are shown on the payroll or wage vouchers if columns are provided. If there are no columns for these payments, they should be itemized on the overtime sheets. For example:

Totals:	Straight overtime (3 sheets)	$1,025.58
	Extra meals, see letter	14.50
	Passenger money, see letter	52.50
	Division of wages, see letter	138.25
	Grand Total	$1,230.83

The total should then be entered in the overtime column of the payroll.

All overtime appearing on the payroll or on a voucher should be supported by overtime sheets, each sheet signed by the seaman, his department head, and you.

OTHER PAYMENTS

War Zone Bonuses

The payroll may have a column for bonuses. If there is more than one, the bonuses may be grouped together and the total sum per man entered. All details should be given in a supporting letter. War zone bonuses are sometimes broken down as follows:

Area Bonus. This bonus calls for wages to be increased, usually by a given percentage, for every day that the vessel is within a war zone. The war zone is usually defined by agreement between the steamship company and the crew unions. Area bonuses have been as high as 100 percent.

Harbor Attack Bonus. This is a payment, provided for under some agreements, whereby the crew will receive an additional sum if they are in a harbor where any vessel is attacked. This is in addition to the area bonus.

Vessel Attack Bonus. This bonus is paid if the vessel itself is attacked. It is either in addition to, or higher than, the harbor attack bonus.

Ammunition Bonus

This generally calls for an extra payment to the crew for each day that the vessel is carrying more than a specified amount of ammunition. The supporting letter should give the dates the ammunition cargo was loaded and discharged, the amount of ammunition (usually in tons), and the number of days it was aboard.

Promotions

If a man is promoted during the voyage he should appear on the payroll twice, once for each rating. It will be easiest for both you and the accounting department if the two entries appear on adjacent lines on the payroll. Dates must not overlap, either on the payroll or on his discharges.

Non-Watch Pay

Non-watch pay should not be added to the base pay but should be entered in a separate column unless instructions from your company state otherwise.

Linen Money

Some union agreements require the crew to be paid a certain amount when they are not issued clean linen as often as stipulated in the agreement. This sometimes occurs when the vessel, on a long voyage, calls at ports that do not have adequate laundry facilities. This payment is seldom necessary if a little foresight is used. If it must be made, a supporting letter may be required to explain the circumstances. Be sure to name the ports where the laundry could not be done or give any other reason why the clean linen was not issued.

Division of Wages for Missing Men

When a member of the crew is missing—because he failed to join on sailing, or he was hospitalized, or the required rating could not be obtained, or he is on board but is ill and laid up—the men who temporarily take over his work either divide his wages or receive overtime. This most often affects the steward's department or the watch-standing licensed officers. If an unlicensed watch stander is missing or laid up, a day worker is usually put on watch and no division of wages is necessary. This, or course, should be in accordance with any union agreement. Write a supporting letter explaining the facts, showing the man's wages per month, the number of days he was missing (with dates), to whom the money was paid, and the amount. It can be paid either by voucher or added to the overtime of the men involved. If the latter, it should be explained on the overtime sheet.

Passenger Money

Some dry cargo vessels carry up to twelve passengers. The union agreement may require that one or two passenger utility men be added to the steward's department according to the number of passengers on board for the voyage, or that a sum of money, at so much per passenger per day, be paid to the men in the steward's department who attend the passengers. As a general rule, only one passenger utility man is carried and if the agreement calls for an additional man, the company, in lieu of taking on a second man, will divide the required sum among the men in the crew who are sharing the work.

The section of the agreement pertaining to passenger money should be thoroughly understood. Note in the logbook the dates, ports, and times the passengers embark and disembark. A supporting letter should show the number of passengers carried, the times, dates, and ports of embarkation and debarkation, rate per day per passenger, number of days on board, total amount payable, names and ratings of the men, and the amount of money each will receive. This sum can be paid by voucher or added to the overtime if a column is not provided on the payroll. If the latter, it should be explained on the overtime sheet.

Extra Meals Served

The union agreement may specify that men in the steward's department who prepare and serve meals to persons other than the crew will receive an extra payment of so much for each such meal served. The procedure varies in different companies but definite instructions are generally issued regarding extra meals. A supporting letter is required to show the total number of extra meals served, the charge per meal, and the total amount, as well as the names and ratings of the men who share the amount and how much each man will get. Some companies issue meal chits that must be signed by the person receiving the meal, in which case a supporting letter is usually not necessary. These amounts can be placed in a spare column on the payroll, or added to the overtime sheet with an explanatory note.

Penalty Cargo

The agreement may call for the crew to receive extra pay if the vessel is carrying a particularly noxious or dirty cargo. These penalty cargoes are listed in the union agreements. The payroll may have a column for this; otherwise, a supporting letter is required showing the date the cargo was loaded, type of cargo, the date and port at which it was discharged, and the total number of days it was on board. This information should also be in the logbook.

Dirty Work

This is an extra payment to crew members who are required to perform especially unpleasant work such as entering boilers, working on sewage disposal machines, etc. Jobs which qualify as dirty work, if any, will be specified in the applicable agreement.

Seaman Receiving Pay of Higher Rating

The union agreement may stipulate that under certain circumstances a crew member will receive the pay for the next higher rating instead of his usual pay rate. For example, when more than a certain number of passengers are carried on a cargo vessel the second cook might receive chief cook's pay during the time the passengers are on board. The difference may be entered on a separate line of the payroll, paid by voucher, or added to the man's overtime, with an explanatory note, depending upon company instructions. You may have to write a supporting letter giving the number of passengers carried, the days they were on board, and the dates of embarking and disembarking.

This is not a promotion as such and need not be entered in the official log. Usually the agreement provides that the man is not actually being promoted to the higher rating, but only that he is receiving the higher rate of pay. Abide by the union agreement or company instructions if different from the above.

PAYROLL DEDUCTIONS

Federal Withholding Tax

This tax is paid by all employees. It is levied on all wages, overtime, and extras—such as bonuses of all kinds, extra meals money, passenger money, and wages for missing men—but not on transportation or subsistence (while on drydock, for example).

The W-4 Form (Employee's Withholding Allowance Certificate). A column on the payroll and a space on the voucher will be headed "Tax Exemptions" or "Tax Status" or the like. The number of tax exemptions and the marital status claimed by the crew members on the W-4 form are entered here. Check to see that the W-4 forms have been properly made out. If a crew member is incapable of writing legibly it will save time and trouble to have the form typed and then signed by the man. Be sure the date and signature are on each form.

A resident alien fills out the W-4 form and also Treasury Form 1078, Certificate of Alien Claiming Residence in the United States, which should be attached to the W-4 form. The resident alien must have a registration card showing proof of legal entry into the United States. Merely claiming residence or showing that he had previously paid full taxes is not enough.

State Unemployment Insurance

An unemployment tax up to a stated amount is paid by each member of the crew, including all aliens. This tax is levied by the state in which the vessel is registered but the entire crew pays this tax regardless of where their homes might be. For example, a seaman living in New York, employed on a vessel that sails between New York and Texas but is registered in Wilmington, Delaware, will pay the unemployment tax of Delaware. The tax varies in different states and the amount is changed from time to time. It is levied on the same amounts that are used in computing Social Security deductions as shown on the payroll or voucher.

Social Security (FICA)

Social Security deductions are levied on all wages, overtime, and other payments except subsistence and lodging.

As seamen often change vessels and companies, and Social Security is deducted for each voyage, up to the maximum amount, it follows that many seamen will overpay their Social Security contribution. A man who changes vessels each voyage, with FICA deducted from his earnings on each vessel, may have paid much more than the required amount by the end of the year. In this case he will apply the amount of overpayment against his federal income tax. The total amount of Social Security paid each year will appear on the W-2 form, Wage and Tax Statement, which is issued by all companies to their employees. Men who change companies often will receive a number of W-2 forms.

Some companies periodically issue a form showing, as far as can be ascertained, the amount of Social Security and unemployment insurance tax already paid by each member of the crew while working for that company. If this information is not available for any member of the crew you must assume that the full amount of taxes is due. Once a crew member has paid the maximum tax due, no further deductions are made.

While working for your company the employee does not receive any credit for Social Security that he paid while he was employed by another company. He is liable for the maximum Social Security amount on wages earned while employed by your company regardless of what may have been withheld by another company. Any excess withheld will be applied to his income tax as explained above.

VOUCHERS

Transportation

Transportation is usually paid and signed for on a voucher separate from the payroll; a few companies include a column for transportation on the payroll. Travel fares are not subject to withholding, Social Security, or unemployment insurance taxes. The usual procedure when transportation is payable is to have your agent ascertain the fare from the ticket office, and also the length of time the journey will take—the last to determine the pay and subsistence the man will receive. Wages, subsistence, and transportation are all paid at the same time.

If the agent pays for the transportation, he may want a travel voucher or a letter from you authorizing him to charge the transportation to your company.

Be sure you clearly understand the transportation clauses of any applicable union agreement and keep an accurate list of where each man joined the vessel. In some companies you will not pay the men transportation; instead your company or the agent will make travel arrangements for the men and will pay the fares directly to the airline or other carrier.

Vouchers Not Paid by Master

When a member of the crew fails to join for any reason, a wage voucher is made up for him and either given to the agent or forwarded to the accounting office, depending upon your company's instructions. Do not give any money to the agent—only the voucher, which should show that the balance has not been paid and is due the seaman. However, you should sign the voucher authorizing payment.

If the voucher is given to the agent, you should instruct him, in case the man turns up after the ship sails, either to have the seaman sign the voucher as a receipt and to pay him his wages, or to give the seaman the voucher to present to the steamship company for payment. Which procedure is used will depend on your company's policy. Be sure to keep several copies, including one for the vessel's file.

Wage Vouchers

When a member of the crew is paid off before the end of the voyage, he is usually paid by wage voucher. Like other forms, these vouchers will vary with the different companies, but the items are more or less the same. If a crew member is paid off after signing on, he is paid by voucher, but his name should be included in the payroll and a note stating that he was paid by voucher inserted in the signature column. Vouchers used in paying off men not on articles (such as men who have quit before signing on), vouchers for overtime which was disputed but has since been determined to be payable, and any other such, are called miscellaneous vouchers. Keep all paid vouchers in a safe place.

Make a sufficient number of copies to provide one for the seaman, one for the vessel's file, and the required number—usually no more than two—for the accounting department. When a man has been paid off in a foreign port, regardless of the reason, the U.S. consul will require the figures shown on the voucher.

If a man fails to join in any port and the vessel sails before the vouchers can be made up, they should be sent back to the agent by pilot, if possible. Otherwise, advise the agent by radio how much the man has coming to him and stop his allotment if he has one. Be sure to make an entry in the official log of any such failure to join, regardless of the reasons. Include the man's wage account in your entry.

The voucher should include overtime but not disputed overtime. The latter should not be paid until settled at the port of payoff or by whatever procedure your company uses. When the vessel arrives at her next port, send the agent copies of the voucher if they have not already been sent back by pilot. Be sure you have the W-4 form, which should have been made up when the man shipped. It could be very disconcerting to find, after a man has failed to join, that you did not have a W-4 form for him. If this should happen, it would be necessary to give "1" as the number of exemptions claimed. The man's Social Security number would be on the articles and on the crew data card, which should also include the exemptions, but if the articles have not been opened and a data card has not been made up, write "Not available" in the space provided for the Social Security number.

Make it a habit to file vouchers as soon as they are paid. A lost or misplaced voucher may be your loss.

Make up a rough list of miscellaneous vouchers and add new vouchers to it as they are made up. This list should show the voucher number, name and rating of the man, and balance paid him. These vouchers should be numbered consecutively, and on your cash statement, or settlement, shown as: "Miscellaneous vouchers, numbers ____ to ____ as per attached list."

Vouchers shown on the payroll for men who have signed articles but were paid off and signed off, or who failed to join before the end of the voyage, need not be included in the above list, but a separate list of such vouchers should be made for your own protection.

The miscellaneous voucher list can be made up as follows:

SS Seven Seas   Voy. 95
MISCELLANEOUS VOUCHERS

No.	Name	Rate	Balance Paid
1.	John Doe	AB	$1,229.00
2.	Joe Slow	OS	528.00
3.	W. T. Door	Oiler	671.20
4.	B. Black	Oiler	1,232.00
5.	I. White	Bosun	835.30
6.	U. Look	OS	497.90
7.	W. Peel	3rd Ck	104.90
8.	E. Slopp	3rd Mate	1,083.80
9.	C. Break	OS	677.00
10.	N. Good	AB	823.20
		Total	$7,682.30

THE SLOP CHEST

Federal law requires that every vessel on a foreign or intercoastal voyage, except a voyage to Canada, Bermuda, the West Indies, Mexico, or Central America, must have a slop chest. The slop chest must contain sufficient clothing for the voyage for each seaman, including boots or shoes, hats or caps, underclothing, outer clothing, foul weather clothing, a complete supply of tobacco and blankets, and everything necessary for the wear of a seaman (46 USC 11103).

When taking command of a vessel in operation, you should have the slop chest inventoried, if possible, before you permit anything to be sold.

When coastwise, most masters use a plain ruled notebook for a slop chest account book and have each seaman sign for his slop chest purchases when they are made. At payoff, the total of each man's purchases are entered on the payroll and on his wage voucher.

On a foreign voyage the slops should be entered and signed for in the official log. Some masters have the crew sign a slop chest account book for purchases during the voyage and then have them sign the official log only for the total at payoff. Other masters have the crew initial the official log for each slop chest purchase at the time it is made and also sign for the total at payoff. The latter is probably the better procedure. Whether in a slop chest account book or in the official log, all sales to a crew member should be initialed by him at the time of the sale.

The above applies only to slops that you sell on credit. A seaman need not sign for his purchase if he pays cash because you will not be deducting the purchase price from his wages.

It seems inevitable that there will always be a shortage in the slop chest at the end of the voyage. Usually the shortage is small and due, most likely, to failure to enter a sale in the account book. When slop chest supplies are received they should be checked carefully, although it is seldom that an error is made at that time. If a shortage is found when supplies are received, it should be reported and noted on the delivery invoice.

The slop chest form—it varies in different companies—shows the quantity and cost of merchandise on hand from the previous voyage, received during the present voyage, sold during the voyage and the price received, and on board at the end of the voyage. You probably won't have a chance to go over it or check it before sailing but it should be checked at the first opportunity.

Make up several price lists and post them on the bulletin boards and in the slop chest room. Also put a copy in the slop chest account book. If possible keep a running inventory and, on a long voyage, check the slop chest several times against the running inventory.

After the slop chest has been opened for the last time on the voyage, take a complete inventory, which should balance with the running inventory. Check the account book for overcharges and undercharges, after which enter the accounts on the payroll.

Never charge the crew more than the amount shown on the slop chest price list regardless of how large a shortage you run into. Federal law requires that slop chest goods be sold to the crew at a profit not exceeding 10 percent of the reasonable wholesale value at the port where the voyage began.

If any profit is taken, it is distributed in accordance with company policy. The profit may be retained by the company, kept by the master as compensation for handling the slop chest, kept by another officer who handles the slop chest, donated to a crew recreation fund, etc. If your company has no policy, it is recommended that you sell slop chest goods at cost and dispense with the profit. The bookkeeping will be simpler and the crew will appreciate it. Slop chest profits are usually very small anyway.

MASTER'S EXPENSES

Keep an accurate account of all money you pay out on company business. Do not rely on memory—get receipts wherever possible and make notes when you can't get receipts. Enter the total on the cash statement and send the original along with the statement. Retain a copy of the completed expense account for your file. Master's expenses should be kept to a minimum.

For accounting purposes, most companies would prefer that you requisition supplies through the company or agent rather than purchase them yourself. Occasionally you may find that time does not permit going through the normal procedure, for example if the vessel has just received a change of orders and is about to sail and you must buy charts for the voyage. Some companies give the master a fixed monthly allowance that he is permitted to spend on incidentals, without prior office approval.

MASTER'S CASH STATEMENT (PORTAGE)

The master's cash statement, also known as the portage, is a statement showing all cash transactions for the payroll period. It includes the beginning balance, all cash received, all cash paid out, and the ending balance. You should start a rough cash statement at the beginning of the pay period and record all receipts and expenditures as soon as they are made. This will avoid any cash transactions being forgotten. Needless to say, the cash statement must agree exactly with the actual cash on hand or you will be liable for any shortage. At the end of the pay period the final copy can be typed from the rough record.

Whenever there is a change of masters, the outgoing master should prepare a cash statement in quadruplicate. The outgoing master and the incoming master each sign the statement after the new master has counted the cash and verified that the amount on hand is correct. One copy goes to each master for his personal records, one goes into the vessel's file, and one goes to the accounting department at the end of the accounting period.

All of this chapter applies to the traditional method of paying seamen, still practiced by most shipping companies. A few companies are experimenting with new systems similar to shoreside operations whereby the men are paid by check from the home office. In these cases, of course, your company instructions should be followed.

EIGHT

OCEAN BILL OF LADING

The ocean bill of lading, abbreviated "B/L," is a very important commercial shipping document. It is the basic document between shipper and carrier, and between shipper and consignee.

Like many commercial documents, the B/L is usually printed in such small type that it is difficult and tedious to read all the terms and conditions. Nevertheless, you should read carefully the B/L issued by your company.

When a cargo is loaded on a vessel, a B/L is issued by the company. Your copies, which are nonnegotiable, will list the cargo loaded on your vessel, with the weights, description, loading ports, and destination ports. If there is any discrepancy between what is shown on the B/L and the cargo manifest or cargo plan, the information shown on the B/L should be used as it is more likely to be correct.

The signed B/L serves several definite purposes in connection with the carriage of goods by sea:

1. It is the final signed receipt from the carrier, both for the goods shown on the B/L and for the condition of those goods. In the United States, both the Harter Act of 1893 and the Carriage of Goods by Sea Act of 1936 (COGSA) require the carrier to issue a B/L as receipt for the goods.
2. It describes the nature, quantity, weight, and packaging of the goods, and any identifying marks or numbers.
3. It represents the contract of carriage (affreightment), defining the terms and conditions of carriage between the carrier and the shipper.
4. It is the document of title for the goods shown on the B/L. If it is made out "To Order" it is negotiable and the goods shown on the B/L may be sold by endorsing and delivering the B/L to another party.

5. It determines the respective responsibilities of the carrier, the shipper, and the consignee. It enables the shipper to arrange insurance against damage or loss for which the carrier is not liable.

KINDS OF BILLS OF LADING

Straight Bill of Lading

This is a B/L showing the goods consigned directly to a person or firm. It is stamped to indicate that it is a "straight bill of lading not negotiable." The goods will be delivered only to the person or company named in the B/L.

To Order Bill of Lading

This type of B/L is negotiable and, because it permits full flexibility of negotiation, is the most common type. It is made "To Order" or "Order Of" a person, bank, or firm, or to order of the shipper so that he may retain title to the goods. As it is negotiable, the title to the goods described on the B/L may be transferred to another party by endorsement of the signed set of originals. A negotiable B/L may be resold several times, each succeeding holder becoming the owner of the goods described in the B/L.

The final holder of the original B/L, or his agent on his order, may claim the cargo at the port of destination by surrendering the B/L. He is entitled to receive the cargo in the condition noted on the B/L and, in some instances, must pay any freight due the carrier. When one of the original bills of lading is presented to claim the cargo, the others become void. This is stated on the B/L.

Through Bill of Lading

A through B/L is issued when goods are to be sent by two or more carriers and the shipper wishes the first carrier to make arrangements for the complete journey. The first carrier may issue a through B/L and undertake to make all the arrangements necessary to get the goods to their final destination. A through bill of lading may be either straight or to order.

The cargo, having been handled by different carriers, should be checked for possible damage or shortage when received and before it is delivered to an on-carrier. The through B/L should contain a clause that limits the issuing carrier's liability for damage to the cargo to the period that the cargo is actually under his control. His liability should end when the cargo is passed on to the next carrier. If there is no such clause, the carrier issuing the through B/L could conceivably be held responsible for damage occurring during any part of the cargo movement.

If your vessel is an on-carrier under a through B/L, the previous carrier should be notified, in writing, of any damage or shortage, and such exceptions should also be entered in the logbook and on the exception lists. Cargo carried on board your vessel should be carefully checked on discharge, any damage or shortage noted, and a receipt requested. If the cargo is in good shape, the receipt should so state. The on-carrier, especially if it is a different company, may find many things wrong with the cargo.

COPIES OF BILLS OF LADING

It is common practice to issue multiple original bills of lading, often three, for the same cargo. In such a case, the B/L will contain a stipulation such as: "In witness whereof the master has signed three bills of lading, all of this tenor and date, one of which being accomplished, the others stand void." All of the originals are negotiable, but the cargo will be delivered to the person who first presents a valid B/L at the discharge port. This is not so that the shipper can sell the same cargo to more than one person; it is to ensure against any possible unreliability of mail service. Usually several originals will be sent to the same consignee by different means.

In addition to the original B/L, a great number of nonnegotiable copies may also be issued. The number varies greatly according to company and trade. These copies, marked "Nonnegotiable" on their faces, are distributed to interested parties. Make certain that you receive copies of all bills of lading covering the cargo on board. Copies may be sent to company agents or consignees at ports of discharge via "ship mail," that is, in envelopes containing cargo papers given to you before sailing. The envelopes bear the names of the discharge ports and may be marked with the agent's or consignee's name. Do not fail to turn these envelopes over to the agent or appropriate person at the various ports.

UNCLEAN BILL OF LADING

A B/L bearing exceptions of any kind is termed "unclean," "dirty," or "foul," or in some ports it may be called a "claused" B/L. In this book it will be referred to as an "unclean" B/L.

An unclean B/L might not be accepted by banks or others when financial transactions concerning the B/L are involved. The bank sometimes requires that the shipper furnish a letter of guarantee holding the bank or other party free from any claims arising from the B/L on which such exceptions are noted. The shipper may be reluctant to do this. Sometimes a letter of indemnity is offered to the carrier, promising to indemnify the carrier for any claims if it will omit the exceptions and issue a clean B/L. If you are ever asked to accept a letter of indemnity in lieu of noting exceptions on the B/L, you should refuse and refer the other party to your office. The decision to accept such a letter is solely the responsibility of the company (see "Letter of Indemnity," below).

If you know the B/L to be incorrect, do not sign it "under protest" unless your company so instructs you. Your signature on a B/L usually means that you have accepted the B/L as correct; to sign under protest puts you in the position of both accepting and disputing the same document. If you believe the B/L to be in error, there is nothing that requires you to sign it. You should insist that the true figures be determined and the B/L corrected. To avoid delay to the vessel, your office may instruct you to sign (possibly under protest) a B/L that you know to be inaccurate. In such a case, abide by the instructions from your company; responsibility for the consequences is theirs.

LETTER OF INDEMNITY

Shippers dislike unclean bills of lading because it is difficult to clear them through a bank, or make other financial negotiations, or arrange the kind of insurance that is so necessary in foreign commerce. Moreover, an unclean B/L is difficult to sell to another party.

This has caused the occasional practice among shippers of requesting a clean B/L in place of an unclean one in return for a letter of indemnity given to the company, agent, or master. The letter states that in consideration of being given a clean B/L, the shipper indemnifies the carrier and the master against all risks and claims arising from the exceptions that made the B/L unclean. This practice, although sometimes used, has been said to be legally wrong. Unless financial or other adequate security is provided with the letter, there is no assurance, other than the good faith of the shipper, that your company will not suffer a loss if the shipper sells the B/L to another party, thereby passing title to the cargo to that party, who may not have been told about the exceptions and the letter of indemnity.

The final holder of the B/L, as owner of the goods shown thereon, would hold your company responsible under the terms expressed in the B/L and, in the absence of any exception, would expect the goods to be delivered in the condition described on the B/L. A master who signs a B/L for so many cases "in good order and condition" when he knows (having accepted a letter of indemnity) that this is untrue, issues a commercial document with a gross misstatement on it, which may be considered nothing less than fraud. If, in the event a suit is brought against his company, he produces the letter of indemnity, he will probably be told in no uncertain terms exactly what he can do with it.

The acceptance of such a letter of indemnity is entirely up to your company or charterer. If in a port where you sign bills of lading such a letter is offered to you, you should refuse it, as acceptance would be committing your company to an agreement which might cause it much trouble and expense. If your agent or the shipper insists that you accept the letter, then notify your home office, make certain they know all the facts, and get their approval. A long-distance telephone call or radio message will be much cheaper than a heavy claim. If the decision is left to you, turn it down.

MASTER'S SIGNATURE ON BILLS OF LADING

In the liner trades it is very seldom anymore that the master must personally sign the B/L. In modern shipping practice it is customary for an official in the company freight department to sign the B/L for the master. However, when carrying bulk cargoes it may be required that the master sign the B/L. There may be a great many copies, all for the same cargo, and they are generally brought on board to be signed only a few minutes before sailing.

In such cases it is sometimes permitted to use a rubber stamp signature on the nonnegotiable copies after signing a number of them by hand. Any changes in these bills of lading, typed or written, must be initialed by the master on each B/L and he may be required to sign in full a few of the bills of lading where the changes have been made.

When under time charter, the charterer may have you sign a letter prepared and presented by him, authorizing him or his agents to sign a B/L on your behalf. An example of such a letter follows.

SS *Seven Seas*

World Shipping Co.
New York, NY

Dear Sirs,
    You, as agents, general agents, and all sub-agents appointed by you
at all the vessel's ports of call, are hereby authorized to enter into and
do all things necessary for the proper execution and signing on my
behalf, in my name, and as my agent, Bills of Lading, Passenger
Tickets, and other documents for the carriage of goods and passengers on board the SS *Seven Seas*.
    This authorization shall remain in full force and effect as long as
you continue to act as agent for the above vessel, unless sooner
terminated by me or whomever shall go for master. Date _____

Yours truly,

Master

Sometimes at tanker terminals a blank B/L is brought aboard
for your signature soon after docking and before loading has
begun, much less finished. The terminal personnel may tell you
that this is to avoid delay to the vessel in that they can fill in the
figures after the ship has sailed and not have to hold the vessel up
while shore figures are calculated. This is accepted practice in some
companies where the vessel and the terminal are both owned by the
same company or where the vessel is time chartered to a company
that also owns the terminal. Be sure to verify with the shipowner or
time charterer, as appropriate, whether or not this practice is acceptable. In all other cases you should refuse unless your company
instructs you otherwise. Remember that when you sign the B/L you
are acknowledging receipt of the cargo listed on the B/L. This could
prove embarrassing if the terminal short-loads the vessel and then
presents a B/L with your signature on it showing that a full cargo
was delivered.
    With packaged goods it is possible to ascertain by actual count
exactly how many packages of each type of cargo are on board. This
is not true of bulk cargoes where the tonnage of cargo on board
must be determined by deadweight survey or, in the case of tankers,
by ullaging. In these cases there will always be a difference between
ship figures and shore figures. Most steamship companies instruct
their masters to dispute the B/L only if the difference between ship

and shore figures exceeds a certain allowance, usually one-half or one-quarter of one percent.

PARCELS OF HIGH VALUE

If you must sign a B/L for very valuable parcels whose contents are shown on the B/L but which cannot be readily verified, have one of your officers check the packages to see that they are intact and have not been tampered with. If possible, the weights should also be checked. The writer recalls one instance where ten cases, rebanded and clean, described on the B/L as containing 100 boxes of nylon hose, were found, when opened on the dock at the discharge port, to be full of neatly folded and boxed pieces of burlap—and old burlap at that! Before signing the B/L you should get a report from the officer making the check. The B/L may be designated as "said to contain" certain articles.

As a matter of caution and good practice, all packages of high value should be checked regardless of who signs the B/L.

In preparing and signing a B/L in any port, you should exercise the utmost care in order to protect the best interests of your company. The quantity or count as shown on the dock receipt or mate's receipt should be the same as that supplied by the shipper, who may have prepared the B/L himself. If the count or weight appears to be less than that given by the shipper, have him add a note to the B/L, "____ cases (or other unit) in dispute, if on board to be delivered," and make a note in the logbook. Make certain that any other exceptions are noted on the B/L. When the B/L is signed and given to the shipper, it is an acknowledgment that the goods shown on the B/L have been received in the quantity and condition stated, which, if no exceptions are noted, may be described as "In good order and condition."

In some ports the shipper may flatly refuse to make, or allow you to make, any exceptions on the B/L. Do not sign the B/L in such a case until you have referred the matter to your office for resolution.

If the vessel is in a foreign port and you are requested to sign a B/L written in a language you do not understand, have the B/L translated, in writing, by your agent, or better still, by the consul's office or someone else not interested in the cargo. A supply of your company's B/L blanks should be kept on board and these should be used whenever possible. In the event of a claim regarding the cargo, the B/L with its notes of exceptions, or lack of them, and its description of the cargo may be of major importance.

When signing a B/L (or documents of any kind) you should be sure, before committing your company to any agreement, that everything is in order and that you know what you are signing. Do not sign a postdated or antedated B/L, or an unclean B/L as a clean one, even if a letter of indemnity is offered, unless so instructed by your company.

CHARTER PARTIES

The B/L, as noted before, is a contract of carriage for the cargo described. If your vessel is chartered, then the charter party, particularly if it is a voyage charter, will also contain clauses that constitute a contract of carriage. If a vessel is chartered to load a cargo, and a B/L is then issued for that cargo, the B/L does not create a new contract and does not end the contract created by the charter party.

Your company will certainly want the charter party to take precedence and they may instruct you to insert a note in the B/L stating that the B/L is issued under the terms of a charter party and that the charter party is to take precedence. If there is a contrary clause in the B/L, one stating that the B/L is to take precedence, you should refer the matter to your company for clarification before signing the B/L.

NINE

CHARTER PARTIES

A charter party is a contract by which a shipowner agrees to lease, and the charterer agrees to hire, a vessel or all or part of her cargo space, on terms and conditions set forth in the charter party. Unless expressly prohibited from doing so by the terms of the charter party, the charterer is generally allowed to enter into subcontracts with other charterers.

The main types of charter parties are bareboat charter party (also known as a demise charter), time charter party, and voyage charter party. There are several general forms of each of these main types of charter party, and many modifications of those general forms.

As master you should be familiar with the basic characteristics of the different types of charter parties. Charter party agreements are often negotiated by telex messages between the shipowner and the charterer or broker while the ship is at sea; you may find yourself having to report to the charterer or his agent at the first loading port before a copy of the charter party can be sent aboard. Unfortunately, many steamship companies are careless about informing their masters of the provisions of particular charter parties, especially if the vessel is in the tramp trade and is making a series of voyage charters for different charterers.

Most charter parties are preprinted documents with blanks for the shipowner and charterer to fill in particulars, such as the name, dimensions, and capacity of the vessel; demurrage rate; laytime allowed; freight or hire rate; etc. Shippers of large quantities of bulk cargo have charter parties with special titles such as "Fosfo," "Baltimore Grain Charter Party," "Gencon," "Intertanktime," etc.

Shipowners and charterers may, and in fact usually do, have clauses added, deleted, or amended to suit their particular needs. These added or amended clauses may be handwritten or typed in, and they are especially important. In cases of lawsuits where a preprinted clause and an added clause conflict, the courts generally hold that the added clause takes precedence.

If your vessel is chartered, it is of the utmost importance that you read the charter party carefully, especially the added clauses, until it is thoroughly understood—no mean feat, considering that charter parties can be many pages of fine-print legalese. You should see that your officers, especially the chief officer, are informed of the more important provisions of the charter party, and it can do no harm to allow them to read it as a matter of information and instruction.

Make notes of clauses referring to time allotted for loading or discharging and compute the laytime allowed. Be sure to note the units given in the charter party—the clause on loading may specify so many long tons (2,240 pounds) or short tons (2,000 pounds) per day and the clause on discharging may specify metric tons (2,204.62 pounds), or vice versa. The correct unit must be shown on the time sheet.

The important clauses may be checkmarked for quick reference. If any refer to dates of notification of ETA to consignee, charterer, or charterer's agent, make a note of the day the message is to be sent and be sure to send it.

CHARTERER'S AGENTS AND CABLE ADDRESSES

If your ship is chartered you should try to obtain a complete list of the charterer's agents and their cable addresses for all ports the vessel is likely to make. Charterer's instructions should state the procedures for sending ETA's to the charterer or his agents. If no such instructions are available, the agent should be advised at least seventy-two hours before arrival.

BAREBOAT CHARTER PARTY

By this type of charter, the shipowner leases his entire vessel and the charterer has the responsibility of operating it as though it were his own. In other words, the charterer becomes a ship operator, but he does so using a vessel that he has rented, rather than by building or buying his own vessel. The charterer becomes the owner *pro hac vice* (owner for a time). The shipowner has, for the period covered by the charter party, relinquished control of his vessel. The charterer pays all expenses: fuel, stores, provisions, harbor dues, pilotage, etc., and he employs and pays the crew. There may, however, be a clause in the charter party that the master and the chief engineer must be approved by the shipowner.

The charterer is responsible for the upkeep, preservation, and safety of the vessel. Before delivery to the charterer the vessel is surveyed by representatives of both parties, and the same is done on redelivery. The charter party will specify that the vessel must be redelivered in the same good order and condition as when delivered, ordinary wear and tear excepted. On redelivery, the owner's representatives, usually a port captain and a port engineer, may check the logbooks for information pertaining to groundings, collisions, or other damage.

Fuel oil and lube oil in the vessel on delivery are usually paid for by the charterer at the current price in the port of delivery; fuel oil and lube oil remaining on board on redelivery are paid for by the shipowner at the current price in the port of redelivery.

Although a bareboat charter party runs for a stipulated period of time, it should not be confused with a time charter party, whereby the shipowner rents out the cargo space but does not relinquish control of his vessel.

The provisions of a bareboat charter party are not of paramount importance to the master; he will be employed by the charterer, who will operate the vessel as if he were the owner.

TIME CHARTER PARTY

By this charter the charterer hires the vessel and her entire cargo-carrying capacity for a specified period of time and for a specified sum per day (called "hire"), payable at designated intervals. All the proper cargo space, including that for deck cargo, is at the charterer's disposal. This is sometimes referred to in a charter party as the "full reach and burden" of the vessel and the charterer invariably assumes it to include any mast or deck lockers available and probably a locker or two in the mate's room as well.

The steamship company is responsible for the physical operation of the vessel and it employs the master and the entire crew. It also pays for the stores and provisions and the upkeep and repair of the vessel. In other words, the shipowner puts at the charterer's disposal a fully equipped vessel and operates her for the charterer's benefit.

The charterer usually pays for fuel, tugs, and pilots; he also pays harbor dues, stevedoring expenses, and entering and clearing fees, but generally not expenses pertaining to the crew, except crew overtime related to the cargo. The charterer pays for any fuel in the vessel on delivery and the shipowner pays for any fuel in the vessel on redelivery, both at current market prices at the port, unless otherwise agreed.

In this type of charter party, unlike a voyage charter party, there is no mention of laytime, dispatch, or demurrage, unless the charterer subcharters the vessel to another shipper on a voyage basis. In that case, it is your responsibility to the time charterer to see that the provisions of the subcharter are complied with and that his interests are protected, so long as they are not in conflict with your own company's interests. A subcharter does not alter the responsibilities between the shipowner and the original charterer.

Reports Required by the Charterer

On time charter you may be required to send the charterer deck and engine room log abstracts, engineer's passage reports, port activity reports, and periodic radio reports giving position, speed, and weather. All of these should be sent promptly as requested by the charterer, just as you would reports to your home office. If any of these reports are to be made on special forms provided by the charterer, request a supply before sailing. The charterer may instruct you that arrival and departure reports for all ports be turned in on completion of the voyage. Do not put these reports off until the end of the voyage, but complete them as soon as possible after the vessel arrives or departs from a port of call and the pertinent details are known. If the job is postponed until the end of the voyage you will have to consult the logbooks and many other papers to get the required information.

As master you are responsible first to your own company, but you should also look out for the best interests of the time charterer insofar as outturn of cargo and quick dispatch are concerned.

Performance Warranties

Speed. Under a time charter party, the shipowner generally warrants that his vessel can maintain a certain speed. If, due to weather or any other reason, this cannot be accomplished, the reason should be noted in the logbook. For example, "Heavy weather, unable to maintain speed" or "In adverse current (named, such as Gulf Stream), unable to maintain speed." An entry claiming inability to maintain speed due to heavy weather should be substantiated by the weather section of the logbook.

Be sure your watch officers log the wind force and direction at least once each watch; most time charter parties excuse the vessel from maintaining her warranted speed if the wind force exceeds a specified level (commonly Beaufort Force 5). If your vessel cannot maintain her speed, except due to heavy weather or other reason excused by the charter party, the shipowner will have to pay the charterer a penalty. On the other hand, if the vessel consistently exceeds her warranted speed the charter party may provide that the shipowner is entitled to a bonus from the time charterer.

Fuel Consumption. Since the time charterer pays for the fuel, the shipowner will also have to warrant that the fuel consumption will not be higher than a certain figure, generally stated as so many tons per day. If the vessel's fuel consumption exceeds the warranted consumption the shipowner will have to pay for the extra fuel used unless, as with speed, the extra fuel consumption is due to weather or other excepted reason beyond the shipowner's control.

Discharge Rate. The owner of a tanker or other self-discharging vessel will have to guarantee the discharging ability of his vessel. It is almost universally agreed that a tanker should be capable of pumping out within twenty-four hours or maintaining 100 psi discharge pressure at the manifold.

Failure to meet any of the vessel's warranties can result in the shipowner having to pay heavy penalties to the time charterer; therefore, you should ensure that a full explanation is given in the logbook any time the vessel is prevented from performing as warranted.

Crew Overtime for the Account of the Charterer

Crew overtime in connection with the cargo is generally for the account of the time charterer and should be kept on a separate sheet. Instructions from your company should specify what overtime, if any, is to be charged to the charterer. In making up these sheets it will greatly facilitate the eventual settlement between your company and the charterer if you describe the overtime work in detail, with a breakdown of each specific operation.

Off Hire

A time charter party contains a clause known variously as the "off hire" clause, the "breakdown" clause, or the "cesser of hire" clause. This clause states that "in the event of loss of time from deficiency of stores or crew, breakdown of machinery, stranding, fire or any damage preventing the working of the vessel for more than ____ hours, the payment of hire shall cease until she is again in an efficient state to resume her service." The time allowed is usually twenty-four hours. If a vessel is broken down for longer than the period allowed in the charter party, then she is off hire for the entire time she is out of service, not just for the time in excess of the allotted time. In addition to breakdowns, off hire also includes periods when the ship is withdrawn from service for dry-docking or overhaul.

Deviation. While at sea on a time charter, if the vessel develops engine trouble or other fault making it necessary for her to deviate to a nearby port for repairs or other assistance, she is usually taken off hire from the time of the breakdown until the time she returns to the geographical position where the breakdown occurred and from which the voyage will be resumed. If her route from the port of refuge to the destination is such that she will not return to the place where the breakdown took place, she is taken off hire from the time of the breakdown until she reaches a position where she is the same distance from her destination as she was when the breakdown occurred and the deviation commenced.

Log the exact time and position of the point of deviation, as well as the amount of fuel oil, diesel oil, lube oil, and water on board at the time, and notify your home office in detail regarding the incident. If the charterer has an agent at the port of refuge he should also be notified, as well as your own agent, if one is in the port. Logbooks, both deck and engine, should carry complete reports of the deviation.

At the earliest opportunity in the port of refuge, make a note of protest before the U.S. consul or a notary public. If the latter, have the agent make the necessary arrangements.

Draw up a statement of facts covering the period from the time the breakdown occurred and the deviation commenced to the time the vessel returned to the point of deviation and the voyage was resumed. This statement should be signed by you and the chief engineer. It is generally sent to the home office from the first port after the voyage is resumed. A typical statement of facts is shown in Fig. 23 for a vessel under time charter, bound from New York to Casablanca. The vessel lost a blade in latitude 39-40N, longitude 70-00W, and returned to New York for repairs.

VOYAGE CHARTER PARTY

This is a charter party for the carriage of a full cargo, not for a period of time, but at a stipulated rate per ton (called "freight"), for one voyage only, between named ports, or to ports to be named on arrival in a given area. This is the most frequently used charter party and most commodities and trades have a particular type to suit their purposes.

In a voyage charter party the charterer assumes no responsibility for the operation of the vessel but generally pays stevedoring expenses in and out. A statement to that effect will be included in the charter party.

The master is particularly concerned with voyage charter parties because of the laytime, dispatch, demurrage, and cancelling clauses and because of the necessity of tendering the notice of readiness to load or discharge. In this type of charter, the charterer contracts to provide a cargo on that particular voyage and he must load and discharge the cargo at a given rate per day. The charter is generally for bulk cargo, stipulated in tons or cubic feet for dry cargo, and tons for liquid cargo, and is usually for the entire carrying capacity of the vessel.

When the full capacity of the vessel is chartered, the charterer must pay freight based on a full cargo even if he ultimately supplies less than a full cargo. In that case the charterer must pay freight on the cargo loaded, and he must also pay "dead freight" (at the same rate) on the difference between the cargo loaded and the cargo that could have been loaded. On tankers, the charterer may sometimes supply a cargo which, due to its light density, fills up all of the cargo tanks but does not bring the ship down to her maximum legal draft. Although the ship is full, the charterer will still have to pay dead freight on the difference between the cargo tonnage actually loaded and the tonnage that would have been required to put the ship down to full draft.

Occasionally a voyage charterer may contract for less than the full cargo capacity of a vessel if the freight rate offered is high enough to satisfy the shipowner. In this instance he will have to pay dead freight only if the cargo supplied is less than the amount contracted for.

On freighters, if the entire carrying capacity is to be used and is stipulated in tons, the stowage should be carefully watched to make certain that all available space is utilized. If the broken stowage is not kept to a minimum, you may find that the vessel is full and there is still some cargo to be loaded, an evidence of poor stowage for which the charterer will probably try to hold the vessel responsible, or he may claim that the wrong cubic measurement was given in the charter party.

Laytime

When the vessel on a voyage charter is in port, the expenses of the shipowner continue. At the same time, the loading or discharging is controlled by the charterer who, if not held to a definite number of days to complete this work, can make the stay in port long and expensive for the shipowner. For this reason the charter party will specify a definite number of days for loading or discharging of cargo, or it may specify a certain number of tons per day to be loaded or discharged.

The time allowed is called laytime (or lay days) and is stipulated in the charter party as working days, weather working days, running days, and excepted days, all of which are explained later in this chapter. Many charter parties now state the allowed laytime in hours, i.e., working hours, running hours, etc. The term "laytime" is preferable to "lay days" because many charter brokers use the phrase "lay days" to refer to the time period during which the shipowner must present his vessel to the charterer for loading (see "Readiness and Cancelling Dates," below).

If the charterer loads or discharges his cargo in less time than the laytime allowed, he earns dispatch money at so much per day or per hour saved. If he takes longer to load or discharge than the laytime allowed, he must pay demurrage at so much per hour or per day. Both dispatch and demurrage may be the subject of much disagreement and argument in which the vessel's logbook can play an important part.

Types of Lay Days. Working days are those days during which work is normally done in the port concerned, the number of hours worked per day depending on the custom of the port. It is eight hours in most ports. Sundays and holidays are excepted if they are recognized as such. In some Latin American and Mediterranean ports you will run into saints' days which are celebrated locally. It may be difficult to get work done on these days. The charter party may stipulate "Sundays and holidays excepted unless worked," sometimes adding "Only hours worked to be counted."

Running days (also called "consecutive days"), if without qualification, means days of 24 hours. All days are counted, including Sundays and holidays and days of bad weather, even if no work was done, unless expressly stipulated to the contrary in the charter party.

Weather working days are the normal working days in the port concerned excluding days when, because of foul weather, it would be unreasonable to expect loading or discharging of cargo. If the vessel is working at an anchorage this may include days when it is impossible to bring, or keep, lighters or barges alongside due to swell, sea, or surf; these are sometimes called "surf days."

Excepted days are those during which no work can be done because of a fault in the vessel, such as a breakdown of boilers or machinery, with consequent loss of power to the winches or cargo pumps; or fire in any part of the ship, if it interferes with loading or discharging of cargo; or because of any other stoppage of cargo work that is not the fault of the charterer. Full details should be entered in the logbook. Excepted days are not counted as used laytime.

Demurrage. A very important clause is the demurrage clause, which states that if the charterer does not complete loading or discharging within the laytime allowed by the charter party, he must pay for the delay at a stipulated sum per day or per hour or pro rata part thereof. Unless otherwise provided in the charter party, demurrage starts from the time loading or discharging should have been completed. All days are counted, whether or not cargo is worked, including Sundays, holidays, and days not worked due to bad weather or other reasons. Once a vessel is on demurrage, it runs consecutively unless otherwise provided in the charter party. Demurrage will be suspended for any period during which the charterer is prevented from working because of any fault of the ship, such as machinery breakdown.

In the tanker trades the charterer is usually allowed a total of seventy-two running hours for both loading and discharging combined; however, under almost all tanker charter parties the shipowner must guarantee that his vessel is capable of pumping out in twenty-four hours or less or maintaining 100 psi discharge pressure at the ship's manifold. If the vessel does not maintain the stated pressure, then any additional discharging time used due to the vessel's failure to maintain her warranted pumping rate will not count against the charterer as used laytime and demurrage will not be payable. If the vessel maintains the required pressure and the discharging still takes over twenty-four hours, the delay will usually be considered to be due to excessive back pressure in the shore pipelines, for which the charterer is responsible, and demurrage will be payable.

Dispatch Money. A clause in the charter party usually stipulates that the shipowner will pay the charterer dispatch money at the rate of so much per day or pro rata for laytime saved in loading or discharging. The amount is usually one-third to one-half of the demurrage rate. When making up the time sheet, it is important to note whether the charter party provides that dispatch money is payable for all time saved or for all working time saved, and to calculate the dispatch money accordingly.

The Time Sheet. This is an abstract showing the times of all cargo operations, the laytime used, and the number of hours for which dispatch or demurrage is due. Time sheets (or laytime statements) are not standard and vary greatly by company and trade. Some are printed forms issued by the company, shipper, or consignee. If none is available the one shown in Fig. 22 may be used, altered as seen fit. In some companies you will not prepare the time sheets; instead, these will be made up by someone in the home office using your log abstracts. The time sheet must be substantiated by the log. If necessary, as it often is, explanatory notes may be added. If your time sheet differs in fact from that of the charterer's agent, both should be checked. It is not always necessary that the vessel's copy—the one made up by you or the chief officer—be signed by the charterer's agent, unless it is required by your company, but a copy should be given to him as well as to your agent and one should be sent to your office. Be sure to keep a copy for your file. You will probably be required to sign the time sheet made up by the charterer's agent but make sure it is correct before signing it and be sure to get a copy for your file.

Disputes over laytime and the amount of dispatch or demurrage due often arise, and the settlement of such is negotiated between the shipowner and charterer. To fully protect your company's interests be sure that the logbook entries in regard to all cargo operations are accurate. It may be advisable, before signing the charterer's time sheet, even if you think it is correct, to append to it the following note: "Signed without prejudice to any of the terms, conditions, and exceptions of governing charter party."

This is especially necessary if the charter party does not stipulate a definite amount of laytime or the number of tons per day to be loaded or discharged. Some charter parties deal in rather vague terms such as: "According to the custom of the port," "Vessel to be loaded or discharged as customary," "With reasonable dispatch." These terms are much too indefinite and, if they do appear, it is advisable to get an interpretation from a responsible party connected with your company.

Readiness and Cancelling Dates

A voyage charter party usually stipulates that the shipowner will present his vessel to the charterer or his agent at the loading port within certain dates. This is commonly a period of three days to a week. Some charter parties refer to this interval as the "laydays"; however, this term is easily confused with the laydays allowed the charterer for loading or discharging (see "Laytime," above).

The first day is called the "readiness date." The charterer is not obligated to accept the ship before the readiness date, although he may do so if he has the cargo ready and a berth available. If the charterer does accept the vessel early, then laytime will start under the provisions of the charter party just as though the ship were not early. It is obviously to the shipowner's advantage to have his vessel accepted early, if possible.

The last day is called the "cancelling date." If the vessel is not presented and the notice of readiness tendered by a certain time on the cancelling date, the charterer has the option of cancelling the charter party by giving notice to the shipowner. Missing the cancelling date is a very serious affair—the shipowner will probably have spent many thousands of dollars in fuel and other operating expenses in getting his ship to the loading port. If the ship is late, the charterer will almost surely cancel the charter party, although he will not necessarily charter another vessel in place of the one rejected. He will probably offer the shipowner a new charter party with terms considerably less favorable than in the original contract.

The Notice of Readiness

When on a voyage charter it is the master's responsibility to advise the charterer or his agent, in writing, as soon as the vessel is in all respects ready to load or discharge. This advice is given in the form of a notice of readiness presented (tendered) to the charterer or his agent. In some cases when a vessel is to load and she is expected at a definite hour, the company or your agent at the port may tender the notice. This is especially likely if the vessel is to go directly alongside on arrival and is not required to be granted pratique or to clear customs. Your agent should advise you if this was done.

Before the notice of readiness may be tendered the vessel must have arrived at the place for loading or discharging as stipulated in the charter party or as near thereto as she can safely get, and she must be actually ready to load or discharge cargo at the specified time.

The above may be modified by the terms of the particular governing charter party.

At the discharge port you should tender the notice without delay. Generally, the charter party will contain a clause stating that "laytime is to commence _____ hours after written notice has been given that the vessel is ready to discharge, whether in berth or not at the place ordered." Sometimes the charter party stipulates that the notice can be tendered during designated office hours only. The time allowed may vary, and different charter parties may require that the notice be tendered by the master only, or by either master, owner, or agent. The time allowed between tendering the notice of readiness and the start of laytime gives the charterer time to make the necessary arrangements for discharging the cargo. However, the clause may add ". . . unless charterer commences to discharge before the _____ hours have elapsed," in which case laytime usually commences when the discharging begins.

The date and time the notice is tendered should be entered in the logbook. If for any reason the notice cannot be tendered after arrival, the reason should be entered in the logbook. If your vessel must anchor to await a berth, send your agent a radio message instructing him to tender a notice of readiness on your behalf. Even if this is done, when the ship finally goes alongside you should still try to get the charterer's agent to sign the notice that you made up on the ship.

The notice may be prepared by your agent and presented on board for your signature. There will be anywhere from four to ten copies—be sure to get one for your file and one to send to your home office. If you are uncertain as to whether the agent will prepare the notice, it is a good idea to make it up before arrival, omitting the date and time, which can be filled in when it is tendered.

Generally, a notice of readiness is required by the terms of the charter party. If there is no one to receive it, the facts should be logged and an attempt made to tender the notice when the charterer or his agent shows up, leaving the original date and time on the notice. If the charterer or his agent refuses to accept the tendered notice, claiming that the vessel is not in all respects ready to load or discharge, make an entry in the log of the reason for the refusal and advise your company at once of the facts. In the absence of other instructions from your company, direct your agent to employ a surveyor to inspect the vessel and inform the charterer or his agent that this is being done. On your time sheet, laytime should be counted from the time stipulated in the charter party as though the notice had been accepted and signed when tendered. Following is a typical notice of readiness which may be changed in any way deemed suitable:

Seven Seas Steamship Corporation
NOTICE OF READINESS

_____

_____

_____

Dear Sirs:
The SS/MV _____, under my command, now at _____, is as of ____ hours this ____ day of _____ 19____, ready in all respects to load/discharge a cargo of _____ in accordance with the charter party dated _____.

_____
Master

Accepted at ____ hours, _____ 19__

Signed _____

Title _____

Arrived Ship. When on a voyage charter and a notice of readiness must be tendered, it is important that you accurately determine the arrival time. For charter party purposes arrival at the bar or pilot station is not necessarily considered arrival time at a port. Generally, arrival is taken to mean the time when the vessel is moored in the harbor proper, at the terminal designated in the charter party, or any place where vessels normally wait for a dock to load or discharge. If a dock or berth is named in the charter party and is available, it is generally taken that the vessel must be made fast to that dock or berth before she is considered to have arrived. It is up to the charterer to secure the dock or berth. If the berth is not available, the vessel is considered to have arrived when she is made fast to a waiting berth or anchored at a place where vessels customarily await berths. Many masters use the time that they ring "Finished With Engines" as the time of tendering the notice of readiness.

The vessel on arrival must be in all respects ready to load or discharge in accordance with the terms of the charter party. This means that the vessel must be ready to work without delay, even if she is not at a dock or berth; otherwise the charterer may refuse the notice of readiness, claiming that the vessel is not ready when, as a matter of fact, he doesn't have a berth ready. A tanker docking at a loading berth in ballast usually is considered to have arrived even though she may not be able to load cargo until she has discharged her ballast, as long as she is otherwise ready to load. In that case you should tender the notice as soon as the vessel is all fast in the loading berth; however, the time spent deballasting and drying or cleaning the ballast tanks will not count against the charterer as used laytime.

If, as often occurs, the vessel must first load or discharge other cargo and then shift to the berth called for in the charter party, laytime does not commence until she has arrived at that berth and the notice has been tendered. When possible, however, the agent will tender the notice a day before the vessel shifts, so that when she arrives at the berth called for she will start work immediately and laytime will begin. If the berth to which the vessel is to shift is not available, the notice of readiness should be tendered as soon as cargo operations at the first berth are complete and the vessel is ready to shift.

The above guidelines may be modified by the relevant charter party and, in some cases, by the custom of the port. If you are in doubt as to whether or not your vessel has arrived under the terms of the charter party, it is best to go ahead and tender the notice of readiness. It is better to tender early rather than late.

If you tender the notice early, laytime will not start until the time stipulated in the charter party even though your notice may have been presented sooner; at least the charterer will have been officially advised of your vessel's presence in the port and readiness to work cargo, and you can always tender another notice at the proper time.

If you tender the notice late, laytime will not start until the specified number of hours after the notice has been tendered, even though it properly should have begun some hours before.

CHARTERER INSTALLING SPECIAL FITTINGS

If the cargo to be loaded requires special fittings and the charter party stipulates that the charterer is to bear the expense of the fittings and their installation, laytime begins when the installation work is started. However, if there is inward cargo remaining in some of the holds and the charter is for all of the space, laytime generally begins after the inward cargo is removed and the holds are cleaned, even though the charterer may have started on the fittings in the space available before the inward cargo was completely discharged. This may be the cause of dispute, so it is important that all times used, both by the vessel in discharging and by the charterer in installing the fittings, are accurately logged.

PREPARING HOLDS

With some dry bulk cargoes the vessel must prepare the holds. This means opening the hatches and spreading tarps or other cloths, if necessary, to protect cargo in the tween decks. Holds must be cleaned, bilges and rose boxes covered, and drain pipes plugged and cemented where necessary. Some companies hire shore gangs to do this work if time permits. If done by the crew, the master is responsible for its completion in time to commence loading or discharging as soon as the vessel is made fast. Any doubt about whether it will be necessary to prepare the holds before arrival should be resolved by asking the company or agent for instructions. Uncovering the hatches or preparing holds may be overtime for the crew. If so they are likely to take their time about it—a contingency not to be overlooked. Generally, the home office or agent will send you a message in ample time, to let you know that the vessel must prepare the holds.

STEVEDORE DAMAGE WHEN UNDER CHARTER

If, as is usual under a voyage or time charter party, the charterer pays the stevedores, you or the chief officer should ascertain who has the authority to sign reports of any damage which may be done by stevedores to the vessel or her cargo. When such damage is discovered, or as soon thereafter as possible, the stevedore's foreman should be notified in writing, and copies sent to the charterer or his agent and to your company. If the damage is not discovered until after the cargo is out but was apparently sustained during cargo operations, follow the same procedure.

In either case, a full accounting must be made on a stevedore damage report (Fig. 26). If no printed forms are on board, a typewritten form is acceptable. Generally this is not a standard form, each company printing its own, but the information called for is practically the same on all versions. Give copies, as complete as possible, to the stevedore and to the charterer or his agent, and send the required number to your office. Be sure to keep a copy for the vessel's file.

Try to get the stevedore's representative to sign a damage report either admitting or denying his liability. It is quite likely that he will refuse to do this; indeed, he may even refuse to accept a copy of the report. The charterer or his agent should also be requested to sign the report, as the charter party usually contains a clause holding the charterer responsible for stevedore damage. Enter all details in the log.

Some charterers issue "Instructions to Master" which will usually include a note on stevedore damage which will specify that the charterer is not responsible for damage to the vessel unless notified by the master at the time the damage occurs; also that the master is to cooperate with the charterer and his agents in giving prompt written notice to the party causing such damage. The instructions may go on to say that claims against stevedores for repair costs are often rejected on the grounds that the damage was not called to the attention of the stevedore when it occurred.

It is apparent that unless the stevedore or the charterer assumes liability for the damage, your company will have to pay for the repairs, which will undoubtedly call for explanatory letters from you and the chief officer.

Signing Damage Letters

Some charterers instruct their agents to present the master with a letter to sign, prior to sailing, stating that notices of responsibility have been served on stevedores and other third parties for damage caused, and that copies of such notices are attached; or that your vessel has been inspected under your supervision and that no damage has been observed. A typical letter is shown below.

CERTIFICATE OF SATISFACTORY LOADING/DISCHARGING

Port _____ Date _____

SS *Seaworthy*

To Whom It May Concern:

This is to certify that the loading/discharging of my vessel was conducted under my supervision and in accordance with my instructions and to my satisfaction.

I further certify that no damage was done to my vessel while loading/discharging this cargo for which the stevedores or others may be liable or responsible.

_____

Master, SS *Seaworthy*

Be wary about signing such a letter, as damages caused by stevedores may not be noticed until a later date. Furthermore, it is common for a vessel to arrive one day and sail the next, or even the same day, having worked cargo continuously. Under these circumstances a thorough inspection would be impractical. Your signature on such a letter might cost your company an expenditure for repairs which rightly should be borne by the charterer's stevedore. If you are pressured into signing such a letter, insist that the following, or a similar note, be added: "Signed without prejudice, in case stevedore damage or other damage, not noted at the time due to fast turn-around or for other reason, is discovered after sailing."

Some companies issue a form letter including the qualifying note, to be given to the charterer or his agent after the master fills in the name of the vessel, that of the charterer, the port, the date, and his own signature.

It sometimes occurs that stevedore damage or other damage is repaired at the expense of the party causing it, or at the charterer's expense. In such cases the damage report should still be made out but a note appended as follows: "Damage by _____ at _____ repaired for their account."

DUNNAGE

When the cargo is discharged, you should ascertain to whom the dunnage, if any, belongs. The consignee may claim the dunnage for the charterer and may try to discharge it with the cargo. Because of the cost of dunnage, this could be a very important item if the vessel is to load another cargo that requires dunnage. If the charterer prepares the holds, he is usually allowed to use any dunnage already in the vessel.

TEN

VESSEL ACCIDENTS

Both at sea and in port the vessel, her cargo, crew, and passengers are subject to a variety of dangers. Marine insurance undertakes to indemnify the steamship company against damage to or loss of the vessel or cargo, and against collision with other vessels. For protection against accidents and losses not covered by marine insurance, many shipowners have joined together in protection and indemnity societies, known as "P and I clubs." These P and I clubs are owned by their shipowner members.

This type of insurance usually covers claims for damage to cargo during loading or discharging; third-party claims for liability to damaged cargo; crew and passenger sickness, injury, or loss of life; pollution liability; and damage to docks, cables, shore installations, aids to navigation, bridges, and other fixed or movable property. P and I clubs do not usually provide war risk insurance, hull and machinery insurance, or insurance for damage to cargo while the cargo is on board the vessel.

Marine insurance companies and P and I clubs will indemnify the shipowner only for damage and losses specified in the policy and only after the shipowner proves that such damage or loss has occurred. This is determined by surveys, entries in the log, reports submitted by the master, and statements of witnesses.

PORT INFORMATION DIRECTORY

Some shipping companies issue a port information directory to their vessels. This directory lists, for each port, the names and telephone numbers used to obtain assistance in case of emergency. It will have the local Coast Guard office, police, fire department, ambulance, agent, harbormaster, etc. If your company does not issue such a directory, you may be able to obtain a similar listing from your agent. Even if you have to make it up yourself, it would be wise to have such a listing available in each port. See Fig. 31 for a sample port information directory page.

ATTORNEYS AND INVESTIGATORS

In the course of your career you will meet with many kinds of accidents to your vessel and cargo, as well as accidents causing injuries to crew, passengers, and stevedores, often resulting in claims against your company. Opposition attorneys, investigators, cargo surveyors, and others may ask to see your logbook or bell book and may attempt to get statements from you, your officers, or crew. Under no circumstances, except by express permission from your company, give any person a statement, either oral or written, regarding an accident, loss, or damage. Do not permit anyone to interview any of the officers or crew or to see the logbook or bell book. As a matter of fact, no such persons should be allowed on board, and if on board they should be summarily ordered ashore.

These men may claim to be "from the office," without saying which or whose office, implying that they are representatives of your company. Attorneys and investigators are persuasive talkers. They may try to convince you that since the damages will eventually be paid for anyway there is no reason why they shouldn't get a statement or be allowed access to the logbook or bell book. Unless such persons have unimpeachable credentials or are vouched for by your company's representative, who is known to you, give them nothing, show them nothing, and tell them nothing—except to leave the vessel—and see that they do so. This, of course, does not apply to Coast Guard investigators, who will be in uniform or will have proper identification.

Names of attorneys and others representing your company, and their firms, should be logged along with the times they board and leave the vessel.

If it is necessary to talk to opposition attorneys—and this should be only with the advice and consent of your company—be careful of what you say. They may try to put words in your mouth and make you think you thought of them yourself. If you must sign any papers, be sure to read them over carefully—every word and every sheet—before signing. Under no condition sign any blank sheets even though they assure you that it will save you time and trouble.

If anyone on board is seriously injured and litigation results, the opposition lawyers will probably claim the injury was due to rank carelessness and gross incompetence on the part of the master and the company. If they can substantiate this claim it will mean a loss to your company and trouble for you.

LOGBOOK ENTRIES

In each case of personal injury or of accident affecting the seaworthiness of the ship, such as fire on board, collision, or grounding, detailed entries should be entered in the official log and in the deck logbook. In case of serious accident it is a good idea to make rough notes on a pad and enter them in the log in proper sequence after they are letter perfect. Do not permit officers to make entries in the logbook haphazardly. If in doubt about whether to make an entry or not, a safe rule is, if it happened, enter it in the log—but not until after it has been roughed out, so that the proper sequence can be followed. Do not trust anything to memory. Write it down as soon as possible after the occurrence, while it is still fresh in mind.

CASUALTY REPORTS TO U.S. COAST GUARD

The Coast Guard is required by federal law (46 USC 6101) to require reports on and, if necessary, to investigate certain marine casualties. Failure to report a marine casualty as required by law or regulation carries a $1,000 civil penalty.

Coast Guard regulations regarding casualty reporting can be found in Subpart 4.05 of Title 46 of the *Code of Federal Regulations*. The reporting requirements apply to all accidents occurring in U.S. waters (including those involving foreign vessels) and to all accidents involving U.S. vessels, regardless of where they occur.

The owner, agent, master, or person in charge of a vessel must notify the nearest Coast Guard marine safety office or marine inspection office as soon as possible in the event of any of the following casualties:

1. All accidental groundings and any intentional grounding which also meets any of the other reporting requirements or creates a hazard to navigation, the environment, or the safety of the vessel;
2. Loss of main propulsion or primary steering, or any associated component or control system, the loss of which causes a reduction of the maneuvering capabilities of the vessel. Loss means that systems, components, parts, subsystems, or control systems do not perform the specified or required function;
3. An occurrence materially and adversely affecting the vessel's seaworthiness or fitness for service or route, including but not limited to fire, flooding, or failure or damage to fixed fire-extinguishing

systems, lifesaving equipment, auxiliary power generating equipment, or bilge pumping systems;
4. Loss of life;
5. Injury causing a person to remain incapacitated for a period in excess of seventy-two hours;
6. An occurrence not meeting any of the above criteria but resulting in damage to property in excess of $25,000. Damage cost includes the cost of labor and material to restore the property to the service condition which existed prior to the casualty, but does not include the cost of salvage, cleaning, gas freeing, dry-docking, or demurrage.

In addition to notifying the Coast Guard when any of these casualties occur, the person in charge must make a written report as soon as possible to the officer in charge, marine inspection, at the port where the casualty occurred or nearest the port of first arrival. This report must be made on Coast Guard Form CG-2692 (Fig. 27).

The requirement to notify the Coast Guard that a casualty has occurred and the requirement to make a written report of the casualty are separate requirements; however, the Coast Guard will accept CG-2692 as both the notice and the report if the form is submitted without delay. If you are involved in a casualty in U.S. waters which presents a hazard to navigation or which results in loss of life, or serious injury or damage, the best procedure would be to notify the Coast Guard immediately by telephone or radio and to follow with the written report as soon as possible.

The required reporting in case of loss of life or injury resulting in incapacitation for over seventy-two hours applies not only to ship's personnel, but also to others who may be on board, such as shipyard or harbor workers. However, you need not report death or injury of such workers if the death or injury was not the result of a vessel casualty or a vessel equipment casualty. For example, if a longshoreman were to suffer an appendicitis attack on board the vessel and die, the death would not have to be reported to the Coast Guard. When in doubt, protect yourself by making a report.

If a death or injury occurs on board that is not required to be reported to the Coast Guard, the vessel is subject to the reporting requirements of the Occupational Safety and Health Administration (see Title 29, *Code of Federal Regulations,* Part 1904).

If a casualty occurs, the owner, agent, master, or person in charge of the vessel must see that all vessel records which might assist in investigating the casualty are retained and made available, on request, to Coast Guard investigating personnel. Such records would include deck and engine room logbooks, bell books, charts, navigation workbooks, compass deviation cards, gyro records, cargo stowage plans, draft records, night order books, radiograms sent and received, radio logs, crew and passenger lists, shipping articles, official logs, etc.

In addition, if your vessel collides with or is in any way connected with a collision with a buoy or other aid to navigation under Coast Guard jurisdiction, you must report the accident to the nearest officer in charge, marine inspection. A written report on CG-2692 is not required unless the accident results in one of the casualties listed above.

REPORTS AND STATEMENTS

Writing reports and statements and getting statements from witnesses in case of accident or casualty to the vessel or cargo, or injury to a person, serve an important purpose in protecting your company's interests. Throughout your career at sea you will have to make up many reports and statements covering a variety of accidents. This is time-consuming labor, but it is a necessary evil, and one which cannot be avoided. You will find yourself on the receiving end of much caustic criticism from management if accident reports are not made promptly or if they are incomplete or inaccurate.

All reports and statements should be completed with the least possible delay. Procrastination will simply cause them to pile up, with the result that when you do get around to them the work will be rushed through with little or no time to check for accuracy. Start all reports and statements early so that you will have ample time to do a good job. You should begin with a rough copy in pencil on which corrections can easily be made. When the report is as letter perfect as you can make it, have it typed.

If your company requires more than four copies of reports or statements, do not type them all in one lot or the bottom copies will be very difficult to read. The reports should be typed no more than three or four at a time and, when it is necessary to use the other side, the sheets should be stacked so that the original is the original on both sides. Too much trouble cannot be taken with these small but important details. All reports and statements should be clear, neat, and legible. Keep in mind that proper and adequate reports and statements will go far toward protecting the interests of your company and will save you the necessity of having to do them over.

Your company may want reports on special forms on all accidents, even those which would not ordinarily require a comprehensive report or statement. If your company does not have special forms for you to use in making the various reports, then the reports may be typed on plain paper in narrative letter form. If no company rules or instructions are available, those listed hereafter may be used.

The reports should be in detail no matter how minor the accident, bearing in mind that the recipients will be many miles away and all they can go by are your reports. If special forms are to be filled out they should be made up as soon as possible after the occurrence, and all questions on the forms answered. If a question is not applicable, draw a line through the space or mark it "N/A." Do not leave it blank or the reader may think that you forgot to answer it. Although reports may be made out by an officer designated by you, you are responsible for their accuracy and you should therefore check all reports before signing them. Keep a copy of each for the vessel's file.

In all cases of accident to the vessel or cargo, or injury to a crew member, passenger, stevedore, or visitor on the vessel, get signed statements from witnesses, in their own handwriting, if practical, with their home addresses. Do this as soon as possible, while the details are still fresh in their minds. If time permits, have the handwritten statements typed and the typed copies signed by the witnesses. This is particularly necessary in case of personal injury. The witness making the statement should be given one of the typed copies.

After a serious accident, your company attorney may come on board to take statements from witnesses. If any seaman asks what he is to say, tell him simply to tell the truth. Through a misguided sense of loyalty a seaman will sometimes make an untrue statement under the illusion that he is helping you or the vessel. Such statements, if found on cross-examination to be false, will harm your company's case.

When writing your own statement, be sure to include all pertinent details but don't make it too long-winded. A clear, concise, absolutely truthful statement will be of greatest assistance to your company's insurance department. Do not attach any reports or statements to the logbook.

When damage to the vessel or other property is the result of coming in contact with a dock, pier, bridge, or other fixed object, your company may want a damage report form. If none is available, the one shown in Fig. 25 can be made up on the vessel.

Make up reports and statements for your company's insurance department when any of the following casualties or accidents occur.

This discussion is by no means complete, as other accidents may occur. Include with your report a copy of any Coast Guard form that is made out and a copy of any notice of liability served on another vessel or received from any source. If surveyors' reports are made they should also be included; however, surveyors will usually send their reports direct to your home office or local agent after the final version has been completed. Draw up a list of all the reports, statements, etc., that will accompany the report and include the list with the report also. Check off all the items on your copy of the list before sealing the envelope.

COLLISIONS WITH OTHER VESSELS OR STRUCTURES

Accidents Going on or Leaving Dry Dock

Regardless of whether or not the shipyard has control of the vessel, if she touches another vessel or craft or the dry dock itself, an accident report should be made out. Due to the close quarters in some dry docks, this type of accident occurs occasionally. If your vessel was using her engine, make copies of the logbook and bell books covering the time period. Show on a diagram the names of tugs used and their positions around the vessel. The pilot should also make a statement. Statements will also be required from the officer on duty on the bridge, the man at the wheel, and the lookout, if one was posted. Usually, however, the chief officer would be on the bow and the statement would come from him.

Collision with Another Vessel

A number of statements and reports will have to be made, so start taking notes immediately or put an officer on the job. Don't forget to serve notice on the master of the other vessel, or her owners, agent, or company representative, that his company will be held responsible for all damage sustained by your vessel. Request the addressee of the letter to acknowledge its receipt. Chances are he will not do this, and he may even refuse to accept the notice.

In all probability he will serve you with a similar notice. Even though you may have hit him amidships on a clear day when his vessel was at anchor, do not admit liability, whether or not you think your vessel is at fault—leave that to your insurance department if they think it necessary. If you do acknowledge his notice, the only thing you should admit is that you received a copy. Do not in any way indicate that you agree with any of the statements contained in his notice. If you do sign the notice, write a statement such as

"Signed for receipt of notice only, fault or liability of any kind denied." Do not put anything else on the notice; any additional statements may compromise your company's position. If in doubt, remember that you are not compelled to sign or even acknowledge the notice. Send a copy of any notice you receive to your insurance department immediately.

Caution your officers and crew not to discuss a collision, or indeed any other accident, with unauthorized persons. Don't give out any information and don't allow anyone, government officials excepted, to examine the logbooks or bell books.

If the vessel is in port your company attorneys will board soon after the accident and they will want to take statements from you, the officer on duty, the man who was at the wheel, the lookout, and any other person likely to have firsthand knowledge of the accident. Always follow the advice of your company attorneys regarding any reports and statements. In a U.S. port the Coast Guard will probably be on board before the attorneys and they too will want statements, and possibly your logbooks, bell books, and course recorder tape also.

It is a well-known fact that when several persons witness the same accident each of them is likely to give a different version of how the accident occurred. If your witnesses ask you what they should say in case of a hearing, advise them to tell the truth in their own words, whether it affects the vessel adversely or not. It will be better for all concerned if no false statements are made.

If you, or any witness, are not sure of a detail or fact, say so—don't make definite statements of fact unless you are sure. Once you are on the witness stand under cross-examination, the opposition lawyers will quickly learn whether or not you are sure of your facts. Be sure the information in your statement, which may be used at a hearing or in court, can be substantiated by log entries.

In your statement or report, do not comment on the possible incompetence of your pilot. Rest assured that the master of the other vessel and the opposition lawyers will take care of that. They may strongly hint that you and your pilot were both stewed and down in the galley dancing a hornpipe with the cook at the time of the collision, but don't let them talk you into saying your pilot was incompetent and not on the job.

Note in the logbook and in your statement:

1. That you made certain as to whether anyone was injured on either vessel.

2. Whether the other vessel was in need of assistance.
3. That you had bilge soundings taken hourly or more often, as thought necessary.
4. The extent of damage to your vessel as far as known.
5. The names of witnesses, such as men who were on deck at the time.

If you see that a collision is imminent, be sure to order the men off the forecastle head and away from danger spots. In a U.S. port, notify the Coast Guard captain of the port as soon as possible, preferably by radio. In a foreign port, have your agent notify the local port authorities.

Don't forget that it is the moral and legal obligation of the master of each vessel, if he can do so without endangering his own vessel or crew, to stand by and render assistance to the other vessel until such time as no further assistance is required. The Coast Guard takes a very dim view of hit-and-run collisions. Be sure you ask the master of the other vessel if he needs any assistance, even if it appears that the damage is slight.

Log the fact that you offered assistance. If the other master states that he requires no assistance, log that as well. If he requests aid of any sort, then of course you must use your best efforts to provide whatever help is asked for. Log the date and time when the other master states that no further assistance is required.

You will require abstracts of the logbook and copies of the bell books for your insurance department. You must make up Coast Guard Form CG-2692. Federal law requires that you make an entry regarding the collision in the official logbook giving particulars of the collision. This entry must be made as soon as practicable after the collision.

You may be required to have a survey made by the American Bureau of Shipping or other classification society. Your agent will make the necessary arrangements.

Have the radio officer make extra copies of all messages sent and received pertaining to the collision.

Check all reports relative to the collision, if made by another person on the vessel, before signing them.

Striking Docks, Shore Installations, Aids to Navigation, etc.

When docking or undocking, vessels will occasionally strike the dock or pier with such force as to cause some damage to the dock and perhaps to dent a plate on the vessel. Quite often the dock or pier is in such dilapidated condition that if the vessel touches even lightly she will cause some damage. It is a common opinion among ships' officers that a number of old docks and piers have been paid for many times over by claims allowed for alleged damage.

If your vessel strikes a dock check its condition and if possible take photographs. If a survey is held pay particular attention to the condition of the dock in general and try to judge what its condition was before the accident. Include this information in your report, to which you should attach any photographs you take.

If you think the case warrants it, ask the pilot to make a statement. If tugs were used, their names and positions around the vessel should be shown on a diagram. You may have to submit copies of the log and bell books to your insurance department.

In U.S. ports, damage by contact or collision with aids to navigation must be reported to the Coast Guard as soon as possible. You will invite trouble for yourself by not reporting such accidents promptly. It also should be reported to your company insurance department, giving the cause of such contact or collision. If in a foreign port, have your agent report the accident to the proper local authorities.

GROUNDINGS

Grounding alongside a Dock or at Anchorage

When docking or anchoring at a berth for the first time inquire from the pilot the depth of water at low tide, or check it on the chart or in the coast pilot or sailing directions. You should always consult these publications when bound for a place for the first time. You are more apt to get into an unsafe berth situation when on time or voyage charters. In order to prevent the vessel from being ordered by the charterer to a wharf, dock, or anchorage where she cannot load a full cargo without touching the ground or resting on the bottom at low water, the "always afloat" clause is inserted in the charter party. This clause usually reads as follows:

> . . . to proceed to _____ or so near thereto as she may safely get, always afloat, and being loaded shall proceed with all convenient speed to _____ or so near thereto as she may safely get and discharge her cargo, always afloat, in any safe dock, wharf, or anchorage.

or

> That the cargo be laden and/or discharged in a dock or at any wharf or place that the charterer or his agents may direct, provided the

vessel can safely lie afloat at any stage of the tide, except at such places where it is customary for similar sized vessels to safely lie aground.

If, in your opinion, your vessel is ordered by the charterer or his agent to a wharf, dock, or anchorage which you consider unsafe, you should immediately inform him by notice of protest, giving the reason why you consider it unsafe. If no change is made you should immediately contact your own agent and your home office. Give the charterer or his agent another written notice of protest holding him liable for all damage the vessel may suffer as a consequence of carrying out his order. Be sure to send copies of these notices, with a note of explanation, to your insurance department and to your agent, and keep a copy for your own file. Send these notices by the fastest means available, usually air courier.

If the charterer does not rescind the order and you get no advice from your home office, and if in your best judgment you think you should not shift to such berth, do not move your vessel. Be sure to enter full details in the log, including the time not worked, if any, while the charterer or his agent decides what to do.

Remember that a berth can be unsafe due to heavy swells coming in that may affect your vessel, especially when there are only a few feet of water under your keel when fully loaded.

Grounding or Stranding

Be guided by your company instructions with regard to forms and reports to be made up. Lacking such instructions, inform your home office and your company agent as soon as possible after the accident and give them the following information:

1. Date and time of grounding and position or exact location in reference to a known object, such as a lighthouse. To save time, include the chart number.
2. Condition of the weather at the time of grounding—clear, fog, etc.
3. Draft on grounding.
4. Type of bottom.
5. Soundings taken around the vessel, stage of tide at that time, and whether rising or falling.
6. Any injuries or loss of life to crew or others.
7. Whether the vessel is in a dangerous position.
8. Whether making water and where, the rate, and whether under control.
9. The location and extent of any damage.
10. Fuel and water on board.

11. Water ballast on board and whether pumping it out. (Observe oil pollution laws.)
12. Assistance at hand, required, requested, or ordered.
13. If refloated, the date and time and whether able to proceed under own power.

There will probably be much to do, so detail an officer to take notes on a scratch pad and put the notes in proper sequence before making a log entry. Be sure to make an entry in the official log giving full details including the position, heading, and condition of the weather at the time of the grounding. Record the names, ratings, and document numbers of the officer on watch, the man at the wheel, and the lookout. You may require statements from these men and it is advisable to get them as soon after the accident as possible. The statements should be signed by the men making them, and should include their home addresses.

Your company insurance department will want a full account of the grounding and the cause. This should be in your statement, which should be in detail and to the point, but not too lengthy.

Notify the Coast Guard at the first port of arrival in the United States after the accident and have Coast Guard Form CG-2692 ready.

Do not forget to make note of protest at the first port after the grounding. Be sure to send a copy to your insurance department.

Reports and Statements. You will require copies of the following reports and statements for your home office:

1. A statement from the officer on the bridge. Get this as early as possible. If the officer was in any way at fault, his statement, if put off, may differ from the actual facts.
2. A statement from the man at the wheel. His statement also may change with time if he was in any way at fault; for example, he may have put the rudder over the wrong way at a critical time.
3. A statement from the lookout or any others having firsthand knowledge of the grounding.
4. A statement from the chief engineer regarding his engine and machinery: when and how long they were used in the attempt to refloat and any resulting damage.
5. Signed abstracts of deck and engine logs.
6. Signed copies of both bell books. The Coast Guard may want the logbooks and bell books for a while.
7. A record of bilge soundings taken after the vessel grounded. These should be taken often.

8. A diagram of soundings around the vessel at the time of grounding. Show the draft and the stage of the tide at the time.
9. A diagram of soundings around the vessel at low water.
10. Lists of deck and engine stores and equipment used in the attempt to refloat the vessel. In both lists mark the items "used," or "new"; do not use the word "old." Fuel, lube oil, and fresh water should be shown on a separate report.
11. A statement of any deck or engine stores jettisoned, lost, or contaminated by water or oil so as to render them useless.
12. Your own statement giving a full description of events.
13. Copies of all letters and messages sent or received relative to the grounding.
14. Personal belongings lost by the crew and in what manner. This does not mean that they will be reimbursed, but the list will be available if required. Get it as soon as possible as it will increase greatly if you let it go too long.
15. If a salvage agreement was made, your home office should be sent a copy. Use Lloyd's standard "No Cure—No Pay" agreement.

In addition you should give your home office the following information, much of which will be in the log:

1. Services rendered by tugs or other vessels, their names, hailing ports, nationality, and owners' names if available.
2. Dangers involved to the salvage vessels at any time.
3. Weather conditions day by day.
4. List of any injured, including members of the salvaging vessels, together with the injury reports and what efforts were made to get badly injured persons to a doctor or hospital. Don't forget statements from injured persons and witnesses. These may be difficult to get at the time.
5. Names of surveyors who boarded and the organizations or classification societies they represent.
6. Names, titles, and organizations of salvage masters or others who assist in any way.

DRAGGING ANCHOR AND CAUSING DAMAGE TO SUBMERGED CABLES, PIPELINES, ETC., OR TO OTHER VESSELS

Such accidents are always expensive and in some ports exact a fine. Generally if there is the least possibility of dragging, the prudent shipmaster will keep the engine ready to maneuver on short notice. Don't forget to enter in the night order book or leave word on the bridge, in writing, that bearings should be taken, and how often, and that you should be called immediately if there is any indication that the vessel may drag.

If your vessel does drag and causes damage you will have a report and statements to make. Your statement should include the time you requested power on the engine, the time the engine was ready, and also what caused the vessel to drag and what you did to stop it. You may have to plot a line on the chart showing the course the vessel took while dragging, from her original position to where she fetched up or was brought under control, and any contacts she made with other vessels, craft, or buoys. You will probably have to make up Coast Guard Form CG-2692. The officer on watch will have to make a complete statement of the circumstances of the dragging.

DAMAGE TO ANOTHER VESSEL OR CRAFT ALONGSIDE A DOCK DUE TO ALLEGED EXCESSIVE SPEED

This is sometimes called wake damage and often occurs in narrow channels. It is a general rule, and a good one, for most ships to slow down when passing moored vessels. It is a regulation in most harbors that vessels must slow down passing a dredge or similar craft working in or near a channel. Enter the reason for such slow bells in the bell book. Such an entry may well disprove a claim for alleged damage.

If any vessel, dredge, or other craft claims damage you probably will not hear about it until your return and you will have to refresh your memory by looking in the bell book for the reason why you had a slow bell about that time. Merely recording a slow bell without also giving the reason for it may not help much. You may have to make abstracts of the log and the bell book covering the time involved. The state of the tide and weather at the time of the alleged damage should also be included in your statement.

It is good practice to have your officers make frequent notes in the bell book of landmarks or aids to navigation passed. That way you can easily later determine where the vessel was at the time of any particular bell. If you pass a vessel whose mooring lines are hanging slack or are otherwise inadequate, the watch officer should note that fact in the bell book, even if you also slow down while passing. If the other vessel claims wake damage, the fact that you noticed and logged the inadequacy of her mooring lines will help to defeat a claim.

MACHINERY AND EQUIPMENT

Accidents Due to Allegedly Defective Material

(See also "Shipboard Injuries and Illnesses," below.) When an injury, however slight, to a crew member, passenger, stevedore, or other person on the vessel is caused by allegedly defective material, gear, or equipment of any kind, it is important, if at all practicable, to label and preserve the supposedly defective gear as evidence. On no account should it be removed from the vessel by an unauthorized person, nor should it be thrown overboard or destroyed. Save it, no matter how much you are tempted to toss it over the side. Do not release it or show it to others until you receive instructions from your insurance department.

Take photographs of the allegedly defective part, particularly if for any reason you will be unable to keep the part on board. Send these photographs along with your report to your company but do not show them to anyone not connected with your company and do not permit anyone to take photographs without proper authority except government investigators making an official inspection or inquiry.

Defective Gear Belonging to Stevedores or Others. If an accident is caused by defective gear or equipment belonging to stevedores or others, make every effort to keep that gear on board. If the owner of the equipment refuses to leave it aboard the vessel, be sure to say so in your report. In any case, try to get a complete set of photographs of the equipment before the owner can remove it from the vessel.

If a rope, chain, or sling parted, make a note of the type of cargo that was being lifted and try to get an estimate of its weight. Have the winch inspected immediately by the chief engineer or one of the assistant engineers. The chief engineer is generally much concerned about his winches and he will have them put in good order at the first sign of imperfection.

Have the chief officer inspect the other gear and equipment involved, such as the runner, blocks, etc. Opposing lawyers are experts at finding something wrong with equipment, especially if no inspections have been made.

If he is able to do so at the time, the injured person should prepare a statement showing how he came to be using the gear or equipment in question. Also get a statement from the person in charge and from witnesses, if any, with their home addresses. If a crew member was injured and will be laid up in excess of seventy-two hours, or was hospitalized, you will have to make up Coast Guard Form CG-2692, a copy of which should be sent to your insurance department.

Accommodation Ladder Accidents

Damage to the accommodation ladder is often caused by barges, lighters, launches, or other craft when the vessel is at anchor or made fast to buoys and working cargo. This can cause a serious injury to anyone who is on the ladder at the time. You should notify the stevedore foreman or person in charge, in writing, that the stevedore will be held responsible for any damage to the accommodation ladder or injury to persons on it caused by his craft. The fact that the warning was given, and to whom, should be entered in the log. Generally, the stevedore foreman will have his own men raise or lower the ladder when there is a danger of it being damaged by his craft.

If alongside a dock, be careful that the accommodation ladder does not become jammed against a bollard or other obstruction on the dock when the vessel surges or the ladder moves along the dock with a falling or rising tide. This can damage the ladder considerably and cause injury to anyone on the ladder at the time. Rollers at the foot of the gangway are particularly dangerous if they are not fitted with a guard.

Accidents Caused by Breakdown of Machinery or Equipment

(See also "Accidents Due to Allegedly Defective Material," above.) These accidents are not rare. The engineers may lose the plant while steaming in a channel or harbor, or a winch may fail when a stevedore is handling a sling of cargo. Losing the plant when underway in harbor may be the cause of various accidents, sometimes a collision, before the vessel can be brought under control.

The chief engineer should make a statement regarding the cause of the breakdown and the engineers on duty may also be required to make statements. If a cargo winch breaks down, the chief engineer's statement should indicate when the winch was last overhauled or repaired. Should the main engine fail and a subsequent hearing be held, the Coast Guard may want the course recorder tape.

Bursting of Steam Pipes

This type of accident is infrequent. When a steam pipe bursts and no one is injured, a report is not generally required. If a man is injured, it will probably be a steam burn which is always nasty. It is urgent that first aid be given and the man sent to a hospital at once if the vessel is in port. If he cannot be moved, have an ambulance brought to the vessel as quickly as possible. Make up an injury report if anyone is injured, even slightly.

It is important to retain the burst section of steam pipe on board for any investigation or until your insurance department takes custody of it or tells you that it is no longer required.

Breakage of Shaft

(See also "Loss of Propeller," below.) Prepare a statement of facts, in rough, as shown in Fig. 23. If on time charter when this type of accident occurs, it will generally mean that the vessel goes off hire. It is therefore necessary that the date and time of the accident and the position of the vessel at that time be accurate, as well as the date, time, and position of the vessel when taken in tow and the date and time she arrives in port. Keep your office and agent at the port of destination fully advised. When sending radiograms regarding the accident, don't skimp on words—make the message clear so there will be no doubt about its meaning.

The chief engineer will be required to furnish an account of fuel on hand at the time of the accident, at the times of arrival in port and departure, and at the time the vessel gets back to the position, or its equivalent, where the accident occurred. This information must be included in the statement of facts, which will probably be the only report required except for Coast Guard Form CG-2692.

Breaking the shaft may cause the loss of the propeller (see "Loss of Propeller," below).

Loss of Blade or Entire Propeller

This accident seldom requires a damage report but a statement of facts should be made up. Usually when either of the above occurs the vessel will start to vibrate and the RPMs will rise. The engineer on duty will cut down the RPMs or stop, by which time the bridge should have put the telegraph on "Stop" and called you. If the vessel is not very deep, you may be able to see what has occurred by putting a pilot ladder over. Whoever goes down the pilot ladder should have a life belt and a line made fast around him. Send a message to the home office informing them of the accident, giving the weather at the time, the weather expected, and where bound, if deviating. If you are sure the propeller struck something, say so. Also enter it in the log and on Coast Guard Form CG-2692. But if you are not sure, say you don't know.

If a blade is lost, it will be necessary for you to proceed to the nearest port with proper repair facilities. If possible proceed to a port in the general direction of the port of destination, keeping in mind the repair facilities and the weather conditions.

If the entire propeller was lost, your company may try to get assistance in the form of a salvage tug, or another company vessel, if one is close by, or they may leave it to you to contact another vessel. In this respect the Coast Guard AMVER system can be of great help. Unless arranged by your company any assistance you take should be on a "No Cure—No Pay" basis. Make an entry regarding the accident in the official logbook, giving the time, date, and position.

Line in Propeller

If a line gets caught in the propeller, call a surveyor, preferably ABS or Lloyd's, to check the blades and shaft. It is generally necessary to employ a diver to clear the line. If the line is cleared by the crew, have a diver check the blades and report his findings to the surveyor, who will then issue a seaworthy certificate if no serious damage is discovered. If the certificate cannot be issued before the vessel sails, he will make an entry in the log that the survey was made, with the result, and that the certificate will be sent to the vessel at a later date.

Make a report describing how the line got caught in the propeller (line parted, tug or linemen let go too soon, etc.) and giving the approximate amount of line caught. The engine movement at the time should be noted in your report. Log the times the diver started work, cleared the line, and left, as well as the time the surveyor came on board and when he left, together with his name and his organization, all in block letters.

Loss of Anchor and Chain

If you lose an anchor take cross bearings immediately to get the exact location. Your statement should include:

1. Time, date, location, bearings, and the number of the chart used.
2. Which anchor and how much chain were lost.
3. The cause of the loss. If another vessel was at fault give her name, hailing port, nationality, and owner's name if available, and whether notice of liability was served.
4. Any injuries to crew, or others, with reports and statements.
5. Wind, tide, and sea conditions at the time.
6. A statement from the officers on the bridge and on the forecastle.

CARGO DAMAGE

Heavy Weather Damage

Cargo damage is a constant problem. It will occur, it seems, regardless of how much care is taken to prevent it. Usually it is the chief officer who must write a statement and make a report giving the reason for the damage. If it was caused by salt water, he should note in the statement that the hatches were properly battened down and the number of tarps used on each hatch. All facts being correct, the statement and report are countersigned by you. You may attribute the damage to heavy weather, but this will avail you little unless a storm carried away a tarp or shoring, or stove in some hatch boards, or caused cargo to shift.

Make up a log abstract covering the period of the heavy weather. The weather must have been extraordinarily heavy—not the rough weather usually expected on a voyage. The log should show what steps were taken to avoid heavy weather damage and to prevent laboring of the vessel—such as slowing down, changing course, or ballasting. These log entries will assist your insurance department in fighting a claim for cargo damage. Any repairs to the vessel for damage attributed to the heavy weather on that voyage should be noted in the logbook and in the statement.

Sweat Damage

The log should show when the holds were ventilated or, if they were not, the reason why not, such as heavy weather or other cause. Many officers fail to make log entries regarding ventilation of the holds, especially on vessels with blower systems. It is important to make a log entry both when the ventilation system is turned on and when it is shut down. Always include the reason for shutting down. On vessels with cowl ventilators which must be trimmed by hand, the log should show each time they were trimmed, and whether to the wind or backed to the wind, and why. The log should also show if the ventilator cowls are unshipped or covered for any reason. This also applies to hatches which are opened for ventilation.

Pilferage

When pilferage occurs a statement is sometimes required from the chief officer and the officer who was on duty when the pilferage occurred or was discovered. The statement should indicate what precautions were taken to prevent pilferage, such as placing guards in the holds, keeping pilferable cargo in special lockers, and so forth. Include the marks and numbers of the cases and the location and manner of stowage.

If pilferage occurs when you are carrying military cargo, the cargo superintendent for the government may want a pilferage report signed by the chief officer or the master. Sometimes, because of the wording, it appears to be an acknowledgment of liability, and many masters refuse to sign such a report and will not permit the chief officer to sign it. However, your company may authorize you to sign it if the following or a similar clause is added: "Acknowledgment of the pilferage, damage, or shortage reported herein is without prejudice to the contractual and legal defenses of the vessel and/or carrier."

Be sure that the report is in duplicate and that you get a copy.

Stevedore Damage

When stevedores or others working on the vessel cause damage to any part of the vessel or cargo, most companies require that a stevedore damage report be made up. One copy should be served on the stevedore foreman or other person responsible for the damage. All the copies should be signed by him, on the appropriate line, either admitting liability or denying it. Although stevedore damage is stressed throughout this section, if any other party such as a drayman, repair gang, or others cause any damage to the cargo or vessel, the same reports should be made.

Any damage caused by stevedores should be called to the attention of the stevedore foreman as soon as damage occurs or is discovered, if the foreman has not already reported it, which would be a rare event. Start a rough copy of the report as soon as the damage is known and make the required number of smooth copies once the report is complete.

The stevedore may deny liability if the damage is not reported immediately. Be prepared to prove that the damage was done by the stevedores, who will most likely claim that the damage was already there. The foreman should be requested to sign all copies, admitting or denying liability, one copy being served on him. If he denies liability, which he probably will, or refuses to sign either way, request that he sign the reports to acknowledge receipt of a copy. It is possible that he will also refuse to accept a copy. If any such difficulties are met with, make a note to that effect on the report and take it up with the port captain or agent at once.

Stevedore damage reports must, if possible, be turned in completely made up before the vessel sails. If the damage is discovered after the vessel sails, the reports should be sent in from the next port. Also send a copy to the agent at the port where the damage occurred, with instructions that he serve it on the stevedore.

Practically all steamship companies issue stevedore damage report forms, all of which have more or less the same items and questions to answer regarding the damage. When making up the report, if any of the questions do not apply, draw a line through the space—this indicates that nothing has been missed or overlooked. In the event that report forms are not available, the one shown in Fig. 26 may be used. Send one copy to the home office, one to the stevedore, and keep one for the vessel's file. Follow your company's instructions regarding distribution, if it differs from that suggested here.

DEVIATION

Deviation in this sense means a departure from the usual route on a voyage. Deviation is justifiable for the purpose of saving life, to put a seriously sick or injured crew member ashore, for urgent repairs, to restow cargo that has shifted so as to be a danger to the vessel, etc.

A deviation to the nearest port sometimes takes the vessel far off its course. For example, a vessel bound from the Panama Canal to Yokohama drops a blade at latitude 42-00N, longitude 152-00W. She would proceed at slow speed to the nearest port—Honolulu. On completing repairs she would not return to the point of deviation but would take the regular route from Honolulu to Yokohama. The difference in distance between the point of deviation and Yokohama on the original track, and between the point of deviation and Yokohama via Honolulu would be the number of miles deviated. The extra fuel used would be computed using the known fuel consumption per mile. A statement of facts should be prepared giving full details of the deviation, including the fuel, fresh water, and lube oil consumed and the extra time and distance steamed (see Fig. 24).

If the deviation was to put a sick or injured crew member ashore or on another vessel it will be necessary to make up Coast Guard Form CG-2692. Also be sure to enter details in the official log and the medical log and make up illness or injury reports. Keep your home office fully advised and notify your agent at the port of refuge.

FIRE ON BOARD

Fire at sea is one of the most dreaded of all marine casualties—always to be feared and always to be guarded against. Damage can be extensive, especially to cargo, not only by the fire itself but by the water or other means used to extinguish it. (See also "General Average" and "Particular Average," below.)

If possible, and time permits, which is doubtful, start taking notes or have an officer do it. If in port, get the names of all tugs and fireboats and the name and rank of the officer in charge of any Coast Guard detail or local fire department detail coming on board to assist.

Men can be very badly injured in a fire on board. Try to avoid sending men into dangerous positions. Many men will be too willing to take an unnecessary chance if given the opportunity.

Inform your home office as soon as possible of the date and time the fire was discovered and its location on the vessel. If the fire is in a hold, give the nature of the cargo. If the vessel is at sea, state the position and weather, if in any immediate danger, whether there are any injuries to crew or others, and whether assistance is required or at hand. Unless you see that the fire can be extinguished almost immediately, you should notify the nearest U.S. Coast Guard station or foreign authority capable of rendering assistance. The Coast Guard AMVER system will, on request, indicate the participating vessels closest to you. When the fire is extinguished, send your home office a general idea of the damage to vessel or cargo. It may be advisable to send an initial report by telex or telephone, followed by a more detailed report by mail.

When making up your statement give a full account of the fire, including when discovered, by whom, assistance rendered and by whom, when such assistance arrived, when the fire was extinguished, and the apparent damage to vessel and cargo. If a Coast Guard fire-fighting detail was on board give them their due. The name and rank of the officer in charge should be entered in the deck log and official log and also on Coast Guard Form CG-2692, which will have to be made up. Make an entry in the official log giving full particulars.

The master of a vessel in port with a fire on board may be ordered by the port authorities to get underway, or the vessel may be towed away from the dock to a place where she will not be a danger to the port or to other vessels. In U.S. ports this order would usually be given by the Coast Guard captain of the port or his representative; however, the local port officials may also have the authority to have dangerous vessels moved. If this occurs, enter full details in the log, including the name, rank, and official capacity of the person giving the order.

If the fire occurs at sea you should note protest on arrival in port. If the fire reached the crew's quarters it is advisable to obtain a list of gear and clothing lost by each crew member. This should be done as soon as possible because if postponed too long the list will increase greatly. This doesn't necessarily mean that the company will pay for such losses, but if the list is asked for you will have it.

In addition to your own statement you will require:

1. Signed abstracts of deck and engine logs.
2. Lists from the chief officer and chief engineer of stores and gear used, or lost, or damaged by fire or water, stating which and whether the items were new or used (do not use the word "old").
3. Signed statements from officers and crew members who have any knowledge of the fire and of attempts to extinguish it, giving their names, home addresses, and document numbers.
4. Signed statements, with home addresses, from any injured persons, and the same from witnesses to accidents causing the injuries.
5. An injury report for every injured person regardless of how minor the injury may be.
6. Coast Guard Form CG-2692.
7. Copies of all messages sent or received relative to the fire.

OIL SPILL IN PORT

This is likely to involve a fine, sometimes a heavy one. Be sure to have someone rope off any oily portions of the deck to prevent injuries due to slipping, even if sawdust or similar material has been used. It is advisable to post a notice at the gangway warning men boarding that the deck is slippery. Longshoremen may refuse to come on board until it is cleaned up, especially if the spill occurs at night.

Many ports issue special regulations regarding oil spills. Have the latest regulations on board; the agent can get them for you.

If you have an oil spill in a U.S. port it must be reported to the National Response Center. This report may be made via the National Response Center's toll-free telephone number, (800) 424-8802. Until recently, the report could be made to either the National Response Center or to the nearest Coast Guard unit. New regulations require that the report be made direct to the National Response Center except when this is not physically possible. In such a case you can satisfy the requirement by notifying the nearest Coast Guard unit provided you subsequently report to the National Response Center as soon as possible. Failure to report an oil spill carries a heavier fine than the oil spill itself.

In some ports failure to report an oil spill is a criminal offense and may result in a fine and/or imprisonment for the master or other responsible officer.

HEAVY WEATHER DAMAGE

All repairs made to an American vessel in a foreign port are subject to a fifty percent duty. However, if such repairs are emergency repairs necessary to make the ship seaworthy, as in the case of damage caused by heavy weather, the duty may be remitted (see chapter 5, "Customs," for details). Entries substantiating the heavy weather must be made in the logbook and abstracts of the logbook covering the period of the heavy weather must be submitted to the district director of Customs. This is usually done by giving the abstracts to the customhouse broker or to your insurance department, depending upon company instructions. The abstracts may be typed on plain paper. It is seldom that a statement is required; however, if the cost of the repairs is $25,000 or more or if the damage affects the seaworthiness of the vessel, Coast Guard Form CG-2692 must be made up. Don't forget to note protest on arrival at the first port after the heavy weather.

If you are asked for a statement it should include:

1. Precautions taken to avoid damage, such as slowing down, changing course, heaving to, or ballasting. (These will have been entered in the log.)

2. Wind direction and force and the state of the sea day by day, from the start of heavy weather to the time it moderates.

3. Damage to vessel or cargo.

4. Any injuries suffered by crew or passengers. This should be in the medical log, and also in the official log if a crew member is involved. Don't forget to make up Coast Guard Form CG-2692, if required, and an injury report with the necessary statements.

5. Any other information that may be of help to your insurance department.

MARINE INSURANCE & AVERAGE

This is a complicated field in the shipping and marine insurance industries and is a study in itself. Many books have been written on the subject. A few highlights, and the master's responsibility in regard to reports and statements required, are given herein.

In shipping and marine insurance terminology "average" is a word meaning partial loss or damage sustained by a vessel and/or cargo during the course of a voyage. In marine insurance parlance, the voyage is often called a "maritime adventure." The origin of the word "average" (which in this sense has nothing to do with averages) is said to be obscure, but legal historians assert that it derives from the Italian word *avaria,* meaning loss or damage.

For our purposes there are two kinds of average—general average and particular average. These terms indicate the character of the loss or damage, and who bears that loss or damage.

General Average

(See also "Particular Average," below.) General average is a voluntary sacrifice, deliberately made by the master, of vessel's gear, equipment, stores, or cargo, or a voluntary stranding. It includes expenses incurred in time of peril to avoid or avert a greater danger or loss threatening the common adventure, and is made for the safety and benefit of all interests concerned in the adventure. Such a voluntary sacrifice is an "act of man" and is called a "general average act"; and the property sacrificed or expenses incurred are called a "general average loss."

All such losses which arise as a result of sacrifices made or expenses incurred for the saving of the vessel and cargo come within general average. These losses must be borne, in proportion to the value saved, by contributions from all interests benefitted. These contributions are called general average contributions. In other words, the property saved must pay for the property sacrificed if the sacrifice was made to save the common adventure. This puts a great responsibility on the master, as the authority to make the sacrifices falls on him.

A peril must exist and must be one which threatens all the interests in the adventure. The danger must be such that there is no escape from it unless a sacrifice is made. The sacrifice must be reasonable and prudent and made in good faith. That is, it should be made with due consideration for the good it will do. And finally, it must be successful—the peril or danger must be overcome and the vessel and cargo, or remainder of the cargo, saved.

Rule A of the York/Antwerp Rules gives a clear and definite picture of a general average:

> There is a general average act when, and only when, any extraordinary sacrifice or expenditure is intentionally and reasonably made or incurred for the common safety for the purpose of preserving from peril the property involved in a common maritime adventure.

The custom of general average is an old established rule of shipping which dates back to the Rhodian Laws of the Sea of many centuries ago. These laws were copied, with modifications, by many other countries in Europe and the Mediterranean. It was the custom at that time for merchants to accompany their goods on the voyage and to dispose of them at the destination, or enroute. Each merchant might have only a few bales of goods, casks or skins of oil or wine.

Most of these ancient vessels were small and had very little in the way of decks or other protection from the elements. The cargo was stowed under whatever shelter was available, such as skins, an old sail, etc. It is doubtful that there was much, if any, supervision of the loading, and even with the small amount of cargo carried the vessels were probably overloaded. It was not until several centuries later that some ports enacted laws to prevent overloading. The vessels were safe enough in fair weather but in heavy weather these small craft must have been extremely difficult to manage.

In time of peril, which was often, jettisoning cargo or spars was the usual remedy, and the master, after consultation with the merchants, would jettison what was most accessible or would do the most good. This practice would also be followed to lighten the vessel if she were chased by pirates, a common occurrence in the Mediterranean in those days. If the jettisoning served its purpose and the vessel made port, the owners of the remaining cargo, by prior agreement and the then existing law, reimbursed the owner of the sacrificed cargo for his loss in proportion to the value of their own cargo saved. If the vessel's spars or gear were jettisoned, they were paid for in a similar manner. At that time it was called "coming into contribution." Today it is called "general average."

The York/Antwerp Rules. Although the principles of general average are recognized by practically all maritime countries, the laws regarding them are not uniform. This lack of uniformity was recognized as the cause of long delays in settling claims. Today most general average claims are settled according to the York/Antwerp Rules. First adopted in 1864 by an international convention of shipowners, merchants, and others interested in the problem, the rules have been revised several times to bring them up to date, the latest revision having been in 1974.

These rules do not change the laws of general average in the maritime countries but they do furnish a common basis for the adjustment of general average. A clause in the bill of lading or charter party will usually provide: "General average to be settled according to the York/Antwerp Rules 1974 at such port or place as may be selected by the carrier, and as to matters not provided in the Rules, according to the laws and usages of the port of destination." Occasionally the clause will omit some of the rules.

Some examples of general average are:

1. A voluntary jettison of cargo, ship's stores, equipment, or gear to lighten the vessel in order to refloat her. These must be thrown overboard, that is, jettisoned—not washed overboard. The mind and agency of man must be employed; it must be an "act of man." However, if time, conditions, and weather permit, and craft are available, the goods should be put into boats or lighters. Bear in mind, but do not be overly hindered by the thought, that cargo interests and underwriters may claim that much, if not all, that was sacrificed was unnecessary and that the master was negligent or overhasty in making the sacrifices.

2. Expenses of discharging and lightering, if used.

3. Cargo, ship's gear, stores, and equipment damaged by water or other means used to extinguish a fire. This does not include cargo or ship's gear actually damaged by the fire itself; that would be particular average. It also does not include damage due to smoke or heat, even if the smoke or heat is a result of attempts to extinguish the fire, rather than a result of the fire itself.

4. Cutting holes in the deck, hull, or bulkhead in order to get at a fire.

5. Damage sustained by ship's engine, propeller, rudder, or other equipment, when used in a manner for which they were not intended in an attempt to refloat a stranded vessel.
6. Fuel consumed in the above attempt.
7. Voluntary stranding for the good of all interests.
8. Ship's material or cargo burnt as fuel to reach a port of safety, provided it can be shown that the vessel sailed from her last port with sufficient fuel for the contemplated voyage. A sufficient supply does not mean a minimum supply or barely enough to reach the destination in good weather. It means the calculated supply necessary for the voyage plus a reasonable amount as a margin for safety considering the season of the year and the nature of the voyage.
9. Loss of an anchor and chain, slipped to avoid a peril.
10. Damage by seawater to the ship or cargo in holds when hatches were opened to jettison cargo.
11. Loss of freight caused by general average sacrifices.
12. Sacrifice of ship's equipment. It must be shown that the gear or equipment was sacrificed, or employed for a purpose for which it was not intended, such as using pumps for pumping water out of a stranded vessel if such water contained sand or other foreign substance in it.
13. Damage to boilers caused by using salt water in an emergency when the supply of fresh water would not enable the vessel to reach a safe port. You will have to show that you sailed from the last port with sufficient water for the contemplated voyage and give the reason why fresh water could not be made on the vessel.
14. Windlass, capstan, or winches damaged in an attempt to pull the vessel off a strand.
15. Putting into a port of refuge to avoid an immediate loss, or to repair damage suffered at sea, or to restow cargo that shifted in heavy weather. Expenses may include towage, pilotage, harbor dues, costs of discharging, warehousing, reloading when necessary, fuel consumed from point of deviation and return (see "Deviation," above), and various other items.

General Average Deposit or Bond. When a general average has been declared the carrier has a possessory lien on the cargo for his share of the general average. The lien is lost upon delivery of the cargo. It is not always practicable or desirable to hold the cargo on board or to warehouse it while the general average statement of how much each interest owes is being prepared, as this generally takes a long time. The average adjuster estimates what each may have to pay and the cargo is released to the owner or consignee on payment of a deposit, called a general average deposit, for which only one receipt is given. No copies are made. Refunds are made as required when the final exact settlement is arrived at. In place of a deposit the company may agree to accept a general average bond guaranteed by the cargo underwriters or by a bank.

It is not likely that you will ever be called on to give a receipt for a general average deposit. If it should be necessary keep in mind that only one receipt is issued; do not make any copies. All the information on the receipt is copied on the stub attached to the form.

General Average Adjustment. The adjustment of general average, meaning determining the amount each interest must contribute, may be a lengthy and complicated job. It is generally handled by independent experts in the field, called average adjusters. The adjuster is supposed to be a fair and impartial arbiter especially trained in the work. He is expected to come up with a disinterested adjustment, fair and equitable, but unfortunately it is rarely satisfactory to all interests in the adventure and there are usually many complaints.

There is an immense amount of detail involved in the work of the average adjuster, depending on the nature of the cargo, the sacrifices made, and the expenses incurred. He may require several months to complete his work, after which he will issue an average statement indicating how much each interest must contribute. The average adjuster will require the following documents:

1. Manifests of the cargo on board at the time of the accident.
2. Copies of bills of lading for the cargo.
3. Vessel's logbooks.
4. Copies of protest noted and/or extended.
5. Accounts of all expenses relative to the general average.
6. List of ship's stores and equipment expended during and in connection with the accident.

The adjuster notes on the manifest which lots of cargo may be released. Copies are given to the vessel, the agent, and others representing the company. The notes are usually made in colored crayon and a code is attached to or explained on the manifest. A typical example follows:

Red: Release cargo. General average contribution guaranteed by (name of bank).
Purple: Release cargo after obtaining consignee's signature on Lloyd's bond.
Yellow: Deposit required.

Blue: May release cargo as required. Have security.
Green: Release cargo.

When cargo is subject to general average, do not release any of it before checking against the coded manifest.

Expense to Vessel. The chief officer and chief engineer should make up lists showing all stores and equipment lost, damaged, or expended as a general average sacrifice in attempting to save the vessel or cargo. In case of fire, one list should show stores and equipment whose loss or damage was caused by the fire itself. Another list should contain stores or equipment lost or damaged in efforts to extinguish the fire. The latter should include bottles of CO_2 or other extinguishing agents expended, fire-fighting equipment damaged in extinguishing the fire, stores and equipment soaked beyond use or damaged by chemicals used to extinguish the fire, and tarps damaged or cut up in an attempt to cover openings or ventilators, or to smother the fire.

Still another list should show any necessary overtime that you authorized for the crew, repairmen, or longshoremen in order to carry out the general average sacrifice. In performing a general average act, the master or officer in charge must use reason and prudence. In this emergency the master is the agent of the cargo owners, consignees, and underwriters, as well as of his company, and he must do all he possibly can to save them from loss. In authorizing overtime bear this in mind.

Particular Average

(See also "General Average," above.) Particular average is a term applied to any accidental loss, less than a total loss of vessel and cargo, by a peril which is not of a general average nature. "Acts of God" are particular average. Accidental stranding, collision, loss of anchor and chain, and damage to vessel or cargo by heavy weather or fire come under particular average. The loss sustained is borne by the owners of the property damaged. It is said of particular average that the loss "lies where it falls." The other interests in the maritime adventure do not contribute to the interest suffering the loss.

The following should illustrate the difference between particular average and general average. Cargo damaged by fire is particular average but cargo damaged by water, chemicals, or other means used to extinguish the fire in order to save the ship and the remaining cargo comes under general average. Damage caused by accidentally going aground comes under particular average. If a vessel accidentally collides with another ship and is badly holed, the damage to the ship and cargo due to the collision is particular average. If the vessel is then deliberately grounded in an attempt to prevent her from sinking and thereby save the vessel and the remaining cargo, the resulting damage is general average.

SHIPBOARD ILLNESSES AND INJURIES

Safety

The frequency of accidents that are so often avoidable results in high costs in claims, care, and maintenance to the company, and pain and suffering to the injured man. Some vessels are found to be "accident prone," and those in charge blame it on bad luck, even though other vessels in the same company and on the same run have far fewer accidents. Investigation usually proves that the accidents are not due to bad luck but to poor or nonexistent supervision.

Many shipboard injuries could be prevented if proper care and attention were paid to accident prevention. Some common causes of needless accidents are grease, oil, and other slippery substances on the deck or gangway; broken or improperly fitting hatch boards; open and unprotected hatchways in dark tween decks; broken or missing rungs on hold or tank ladders, pilot ladders, and others; and broken gangway steps. But perhaps the greatest cause, and the easiest to correct, is poor crew supervision or even rank indifference on the part of the officers. That puts practically all accidents on the vessel right in the lap of the master who is, in the final analysis, responsible for what happens on his vessel.

Many shipowners have an accident prevention program supervised by a shoreside safety manager. Circulars and pamphlets are issued dealing with accident prevention and safety. These should be kept on file, read by all crew members, especially the officers, and discussed until they are thoroughly understood. Books on safety and accident prevention can be obtained from the Department of Labor and various other sources. The U.S. Coast Guard publication *Proceedings of the Marine Safety Council,* published monthly, should be obtained and read by all the officers and crew. It contains interesting and informative articles on safety and other matters of importance to seamen. If possible, keep a file of back issues.

An injured crew member on the vessel does no one any good. Others must do his work; an officer must give medical treatment, sometimes for an extended period; there are forms to make up, statements to get, and letters to write regarding the accident; and finally, it is usually necessary to hold an investigation to learn the cause of the accident. All this because someone in charge failed to make sure that the injured man was working in a safe place, with safe and proper tools, and knew what he was doing.

Sick or Injured Seaman Working

It is poor economy, dangerous to the seaman, and possibly expensive to your company to make a sick or injured seaman work, regardless of the cause of the illness or injury. It could also result in a great deal of trouble for the officer who ordered him to turn to, and probably much correspondence on your part explaining why it was done. As soon as a seaman reports himself ill, or is reported ill, he should be taken off duty if the illness or injury is serious enough that he should not turn to. A day or two off duty at the onset of an illness may save time, from several days to a week or more, later on. Generally a seaman dislikes laying up unless he is actually sick. Malingerers, as a rule, are few and far between.

Injuries in Port

When an accident occurs on your vessel while in port and a crew member, longshoreman, or other person is injured, regardless of how it happened, it is of the utmost importance that the injured person be given first aid immediately and, if necessary, sent to a hospital or put under a doctor's care. Everything possible should be done for the injured person. Some docks and practically all ship-yards have first-aid stations to which an injured man can be sent.

Enter in the medical and official logs all cases of injury to or illness of a crew member. Also enter in the medical log any injury or medical treatment to persons on board who are not crew members. Fill out Coast Guard Form CG-2692 if anyone is hospitalized or is laid up for over seventy-two hours, and send a copy of this report to your insurance department. In all cases of illness or injury to anyone on board, make up injury or illness reports for your company insurance department.

Injuries and Illness at Sea

If when at sea an accident causes a serious injury, or a serious illness occurs, you should apply for assistance by radio to a passenger ship having a doctor or to any of the many hospitals in the various countries that supply radio medical advice through a system that is described in detail at the end of this chapter. If you are advised to get the sick or injured person to a doctor, the Coast Guard AMVER system will, on request, send you the names and positions of the closest participating vessels carrying a doctor.

Deviating. If, due to an injury or illness at sea, expert medical attention is required or if there is any danger to life which could possibly be averted by proceeding to the nearest port, you would be justified in deviating. In fact, it is your duty to deviate if there is even a slim chance of saving a life by doing so. In the meantime you should advise your agent at the port bound for, giving him an ETA. If there is no agent in that port, the port authorities should be notified so that a boat or ambulance will be on hand to transfer the sick or injured person to a hospital. A doctor may come on board with the authorities.

Be sure to send a message to your home office informing them of the deviation and the reason. Any time a serious accident occurs the home office should be notified by radio, telex, or telephone, followed by a detailed letter from the first port after the accident, with copies of the injury reports, statements, and photographs. Promptness in thus reporting serious accidents is particularly important; it will enable the insurance department to have an investigator on the vessel to take statements or depositions if necessary.

Have your agent at the port where the person was hospitalized send you a message informing you of the doctor's diagnosis, if you were unable to get it before sailing. This is important, as the man may later claim he was hospitalized for an entirely different reason— conceivably one involving an alleged injury or illness he had several months before, which may or may not have been reported. This is another argument for making up reports for all injuries and illnesses, however slight, and also entering them in the official log and medical log. In so doing you will serve the best interests of your company and may help to defeat an expensive claim which could not otherwise be disproved. This is especially true of claims made by what are known as "claim-happy" seamen. It in no way prevents a seaman from claiming and receiving fair compensation for a legitimate injury.

If it is necessary to deviate, a statement of facts should be made up giving the date, time, and position where the deviation commenced and the date and time the vessel returned to the same or an equivalent position. Fig. 24 can be used. Data entered in the statement of facts should be substantiated by the entries in the log.

The Reports

In all cases of injury or illness, regardless of how caused or how minor, you should make up the required reports and obtain the necessary statements. Even if a person who has no right to be on the vessel gets hurt while aboard, an injury report should be made up and an entry made in the medical log. Shore people working on the vessel are more likely to have accidents due to their inexperience and their lack of shipboard safety consciousness.

Start a rough injury report as soon as possible and type the final copies once all the facts are known. As soon as he is able to do so, the injured person should be requested to give you a signed statement giving his version of how the accident occurred. It is important that the report be as complete as possible, omitting no detail that could be of some assistance to your insurance department. All the above applies regardless of how slight the injury may be.

Enter the name and address of the doctor or hospital in the official log, medical log, and on the report, along with the diagnosis and treatment. If in a foreign port, request the agent to have the diagnosis and treatment prescribed written in English. Copies of the diagnosis and the doctor's recommendations should be attached to the report.

When there is an accident on the vessel caused by tripping, slipping, or falling, you and the chief officer should personally examine the scene as soon as possible after the accident and note the conditions. Was there grease, oil, or other substance on the deck? Were ropes, wire, dunnage, or hoses of any kind cluttering the deck at the scene of the accident? Or were the ropes faked down, wires coiled, dunnage stacked, hoses safely out of the way? What you find should appear on your report and in your statement. If the accident occurred in the engine room, the chief engineer should accompany you when you make the inspection.

The scene of every shipboard accident causing an injury should be photographed if possible. Type or block print the date and the name of the vessel on the back of each photograph and send them in with your report. This is often overlooked.

Do not wait until the end of the voyage to complete reports and statements. It is important to do this as early as possible. If an injured man is paid off in the port where the accident occurred, the report should be sent in from that port, if possible. It can be taken for granted that a crew member, longshoreman, or other person who is injured on the vessel, or asserts that he was injured, will put in a claim; the chances are that his claim will be in the insurance department before your reports arrive. If any additional information comes to your attention later, it can be sent in by letter.

When making up illness or injury reports, give full particulars so that nothing is left in doubt. Reports are often completed with important details missing, usually because the officer responsible put them off to a more convenient time, forgot all about them until the end of the voyage, and then had to make them up in a hurry. Avoid procrastination. The importance of making up reports promptly and forwarding them to your insurance department immediately after an illness or injury is discovered cannot be too strongly stressed.

Statements

Always try to get signed statements from witnesses to any accident causing an injury, and from the injured person, regardless of how slight that injury may be. The statement should be dated and signed by the person making it and include his home address and the name of the vessel. This is sometimes overlooked. Give a copy of the statement to the person making it.

Statements should be obtained from all persons able to give any information on the cause of an accident as soon as practicable after the accident, while the facts are still fresh in their minds. A seaman will be more likely to state the true facts concerning an accident immediately after it happens and before he can discuss it with others. If the statement is put off he will undoubtedly talk about it with his shipmates, probably with a sea lawyer or two, and perhaps with the injured man's lawyer. His statement after that, if given at all, may differ widely from the actual facts.

The Master's Statement. If you can supply any information on the cause of an accident, you should make up a statement. The master's statement is always considered important. Be sure to state if you personally examined the scene of the accident, and what you found; this is an important part of your statement. Include any suspicious circumstances concerning the accident.

If any letters or notes were written to or received from others regarding an injury on the vessel, send copies in with your statement. As a matter of policy, you should be cautious about writing to others regarding an accident on the vessel unless you are requested to do so by your office. This also applies to interviews and statements, oral or written, requested by reporters and the like. Never discuss the facts except with company officials or government investigators. Never make a statement admitting liability, even if you think your vessel may have been at fault. Leave that to your insurance department. When unauthorized persons, including reporters, request information or your opinion, refer them to your office. Do not offer an opinion one way or the other—you may be rudely and unpleasantly surprised when you later read what is quoted as your opinion.

If you believe the injured man had been drinking or using drugs, your statement should mention this. Do not say he was drunk—that may be difficult to prove. Did his breath smell of alcohol? Was he staggering? Was his speech incoherent or belligerent? Did he admit having had too much to drink or that he had been drinking just prior to the accident? These are points to bring out in your statement. The same applies to those who were helping him or working with him. As a matter of safety, his own and that of others, a man under the influence of alcohol should not be permitted to turn to.

If the injured person has suffered similar injuries before, bring it to the attention of your company, but do not mention the earlier accident in your report about the current injury. Some seamen make a habit, and a profitable one, of getting hurt on a vessel, and you may find that the alleged accidents bear a surprising similarity.

If photographs, diagrams, or sketches are sent in with your report, the date and name of the vessel should be shown on the back.

The Medical Log

A medical log, which can be an ordinary ledger, should be kept up-to-date by the officer charged with first aid all the time the vessel is in service. All cases of injury or illness on the vessel, however slight or minor, to a crew member, passenger, longshoreman, or other person should be entered in the medical log, with the treatment given and any other pertinent data. The medical log must be signed by the person giving treatment; it is good practice also to have the ill or injured person sign the medical log.

A well-kept medical log will often save your company a claim and you much correspondence. Make it a practice to read the medical log weekly. The entries should be legible—block printing them is one way to ensure this. Remember that every case of injury to or illness of a crew member must also be entered in the official log with the treatment given.

Hospitalized Seaman's Clothes and Effects

When a seaman is hospitalized in any port, send his gear with him; another seaman can accompany him to assist, if necessary. Try to avoid taking his gear back to the United States. If you keep it on board, the vessel becomes responsible for its safety. If the hospitalized seaman needs only a few items and wants to leave the rest on board with another seaman, the sick man should be instructed to write a note naming the seaman who is to take charge of the gear. The seaman named should read and sign the note; otherwise the vessel may still be responsible for the gear. In any case, take an inventory of all the gear. Send one copy to the seaman in the hospital and one with the report to your company, put one with the gear, and keep one for your file. It is also likely that the consul and the agent will each want a copy, so make plenty of copies.

If it is impractical to get the gear to the hospital or to put it ashore in charge of the agent, the vessel will be responsible for it. Lock the gear up in a safe place with a copy of the inventory attached.

It is important that the man in the hospital gets the things he will need—shaving gear, underwear, etc. If not taken with him, these items should be sent to the hospital; or if that is impractical, they should be left with the agent to be delivered later. Some cigarettes, books, and magazines will be welcome, especially in a foreign port. Customs in most foreign ports will usually permit these things to be taken off the vessel. If there is any difficulty with customs, the consul's office can probably help in having the items cleared.

Seamen Going to Private Doctors

Occasionally a crew member will ask to see a doctor or dentist of his own choosing. This practice should be discouraged and he should be offered treatment by the doctor employed by the company or agent at that port; naturally, you cannot prevent a man from going to his own doctor if he insists on doing so. If hospitalization is indicated, do not waste time trying to contact the agent or home office, but get the man to a hospital without delay.

If a seaman refuses the offer of treatment by a company doctor and consults a private doctor, enter the facts in the medical log, the official log, and on the illness or injury report, which is made up regardless of where he gets treatment. The bill for treatment by a private physician or dentist should be paid by the seaman. Do not, however, fail to offer a seaman medical aid any time he requests or requires it, and this includes certain types of dental aid as well.

Bills for medical attention by private doctors or dentists should be returned to the seaman for payment. Do not sign these bills. If the bills must be paid before the vessel sails and the seaman has no money, he should sign the official log for the amount as an advance. If he refuses to sign for the amount and local officials require that the bill be paid before the vessel sails, make an entry in the official log that the seaman will be charged with the amount. Be sure to read the log entry to him and give him a copy.

Any or all of the foregoing procedures may be disregarded if they are in conflict with your company instructions or union agreement.

Even if a seaman pays his own doctor bill, an injury or illness report should still be made up with a note to the effect that he paid the doctor. This fact should also be entered in the official and medical logs. Try to obtain a signed statement from the seaman stating that he refused the treatment offered and that he preferred to see a private doctor.

It may be difficult to get a report or diagnosis from the private doctor, especially if the seaman was treated for alcoholism or a sexually transmitted disease. Have your agent procure the diagnosis, if possible. Failing that, make an entry in the logs and on the report stating the reason why the diagnosis was not available.

Even if a seaman has seen a private doctor, if you are in serious doubt as to his medical condition and you believe that his health could be endangered by being at sea and away from ready access to professional medical attention, send him to the company doctor. You cannot force a seaman to accept medical treatment against his will, but you are probably within your rights to require that he be examined, for his own protection as well as yours and that of your company.

Medical Advice by Radio

It is the definite duty and responsibility of the master of a vessel to seek medical advice by radio whenever the welfare of his crew or passengers requires it. Many countries offer medical advice by radio to ships, usually free of charge, and you should take advantage of it.

A medical radio advice service was begun by the United States in 1921; enough other countries have adopted similar services that the system now offers worldwide coverage. This system is often referred to as the "medico" system because messages sent through U.S. coast radio stations are prefixed DH MEDICO. DH stands for "deadhead," a radio service term meaning that the message is free.

Hydrographic Office Pub. No. 117A, *Radio Navigational Aids (Atlantic and Mediterranean Area),* and Pub. No. 117B, *Radio Navigational Aids (Pacific and Indian Oceans Area),* contain a listing, by country, of radio stations which will transmit medical advice by radio. The information in these publications is extracted from the *List of Radio Determination and Special Service Stations,* published by the International Telecommunications Union, which may be consulted if more detailed information is needed. All ships should have a copy on board.

Although radio medical advice is available worldwide, it is not actually an international system. Each country that offers medical advice by radio operates its own independent system with its own requirements. You should therefore consult one of the above publications before sending a medico message. For example, some countries insist that messages be in the official language of the country, while others will accept several different languages.

Messages regarding medical advice should be in plain language whenever possible, but in case of language problems the signals from the medical signal code of the *International Code of Signals,* Pub. No. 102, may be used. The medical signal code is also reprinted in Chapter XII of *The Ship's Medicine Chest and First Aid at Sea,* published by the U.S. Department of Health and Human Services.

All U.S. coast radio stations offer free medical message service to all vessels if the message is headed DH MEDICO and is signed by the master. Medical advice may also be obtained from any U.S. Coast Guard radio station. Messages to the Coast Guard will be handled either by a Coast Guard medical officer or by a hospital with which the Coast Guard has an agreement.

There are now commercial firms which offer medical advice by radio. Shipping companies may subscribe to these services for a fee. Such a firm will have its own doctors on duty twenty-four hours a day, and will usually have its own communications facilities. The doctors at these companies are especially trained in dealing with nonmedical personnel by radio and they are aware of the limitations of shipboard medical treatment. They are also usually aware of the facilities available for evacuating a seaman from a ship in different parts of the world. If your company subscribes to such a service, you will of course obtain your medical advice from that company whenever communications permit.

The more information and symptoms contained in your message, the easier it will be for the doctors to prescribe treatment. If you request medical advice by radio from any source, keep copies of all messages sent and received relative to the illness or injury.

ELEVEN

PANAMA CANAL

Regulations of the Panama Canal Commission, the agency that is responsible for operation of the canal, are found in Title 35, *Code of Federal Regulations*. These regulations, as they may be amended from time to time, will remain in force until midnight December 31, 1999. At that time the Panama Canal Commission will be disbanded and responsibility for and authority over all Panama Canal operations will be turned over to the government of Panama in accordance with the Panama Canal Treaty of 1977.

Not less than forty-eight hours before arrival you must send a radio message to the navigation division of the Panama Canal. The message should be in the following format with each item identified by a heading from the phonetic alphabet. The word "NEGAT" should be used after each item that can be answered "no," "none," or "not applicable."

ALFA—The Panama Canal Identification Number of the vessel.

BRAVO—Estimated date and time of arrival, port of arrival, and request for canal transit if desired.

CHARLIE—Estimated draft upon arrival, in feet and inches, fore and aft, in tropical fresh water (density 0.9954).

DELTA—Any changes in the vessel's name, country of registry, structure, or use of tanks that have occurred since the vessel last called in Panama Canal waters.

ECHO—Will the vessel dock at Balboa or Cristobal? What is the reason for docking? If it is for cargo operations, fuel, or water, give the tonnage involved in each case. Is there any reason the vessel will not be ready to transit upon arrival? What is the reason?

FOXTROT—The nature and tonnage of any deck cargo.

GOLF—If the vessel is carrying any explosives or dangerous cargoes in bulk, state the correct technical name, quantity (in long tons), United Nations number, and the International Maritime Organization class for each dangerous cargo carried. If the vessel is a tanker in ballast condition and not gas-free, state the correct technical name, United Nations number, and International Maritime Organization class of the previously carried cargo.

HOTEL—If the vessel is carrying any packaged dangerous goods other than explosives, state the International Maritime Organization class and the total quantity (in long tons) within each class.

INDIA—Quarantine and immigration information:

1. Is radio pratique desired?
2. The ports at which the vessel has called within 15 days preceding its arrival at the canal.
3. All cases of communicable disease aboard and the nature of the disease or diseases, if known.
4. The number of deaths which have occurred since departure from the last port and the cause of each death, if known.
5. The number of passengers disembarking and their port of destination.
6. The number and ports of origin of any stowaway and a brief description of the identity papers of each stowaway.
7. The number, kind, and country of origin of any animals aboard. Are any animals to be landed?
8. The country of origin of all meat, whether carried as cargo or as ship's stores.
9. Has the vessel called at a port in any country infected with foot-and-mouth disease or rinderpest during its present voyage? Countries considered to be infected are:

   (a) All countries east of the thirtieth meridian west longitude and west of the international date line, except Australia, Channel Islands, Fiji, Greenland, Iceland, Japan, New Zealand, Northern Ireland, Norway, Republic of Ireland;
   (b) All countries of South America;
   (c) Curacao (the leeward islands of the Netherlands Antilles);
   (d) Martinique;
   (e) Cuba;
   (f) Guadaloupe.

10. Specify whether the vessel has a valid deratting certificate or a deratting exemption certificate issued within 180 days prior to arrival.

The exact format and requirements of this message are changed from time to time; check Section 123.4 of the latest Panama Canal regulations for the current requirements. You can send this message directly to the navigation division of the Panama Canal, or you can send it to your agent with instructions for him to pass it to the canal authorities.

A vessel approaching from the Atlantic must report by radio, at least twelve hours prior to arrival, any change in ETA of one hour or more. A vessel approaching from the Pacific must report the time of passing the latitude of Cape Mala and the speed being made good.

DOCUMENTS REQUIRED ON ARRIVAL

The following documents must be ready for presentation to the boarding officer on arrival:

1. Ship's Information and Quarantine Declaration, Panama Canal Form 4398, 1 copy (Fig. 32).
2. Cargo Declaration, Panama Canal Form 4363, 1 copy (Fig. 34).
3. Crew List for Incoming Vessels, Panama Canal Form 1509, 2 copies (Fig. 35).
4. Passenger List, Panama Canal Form 20, 1 copy.
5. Dangerous cargo manifest, 1 copy (only if carrying packaged dangerous goods).
6. Loading plan, 1 copy (only if carrying dangerous cargo in bulk).
7. Panama Canal tonnage certificate (only if transiting canal, and see Chapter 3).
8. Ship's plans (general arrangement, engine room, capacity, midship, etc.), 1 copy (only if transiting canal).

The plans listed in item 8 are almost never asked for by the boarding officer, but the regulations require that they be available. They are not required if the vessel is calling at a canal port but is not going to transit the canal.

In addition, the following documents must be available for inspection if requested by the boarding officer:

1. Ship's log.
2. All ship's documents pertaining to cargo, classification, construction, load lines, equipment, safety, sanitation, and tonnage.
3. SOLAS certificate, for ships carrying dangerous cargo in bulk.
4. An international oil pollution prevention certificate, for ships carrying dangerous cargo in bulk.
5. Certificates showing compliance with the International Convention on Standards of Training, Certification and Watchkeeping for

Seafarers, 1978, if the nation of registry has implemented the convention standards.

Draft and List

On a vessel with excessive draft, list, or trim, or over her marks, you may have to sign a release to the Panama Canal Commission and employ an extra tug for part of the canal transit. A vessel with a list exceeding ten degrees will not be allowed to transit the canal. A vessel with a list of between three and ten degrees may be allowed to transit, but only at her own risk and at the discretion of the canal authorities.

MAKING UP THE CANAL FORMS

Forms used at the canal are sometimes changed. Generally, if the old forms have already been made up, they will be accepted up to a certain date. When you receive new forms you should destroy the obsolete ones. If you are bound for the Panama Canal and there are no canal forms on board, have your company request several sets from their agent at the canal, time permitting. In some U.S. ports your local agent may have a supply. At the canal, the boarding officer will give you a set for your next transit. Have your agent at the canal supply you with several additional sets. Also request a copy of the latest canal regulations.

Most of the forms are self-explanatory and simple to fill out. Start making them up early on the voyage, especially the cargo declaration form, which may take a little time. Many of the items can be filled out before arrival. A few details, such as date and time of arrival, draft, and fuel must be entered after arrival.

CANAL CLEARANCE

Before sailing from the canal you will be given a canal clearance. This is usually sent on board when the transit is completed and the pilot disembarks. This clearance is given to the officials at the next port, if required. If the next port is a U.S. port, Customs will want the clearance.

TWELVE

THE OFFICIAL LOGBOOK

There are few documents on the vessel that are as important to the master as the official logbook. It is required by law and must be kept in strict accordance with law and regulation. You personally are held responsible for the proper keeping of the official logbook and this duty should not be delegated to anyone else. If for any reason entries are made by another person you should check them carefully. You must sign all entries and a member of the crew, usually the chief mate, must sign as a witness. When an entry is made concerning a crew member, the head of his department should also sign as a witness.

An official logbook is required on every U.S. merchant vessel making a voyage from a U.S. port to a foreign port (except a Canadian port), and on every vessel of 100 tons or more making an intercoastal voyage. An official log is not required on vessels in the coastwise trade, or vessels trading between U.S. and Canadian ports.

Official logbooks can be obtained from any Coast Guard officer in charge, marine inspection. At the end of a voyage on which an official log is required, the log should be deposited with the nearest officer in charge, marine inspection.

MANNER OF MAKING ENTRIES

Make entries in the official log in ink in a clear, legible, and careful manner. They should be in chronological order with not more than one line left blank between entries. Correct errors in the same manner as for the deck log: draw a thin line through the error and initial the correction. Do not erase or obliterate the entry. It is best if you block-print all entries. Keep in mind that the logbook may be read by an official who is totally unacquainted with the facts. There should be no need for him to have to decipher any part of it because of illegible entries.

Each entry in the official logbook is to be made as soon as possible after the occurrence to which it relates. If the entry is not made on the same day as the occurrence, then the entry must show both the date of the entry and the date of the occurrence. If the entry is about an event happening before arrival at the final port of discharge, it must be made within twenty-four hours of such arrival. Each entry must be signed by the master and by the chief mate or another seaman.

Failure to maintain the official logbook as required by law, or failure to make a required entry, is punishable by a $200 fine. Making an entry more than twenty-four hours after arrival at the final port of discharge is punishable by a $150 fine if the entry is about an occurrence happening before arrival.

ENTRIES REQUIRED BY LAW

The following entries in the official log are required by 46 USC 11301:

1. Each legal conviction of a seaman and the punishment inflicted.
2. Each offense committed by a seaman for which it is intended to prosecute or to enforce a forfeiture, together with statements about reading the entry and the reply made to the charges.
3. Each offense for which punishment is inflicted on board and the punishment inflicted.
4. A statement of the conduct, character, and qualifications of each seaman or a statement that the master declines to give an opinion about that conduct, character, and qualifications.
5. Each illness of or injury to a seaman, the nature of the illness or injury, and the medical treatment given.
6. Each death on board, with the cause of death. If the deceased is a seaman, the master must take charge of the seaman's money and property and must make an entry containing an inventory of that money and property and a statement of the wages due the seaman and the total deductions to be made from his wages. This entry must be signed by the master, the chief mate, and an unlicensed seaman.
7. Each birth on board, with the sex of the infant and the names of the parents.
8. Each marriage on board, with the names and ages of the parties.

9. The name of each seaman who ceases to be a crew member (except by death) with the place, time, manner, and the cause why he ceased to be a crew member.
10. The wages due to a seaman who dies during the voyage and the gross amount of all deductions to be made from his wages.
11. The sale of the property of a seaman who dies during the voyage, including a statement of each article sold and the amount received for the property.
12. When a marine casualty occurs, a statement about the casualty and the circumstances under which it occurred, made immediately after the casualty when it is practicable to do so.

Item 11 above, while still law, is a holdover from the days when the master was allowed to sell the property of a seaman who died during the voyage. Current law requires that a deceased seaman's effects be given to the U.S. consul if the next port is a foreign port, or be delivered as detailed in Coast Guard regulations if the next port is a U.S. port. The master is no longer allowed to sell the seaman's effects.

In addition to the items which are required to be logged by the statute cited above, the following entries must be made in accordance with Coast Guard regulations.

1. Weekly fire and boat drills.
2. Lowering each lifeboat to the water at least every three months.
3. Examining electric power-operated lifeboat winches, motor controllers, emergency switches, master switches, and limit switches at least once every three months.
4. Testing steering gear, whistle, and means of communication prior to departure from port. This is not the same as the test of steering gear, vessel control communications and alarms, emergency generator, storage batteries for emergency lighting and power systems, and main propulsion machinery (ahead and astern) that is required prior to entering into or getting underway in U.S. navigable waters (see Title 33, *Code of Federal Regulations*, Section 164.25).
5. Drafts and load line markings prior to leaving port.
6. The time and circumstances of opening and closing at sea watertight openings such as exposed cargo hatches; gangway, cargo, and coaling ports fitted below the freeboard deck; and port lights that are not accessible during navigation.
7. Testing line-throwing apparatus every three months.
8. Testing emergency lighting and power systems weekly.

9. Timed load test of batteries for emergency lighting and power system every six months.

10. Fuel oil data upon receipt of fuel on board: quantity received, name of vendor, name of the oil producer, and the flashpoint for which the oil is certified by the producer.

11. Visual inspection of cargo gear by a ship's officer at least once a month.

12. Tests and inspections of all portable fire extinguishers, semiportable fire-extinguishing systems, and fixed fire-extinguishing systems annually.

OFFENSES AND PENALTIES

To assist the master in maintaining discipline on board his vessel, 46 USC 11501 specifies the following loggable offenses and the penalties for them:

1. For desertion the seaman forfeits any part of the money or property he leaves on board and any part of earned wages.

2. For neglecting or refusing without reasonable cause to join his vessel or to proceed to sea in the vessel, for absence without leave within twenty-four hours of the vessel's sailing from a port (at the beginning or during the voyage), or for absence without leave from duties and without sufficient reason, the seaman forfeits from his wages not more than two days' pay or a sufficient amount to defray expenses incurred in hiring a substitute.

3. For quitting the vessel without leave after the vessel's arrival at the port of delivery and before the vessel is placed in security, the seaman forfeits from his wages not more than one month's pay.

4. For willful disobedience to a lawful command at sea, the seaman, at the discretion of the master, may be confined until the disobedience ends, and on arrival in port forfeits from his wages not more than four days' pay or, at the discretion of the court, may be imprisoned for not more than one month.

5. For continued willful disobedience to lawful command or continued willful neglect of duty at sea, the seaman, at the discretion of the master, may be confined, on water and 1,000 calories, with full rations every fifth day, until the disobedience ends, and on arrival in port forfeits, for each twenty-four hours' continuance of the disobedience or neglect, not more than twelve days' pay or, at the discretion of the court, may be imprisoned for not more than three months.

6. For assaulting a master, mate, pilot, engineer, or staff officer, the seaman shall be imprisoned for not more than two years.

7. For willfully damaging the vessel, or embezzling or willfully damaging any of the stores or cargo, the seaman forfeits from his wages the amount of the loss sustained and, at the discretion of the court, may be imprisoned for not more than twelve months.
8. For smuggling for which a seaman is convicted causing loss or damage to the owner or master, the seaman is liable to the owner or master for the loss or damage, and any part of his wages may be retained to satisfy the liability. He also may be imprisoned for not more than twelve months.

As provided by 46 USC 10509, a seaman who fails to be on board at the time specified in the shipping articles, without giving twenty-four hours' notice of inability to do so, forfeits one-half of one day's pay for each hour's lateness, provided the lateness is recorded in the official logbook on the date of the violation. A seaman who does not report at all or who reports on board and subsequently deserts before the voyage begins forfeits all wages.

The requirements for making entries relating to offenses and punishments are even more detailed than for other entries. These requirements must be followed exactly for the entries to be valid. If any offense becomes the subject of a legal proceeding and the entries have not been made exactly as prescribed, the court may refuse to receive the official logbook as evidence.

When any of these offenses is committed you must make an entry, stating the details, on the day of the offense. This entry must be signed by you and by the chief mate or another seaman. Before arrival in port, if the offense was committed at sea, or before departure, if the offense was committed in port, you must read the entry to the offender, you must give him a copy of the entry, and you must give him an opportunity to reply to the charge.

You must then make another entry in the official log stating that the entry about the offense was read to the offender, and that a copy was given to him, and stating his reply. His reply should be logged word-for-word; if no reply is made, so state.

You should request the seaman to sign the entry stating that the logging was read to him. Tell him that signing this entry merely confirms that the logging was read to him and that he was given a copy; it is not an admission of guilt. More than likely he will refuse to sign, in which case note "refused to sign," after which you and a witness sign the entry.

Money, property, and wages forfeited for desertion may be applied to compensate the owner or master for expenses caused by the desertion. The remaining balance, if any, must be transferred to the secretary of the department the Coast Guard is operating under, currently the Department of Transportation. All other forfeitures from the seaman's wages are retained by the shipowner.

ADVANCES AND SLOPS

The back of the official log provides a section for each crew member to sign for cash advances and for credit purchases from the slop chest. You should open an account for each man as soon as he signs on.

If an error is made in entering an amount, or if the seaman decides to change the amount, do not alter the figure already entered but draw a line through it and enter the new figure on the next line. Never alter any figures after they are entered.

Try to avoid giving an advance to a seaman who is under the influence of alcohol to such extent that he doesn't seem to know what he is doing. If possible, put off the advance until the man is sober. If you do give the advance, have it witnessed by another crew member and the chief mate, both of whom should write their initials after the man's initials.

Most masters open the slop chest weekly. The items purchased by each crew member should be totaled and entered in the official logbook. If on a long voyage during which many ports will be made, each man could be allotted two sections, on opposite pages—one for advances and the other for slops. There will probably be many advances.

PROMOTING A SEAMAN

If a man is promoted he must be signed off the articles from his old rating and signed on in his new rating. Make an entry in the official log for both events. If a man is offered a promotion and refuses, it is wise to enter that fact in the official log for your own protection.

DISRATING A SEAMAN

Given cause, the master has the right to disrate a seaman, subject to the provisions of any applicable union agreements. This is a very serious step that should be taken only after due consideration and after talking it over with the seaman's department head. Disrating is purely a corrective measure; it should never be used as punishment. A man should be disrated only if he is incompetent or almost totally unable to perform the duties of his rating. Do not disrate a man below his next lower rating. To disrate a seaman in a foreign port it is necessary to get the approval of the U.S. consul.

Disrating is seldom, if ever, done anymore. A disrated seaman and his union will almost certainly dispute the action. He may even appeal to the courts, which will cause you much lost time and inconvenience in court appearances, with the chance that the disrating will not be upheld after all. It is doubtful whether your company will give you any help. If the seaman's conduct does not actually endanger the crew or vessel, it is wiser to log him for each breach of discipline and to get rid of him at the first opportunity.

ITEMS FREQUENTLY NEGLECTED

Some common faults in keeping the official logbook which must be guarded against are:

1. Failing to sign entries.
2. Failing to have a witness sign entries.
3. Failing to enter drafts and load line marks leaving port, or omitting ports.
4. Entering mean draft instead of position of load line mark.
5. Omitting governing load line season from draft and load line entry.
6. Omitting date and time of closing hatches and openings before sailing.
7. Failing to enter testing gear before sailing, or omitting the time.
8. Failing to enter fire and boat drills, or entry inadequate.
9. If weekly fire and boat drills were not held, failing to enter the reason why.
10. Failing to make entries regarding injuries and illnesses to the crew and medical care afforded them, or entering them insufficiently. You should instruct the medical officer to notify you of the details as soon as possible after a seaman has reported himself sick or injured.
11. Omitting entries regarding seamen who leave the vessel for any reason before the end of the voyage, or making inadequate entries.
12. Omitting wage accounts of such seamen.
13. Failing to enter disciplinary loggings in detail.
14. Assessing excessive or unlawful fines against seamen.
15. Failing to enter having read a logging to a seaman, furnished him a copy, and his reply.
16. Failing to log fuel oil taken and required data.
17. Omitting weekly tests of emergency lighting and power system.

COMPANY LOGBOOK

For vessels that are not required by law to maintain official logbooks, the steamship company may supply its own logs or records in whatever form it desires. These records will be considered to take the place of the official logbook and may be used for making the required entries. In this case, the records are not surrendered to the officer in charge, marine inspection, at the end of the voyage, but they must be kept on board available for review by a marine inspector for at least one year, except for separate records of tests and inspections of fire-fighting equipment, which must be kept with the vessel's logs until her certificate of inspection expires.

EXAMPLES OF LOGGINGS AND LOG ENTRIES REGARDING THE CREW

Manila, P.I.
5 Jan. 19___
1730 hours

John Doe, AB, 123-45-6789, was absent from duty without leave today from 0800 hours to 1700 hours. For this offense Doe is fined by forfeiture from his wages one day's pay amounting to $_____.

/s/ John Black
Chief Mate

/s/ Frank White
Master

Manila, P.I.
6 Jan. 19___
0800 hours

The above entry has been clearly and audibly read to Doe and a copy furnished him. His reply to the charge was: "I have nothing to say."

/s/ John Doe

/s/ John Black
Chief Mate

/s/ Frank White
Master

Genoa, Italy
15 July 19___
1900 hours

Walter T. Door, OS, 111-22-3333, returned to the vessel at 1000 hours under the influence of alcohol, unfit for duty and unable to turn to for his 1200 to 1600 watch. He was in his bunk and unable to turn to at 1800 to secure for sea. For these offenses Door is fined by forfeiture from his wages two days' pay amounting to $_____. Because of his intoxication, Door was in no condition to have this logging read to him before putting to sea.

/s/ John Black
Chief Mate

/s/ Frank White
Master

Lat. _____N
Long. _____E
16 July 19__
0800 hours

The above entry has been clearly and audibly read to Door and a copy furnished him. His reply was: "I think I drank too much."

/s/ W. T. Door

/s/ John Black
Chief Mate

/s/ Frank White
Master

Note: Normally this logging must be read to the seaman before departure from port. If for any reason this cannot be done, as in this example, include the reason in the log entry, otherwise the logging will not be valid.

Piraeus, Greece
1 Aug. 19___
1700 hours

John Doe, AB, 123-45-6789, was absent from duty without leave from 0800 to 1700 hours. For this offense Doe is fined by forfeiture from his wages one day's pay amounting to $_____.

/s/ John Black
Chief Mate

/s/ Frank White
Master

Lat. _____N
Long. _____E
2 Aug. 19___
1200 hours

John Doe, AB, 123-45-6789, failed to be on board when vessel sailed for Barcelona at 1000 hours. For this offense Doe is fined by forfeiture from his wages two days' pay amounting to $_____. Agent at Piraeus told that if Doe shows up to inform him his transportation and all expenses involved in returning him to the vessel will be charged to Doe and to have Doe sign a statement to that effect. Agent told to notify U.S. consul at Athens.

Wages due Doe as of 2 Aug. 19___:
Earnings:

Wages due, 55 days	$
Overtime	$
Total earnings	$
Deductions:	
Allotments (3)	$
Advances	$
Slops	$
Soc. Sec.	$
Fed. Inc. tax	$
Unemployment ins.	$
Fines	$
Total deductions	$
Total earnings	$
Total deductions	$
Balance Due	$

Doe's allotment stopped 2 Aug. 19___.
Doe's pay stopped effective 3 Aug. 19___.

/s/ John Black
Chief Mate

/s/ Frank White
Master

/s/ F. Water, AB
Crew Delegate

Note: The man's allotment should always be stopped for your own protection. If he returns at another port he can request that the allotment be reinstated.

Barcelona, Spain 7 Aug. 19__ 1800 hours	John Doe, AB, 123-45-6789, rejoined vessel after failing to join at Piraeus on 2 Aug. 19__. Doe's pay stopped from 3 Aug. to 7 Aug. inclusive. Doe told to turn to in the morning. The following bills, paid by agents at Piraeus and Barcelona, to be charged to Doe. Doe did not want his allotment reinstated. Pay to start again on 8 Aug. 19__.

Hotel and meals, Piraeus	$ 25.30
Taxi to airport, Piraeus	7.50
Plane fare, Piraeus to Barcelona	120.00
Hotel and meals, Barcelona	35.40
Taxi to vessel, Barcelona	15.00
Total expenses	$203.20

/s/ John Black /s/ F. Water, AB /s/ Frank White
 Chief Mate   Crew Delegate   Master

Barcelona, Spain 8 Aug. 19__ 0900 hours	The log entry of 1 Aug. has been clearly and audibly read to Doe and a copy furnished him. When asked for his reply to the charge, Doe remained silent.

                /s/ John Doe
/s/ John Black /s/ F. Water, AB /s/ Frank White
 Chief Mate   Crew Delegate   Master

| Barcelona, Spain
8 Aug. 19___
0900 hours | The above log entries of 2 Aug. and 7 Aug., including list of expenses, have been clearly and audibly read to Doe and a copy of each given to him. His reply to the charges was: "I guess I'll have to pay it." |

/s/ John Doe

| /s/ F. Water, AB
Crew Delegate | /s/ John Black
Chief Mate | /s/ Frank White
Master |

When a man misses his vessel and rejoins at another port he should not be logged for the time the vessel was at sea, but his pay should be stopped for those days.

| London, England
20 Sept. 19___
1430 hours | At 1000 hours John Doe, AB, 123-45-6789, slipped on deck. He complained of pain in his right knee and back. Doe sent to Mercy hospital, Burdett Rd., by taxi. Doe returned to vessel at 1400 hours. He had a note from the doctor saying that he should be taken off duty for five days and also prescribing medicine, which was ordered through the agent. Witness to accident S. M. Spike, Bosun, address |

| /s/ John Black
Chief Mate
/s/ S. M. Spike
Bosun | /s/ Frank White
Master |

Rotterdam, Holland John Doe, AB, 123-45-6789, returned to duty.
26 Sept. 19___

| /s/ John Black
Chief Mate
/s/ S. M. Spike
Bosun | /s/ Frank White
Master |

In the above incident the details should be entered in the medical log and Coast Guard Form CG-2692 made up.

Lat. _____N	John Doe, AB, 123-45-6789, set fire to his
Long. _____W	mattress while smoking in his bunk. Fire extin-
30 Sept. 19__	guished by wiper Joe Grease. Mattress and
1400 hours	sheets damaged beyond repair. Doe to be

charged with cost of mattress and 2 sheets as
follows:

1 innerspring mattress	$47.50
2 white sheets at $4.50 each	$ 9.00
Total	$56.50

/s/ John Black   /s/ Frank White
    Chief Mate   Master
/s/ J. Johnson
    Steward

Lat. _____N	The above entry has been clearly and audibly
Long. _____W	read to Doe and a copy given to him. His reply
30 Sept. 19__	to the charge was: "I must have fallen asleep."
1500 hours	

                /s/ John Doe
/s/ John Black   /s/ Frank White
    Chief Mate   Master
/s/ J. Johnson
    Steward

Bremen, Germany	0900 hours. Harbor police came on board and
4 Oct. 19__	reported that Joe Grease, wiper, Z-00001, was
	arrested at 0500.

Bremen, Germany	Joe Grease, wiper, Z-00001, absent from duty
4 Oct. 19__	without leave from 0800 to 1700. For this
1700 hours	offense Grease is fined by forfeiture from his

wages one day's pay amounting to $_____.
Grease not available to have logging read to him.

/s/ John Black   /s/ Frank White
    Chief Mate   Master
/s/ F. Water, AB
    Crew Delegate

Hamburg, Germany
5 Oct. 19___
1500 hours

Joe Grease, wiper, Z-00001, in custody of police at Bremen, taken off articles by U.S. consul, Hamburg, as of this date, 5 Oct. 19___. Pay stopped effective this date. Grease not available to have logging read to him. Allotment stopped 4 Oct. 19___. Wages due Grease:

Earnings:
  Wages due, 118 days $
  Overtime $_____
  Total earnings $
Deductions:
  Allotments (4) $
  Advances $
  Slops $
  Soc. Sec. $
  Fed. Inc. tax $
  Unemployment ins. $
  Fines $_____
  Total deductions $
Total earnings $
Total deductions $_____
Balance Due $

/s/ John Black   /s/ Frank White
    Chief Mate   Master

Lat. _____N
Long. _____W
15 Nov. 19___
1600 hours

Pintle N. Gudgeon, oiler, 222-33-4444, disobeyed a direct order from the chief engineer. Gudgeon was told to clean up spilled oil from the deck around the evaporator. He refused, saying: "That's not my job, get the guy who spilled it to clean it up." For this offense Gudgeon is discharged for cause on arrival at the next port.

/s/ John Black   /s/ Frank White
    Chief Mate   Master

Lat. _____N
Long. _____W
15 Nov. 19___
1700 hours

The above log entry has been clearly and audibly read to Gudgeon and a copy given to him. His reply to the charge was: "You can't fire me. I'll see the union about this."

/s/ John Black   /s/ Frank White
    Chief Mate   Master

Kingston, Jamaica	Signed off Pintle N. Gudgeon, oiler, 222-33-4444,
18 Nov. 19___	discharged for cause. Wages due Gudgeon:
1300 hours	Earnings:

Earnings:

Wages due, 67 days	$
Overtime	$_____
Total earnings	$

Deductions:

Allotments (3)	$
Advances	$
Slops	$
Soc. Sec.	$
Fed. Inc. tax	$
Unemployment ins.	$
Fines	$_____
Total deductions	$
Total earnings	$
Total deductions	$_____
Balance Due	$

/s/ John Black   /s/ Frank White
    Chief Mate   Master
/s/ F. Water, AB
    Crew Delegate

Note: In this example, Gudgeon could also have been fined up to four days' pay for disobedience.

Kingston, Jamaica 19 Nov. 19___ 1400 hours

Signed off Joe Conrad, AB, 333-44-5555, mutual consent. Wages due:

Earnings:

Wages due, 115 days	$
Overtime	$_____
Total earnings	$

Deductions:

Allotments (3)	$
Advances	$
Slops	$
Soc. Sec.	$
Fed. Inc. tax	$
Unemployment ins.	$
Fines	$_____
Total deductions	$
Total earnings	$
Total deductions	$_____
Balance Due	$

Signed on J. London, AB, 999-88-7777, as replacement.

/s/ John Black   /s/ Frank White
   Chief Mate   Master

/s/ F. Water, AB
   Crew Delegate

THIRTEEN

FOREIGN PORTS

Information on foreign port requirements can be given only in general. The first port of call in a foreign country usually requires the most papers.

When approaching a foreign port for the first time, check the sailing directions and your company port information file for special port requirements. Check whether it is necessary to notify the harbormaster, captain of the port, or other authority regarding your ETA, draft, or other matters. Generally, your ETA to your agent is sufficient as he will notify the required authorities, but a few ports insist on a message direct from the ship. The *Guide to Port Entry,* published by Shipping Guides Ltd., of England, is especially useful for paperwork requirements and it also has diagrams of many docks in all parts of the world.

THE CLEARANCE

On entering some ports you must produce a clearance from the last port of call. On entering the first U.S. port from foreign, you must produce a clearance from the last foreign port. Depending upon the practice in each port, this clearance may be issued by customs, the harbormaster, or the harbor police. Your agent will bring it on board before sailing. If the port you are departing does not issue clearances, have your agent furnish you with a letter stating that fact. The letter is given to the authorities at the next port in lieu of the clearance.

QUARANTINE

The quarantine officer, sometimes called the sanitary or health officer, boards the vessel in the first port of call in the country. Bills of health are very rarely required anymore but if your vessel calls at

175

an infected port, it may be necessary to get a bill of health from the consul of the country she will visit next and, in some cases, for subsequent ports in other countries. Your agent in the infected port will know.

The quarantine officer will want to see the derat certificate and he may ask you to fill out a maritime declaration of health. This is an international form, usually printed in the language of the country with an English translation. It deals with such items as ports called at by the vessel in the previous three months, with dates of sailing, and reports of any sickness aboard suspected of being contagious. It requires a yes or no answer to several questions about any sickness currently on board or occurring during the voyage. The quarantine officer may want a crew list, passenger list, and stores list.

He may also want to see the shot records of the crew and passengers. Any person on board not having a shot record, or having one with the vaccination outdated, or lacking various shots, may be required by the health authorities to receive the shots at that time. If the crew's shot records are collected, be sure to return them before the vessel pays off.

In practice, due to the great advances made worldwide in eradicating various diseases over the last several decades, shot records are very rarely called for and shots are seldom required. Many seamen do not even carry shot records anymore.

VISAED DOCUMENTS

Some countries, especially in Latin America, require that crew lists, passenger lists, stores lists, and manifests be visaed by their consuls. Some countries also require that the crew list be on a special form, issued by them, which must be procured from and visaed by their consul, usually at the last port prior to arrival in the country. When a special crew list or other forms must be visaed, the agent or broker will attend to it, but regardless of who gets the required visas or makes up the forms, it is your responsibility to see that it is done and that the papers are on board before you sail; or, if not ready before sailing, that the agent or broker knows where to send them. Some countries fine the vessel if the visaed papers are not on board as required, or impose a fine for each member of the crew omitted from the visaed crew list. In large ports, special customhouse brokers are employed to make up these papers. They are familiar with the numerous details, understand the language, and are up-to-date on any changes in the many rules and regulations of these countries. They also have a supply of the necessary forms.

Crew Lists

Crew lists are required in all foreign ports. These must be given to the customs, quarantine, and immigration officers when they board. The agent always wants a copy and the terminal may want one for the gate guard. You will require a half-dozen to a dozen crew lists in most ports. Sometimes officials other than those noted request copies. Most countries require you to sign several of the crew lists.

Passenger Lists

In all foreign ports, at least two passenger lists will be required and it is advisable to have a number of extra copies. The list should indicate which passengers are landing and which are in transit, or in some ports two separate lists may be required. It is helpful but not necessary to use Form I-418; ordinary paper will do, unless the country requires special forms. Passenger lists should include the full name, sex, age, nationality, passport number and country of issue, port of embarkation, and destination.

The immigration officer may want to see the passports of the passengers in transit. If so, it is a good idea to collect these passports in advance, so that if the vessel enters port at night it will not be necessary to awaken the passengers. Usually if the passports are available the officials will not require you to wake the passengers. If the officials do want to see the passengers, it is sometimes possible to make arrangements for them to return during daylight hours rather than disturb the passengers' sleep.

Stores Lists

A stores list is required in all ports except free ports. Be especially careful that the quantities shown for cigarettes and other tobacco products, alcoholic beverages, ship's weapons and ammunition, and narcotic drugs in the medicine chest, are accurate. All tobacco and alcohol products in the slop chest, and therefore belonging to the ship, should be shown on the stores lists. All tobacco and alcohol in the crew rooms and belonging to the crew should be shown on the crew effects list.

Customs will probably seal the slop chest. Do not under any circumstances break the seal or sell any tobacco or alcohol to the crew, no matter how long the vessel's stay in port, without written permission from customs. If the vessel's stay is especially long, your agent can apply to customs to open the slop chest and reseal it after the allowed sales.

IMMIGRATION

The immigration officer usually comes on board soon after docking or anchoring, or possibly before if the vessel passes through locks. He may want to see the passports of any passengers whether landing or not. Be sure to ask him whether shore passes are required and if so, whether they must be collected and returned before sailing. He will want a crew list and passenger list.

CUSTOMS

The customs officer boards the vessel at each port except free ports. However, if the vessel leaves the free port and enters a customs port or area, it will be necessary to observe customs rules in regard to stores lists and crew declarations. Often what is termed a free port may be only a section or area of the port proper. The customs officer will require stores lists and a crew effects declaration and may seal up excess cigarettes and other tobacco products, spirits, and perhaps some other goods of high duty value. It is possible that he will want to count the cartons of cigarettes and bottles or cases of alcohol products.

In some countries one or more customs officers may be assigned to the vessel and stay on board all the time the vessel is in that port. They should be given a comfortable room, allowed to eat in the officers' mess, and receive courteous and considerate treatment.

The customs boarding officer will want to see the register (certificate of documentation) and load line certificate and perhaps also the safety equipment and safety radiotelegraphy certificates. If you are required to enter at the customhouse, it may be necessary to send these certificates ashore with the agent. In some ports the customs boarding officer will take the register, giving a receipt for it. Be sure to get the register back before sailing and check to see that it is the correct one.

The customs boarding officer will want copies of the stores lists, crew effects list, crew list, passenger list if any are on board in transit, list of passengers landing, cargo manifest, and possibly the clearance from the last port.

Tonnage Tax

At the first port of call in some countries, you may have to pay a tonnage tax (also called tonnage dues or light dues) for which the customs officer will give you a tonnage tax receipt. This receipt may be good for a certain length of time during which the vessel may call at other ports in that country without the payment of additional tonnage tax; or it may be good for a definite number of calls over a stated period. The period of its validity dates from the day the tonnage tax receipt is issued. Keep the receipt in a safe place; you may have to produce it on arrival at subsequent ports in the same country. If it is taken up by the agent or by the customs officer, make certain it is returned before you sail. The customs officers at each port in that country may want to see it.

Crew Effects Lists

Before arriving at the first port of call in any country, make up a crew effects list. This list must show the cigarettes, other tobacco products, alcoholic beverages, and items of high duty value (such as cameras, radios, jewelry, etc.) owned by the crew. Other than to-bacco and alcohol, the rules are usually rather vague regarding just what must be declared. It is best to tell the men that if there is any doubt about whether or not an item is declarable, to declare it.

Each country has its own rules regarding the amount of tobacco or alcohol products that may be kept out by the crew for personal use. A common allowance is 200 cigarettes (one carton) or an equivalent amount of other tobacco products, and one quart or liter of spirits per person. A very few countries require that all tobacco or alcohol products over the allowed amount be collected and stored in a sealed room or locker; however, this practice is rare nowadays. If it is necessary to place any of the crew's personal belongings under seal, have each man write his name on the pack-ages he places under seal.

The Searchers

Although it is unusual for a merchant vessel to be searched these days, practically all customs agencies do maintain teams of searchers for use when the need arises. Some ports may occasion-ally pick vessels at random to be searched in order to verify compli-ance with customs laws. They are especially likely to give your vessel a complete search if they have ever had any trouble, such as smug-gling, with your ship in the past, even though there may have been a complete change of crew in the meantime. These searchers, either because they are ex-seamen or through long experience, are very thorough, and rarely miss concealed articles. They know all the tricks. The vessel is subject to a fine, sometimes a heavy one, if any undeclared articles or contraband are found. If any of your crew are suspected of drug smuggling, the searchers will very likely bring with them dogs that are trained to sniff out drugs of all types.

The Customs Seals

The customs laws and regulations in all countries should be strictly complied with, particularly in regard to customs seals. Once a customs seal is on a locker or room it must not be broken or tampered with. If the vessel is to proceed to another port in the same country, the seals should be left intact until permission is given, in writing if possible, to break them at sea after leaving the first port. The only time a seal may be broken without permission is when the vessel leaves her last port of call in a country, is outside port limits, and has dropped the pilot. The customs laws in all countries are very strict about this and a seal broken without authority may result in a very heavy fine. Don't take chances—it isn't worth it.

TRADITIONAL COURTESIES

Treatment of Officials

In all ports, foreign and domestic, treat officials courteously and with consideration. Above all, do not cross them or argue with them. Generally they will have the last word and it may turn out to be an expensive one for your company and a troublesome one for you.

Gratuities to Officials

Gratuities of some kind, usually cartons of cigarettes or bottles of whiskey, are generally given to the officials in foreign ports. Usually the master keeps a few extra cartons of cigarettes in his room, which are not shown on the stores list, for gratuities. You may find that the officials will help themselves when they inspect the storerooms. If you are in doubt about what gratuities should be given, consult your agent; he will be familiar with the local customs. Sometimes the agent will also expect a gratuity—whether he gets one or not is entirely up to you.

Courtesy Flag

When entering a foreign port it is customary to fly the national flag of the country you are visiting from a conspicuous place on the vessel, usually the starboard yardarm. In many ports, flying the courtesy flag is required by law. In certain countries the officials are very sensitive about this and you may get a rough reception or even a fine from the authorities if the courtesy flag is not properly flying on arrival.

When you receive orders to a foreign port for which you do not have a flag, be sure to have your agent at a previous port supply you with one. If you are diverted at sea and are thus unable to obtain a courtesy flag before arrival, radio your agent at the foreign port to have one for you on arrival.

AGENT'S REQUIREMENTS

In all foreign ports your agent will want fuel, water, and draft on arrival and on sailing, an ETA for the next port, crew lists, and passenger lists. Check with him whether a notice of readiness, if required, has been prepared.

SHORE LEAVE

Union agreements often contain a clause specifying that if shore leave is denied the crew, they may claim overtime for the number of hours of shore leave they were denied, unless you have a letter from a government authority stating that shore leave was prohibited by law, regulation, or government order. The crew may claim that shore leave was denied them if a launch is not provided as called for in the agreement.

When the vessel arrives at the first port of call in that country, she must generally comply with various formalities before any crew members or passengers will be allowed ashore. These include granting pratique, and immigration and customs clearance. If the vessel arrives at night, these formalities may not be completed until the following morning. If the vessel must anchor, the agent will usually be on the job and have a shore-leave launch waiting.

In some cases, the immigration and customs officers will give permission for the men to leave as soon as pratique is granted, unless passes have to be made up. In other cases, the vessel may remain at anchor for several days awaiting a berth. Even though pratique may have been granted, customs and immigration may not clear the vessel until she docks. Regardless of this, the crew may claim overtime for the time they were not able to go ashore while the vessel was awaiting clearance. Such overtime should be disputed.

On arrival at a port where the vessel may have to remain at anchor under the above conditions, it is important to have the agent get a letter from customs, immigration, or other authority, stating the reason why shore leave was prohibited.

Shore Launch

In some ports the vessel may anchor or tie up to buoys, making it necessary for the crew to use a launch for shore leave. Make up a boat schedule as soon as possible after arrival and post it on the bulletin boards. Your agent should give a copy to the boat operator and another to the launch office at the landing. Usually boats are run every four hours, at the change of watch, with possibly an extra boat on the 4-8 watch for the steward's department.

DANGEROUS OR FLAMMABLE CARGO

What you think is safe cargo may not be considered so by the local port officials. Should the authorities consider any of the cargo dangerous and/or flammable, they may require you to run out hoses at each hatch or area where such cargo is stowed. They may also have a detail from the fire department stand by with equipment as long as the vessel is in port with that cargo on board. Check with the agent as to whether it will be necessary to fly "Bravo" during the day and display a red light at night. The vessel may be fined for not doing so if it is required.

DUNNAGE AND SCRAP

Unless authorized by your company, do not permit any dunnage, old rope, or scrap metal to be sold. In many foreign ports, junk dealers will board to buy dunnage, old rope, tarps, etc. Shipowners generally issue instructions regarding this. You are usually permitted a wide use of discretion. If, in the absence of instructions to the contrary, you consider it to be in the best interests of your company to get rid of dunnage or junk, you should do it through the agent and obtain proper receipts.

U.S. CONSUL

Most major foreign ports have a U.S. consul. The consul's office performs various services for U.S. vessels and seamen.

If any seamen are shipped or discharged in a foreign port, they must be signed on or signed off before the consul, if there is one in the port (see Chapter 2, "Shipping Articles," for details). The consul will also make arrangements for the repatriation of destitute seamen.

If you desire to note protest because of some extraordinary occurrence on the voyage, the consul's office will accept the protest (see Chapter 14, "Noting Protest").

Federal law requires you to deposit your register (certificate of documentation) with the U.S. consul or vice-consul upon arrival in a foreign port, if there is a consul or vice-consul in the port. The consul will return the register when you receive your clearance from the port authorities, provided you have complied with the law regarding shipment and discharge of seamen. Failure to deposit the register with the consul carries a $500 penalty.

The federal courts have ruled that "arrival at a foreign port" means an arrival for ship's business that requires an entry at the customhouse. You will not be required to deposit your register if your vessel calls at a foreign port only incidentally, for example for orders, and the local officials do not require you to enter at the customhouse. You will have to deposit your register if you are required to enter, regardless of the purpose for entering port.

The consul's office may have a form for you to fill out giving various information. The consul is required by law to make reports to the secretary of commerce of seamen shipped or discharged before the consul and the wages paid them, the registered tonnages of U.S. vessels calling at the port, the number of their crew and the number who are U.S. citizens, and the nature and value of the cargo.

SAILING OR DEPARTURE PERMIT

In some ports you cannot depart until the immigration officer, harbor police, or other local authority has issued a permit. You may have to show or give this permit to the pilot before the vessel can sail, so keep it in a handy place. This is for local use and is not the same as the clearance.

FOURTEEN

NOTING PROTEST

A note of protest is a declaration or deposition by the master, made under oath, giving full particulars regarding heavy weather or other incident which may have caused damage to the vessel or cargo. Its purpose is to state that the master and crew performed their duties in protecting the vessel and cargo, and that any damage sustained was not due to any fault of the vessel, her officers, or crew, but to circumstances beyond human control. The full extent of the damage may or may not be ascertained at the time protest is noted.

Always note protest after any accident, such as collision or grounding. A good rule to follow is, if in doubt, note protest. Protest should be noted within twenty-four hours after arrival.

Always leave a copy of the protest for your agent, send one to your insurance department, and keep one for your file. In a foreign port, the consul will make the required number of copies.

IN THE UNITED STATES

In the United States, protest is noted before a notary public. Very often the agent or customhouse broker will be a notary and may even help you make up the note. He may have a printed form or, if necessary, you may make up a general form on the vessel.

IN A FOREIGN PORT

Before a U.S. Consul

In foreign ports, protest is noted before the U.S. consul, who will issue a special form (Fig. 28). Department of State regulations require the master to appear personally before the consul. This duty may not be delegated unless the vessel operators furnish the consul with a written statement authorizing a vessel officer other than the master to note protest (see Title 22, *Code of Federal Regulations*, Part 82.12).

Before a Notary

If there is no consul, protest can be noted before a notary public or a magistrate. If this is necessary, consult your agent for assistance. It may be necessary to bring the logbook and several witnesses; the agent will tell you how many. All the witnesses must do is swear that the vessel encountered the conditions shown in the log and that the entries in the log are true facts. This may take several hours, as the logbook entries may have to be translated into the language of the country. Keep track of your witnesses or they may get tired of waiting around and end up in a bar, especially on a hot day. See Fig. 30 for a sample form for noting protest before a notary or magistrate when no official form is prescribed.

EXTENDING PROTEST

No witnesses are required if you note protest before a U.S. consul, but witnesses are required if you extend protest (Fig. 29). This may be done if further damage is found after noting protest. When such action is taken, whether before a U.S. consul or a notary, bring the logbook and several members of the crew as witnesses. If you deem it necessary to extend protest, advise your company before doing so.

FIFTEEN

THE LOGBOOKS

THE DECK LOG

The deck log, or bridge logbook, is a continuous record of the activities of the vessel while she is in service, both at sea and in port.

It is very important to you and to your company that the logbook be clear, complete, and correct. The book must reflect a true and accurate record of the voyage and of activities in port. It is your responsibility to see that entries are made of all important matters. The essential thing is that a correct record of what took place on the voyage is entered in sufficient detail to present a true picture.

All names and titles should be clearly and legibly block-printed. This includes pilots, Coast Guard officials, classification society surveyors, and others boarding the vessel. Enter arrival and departure times in red ink, as well as drills and testing of gear.

If a statement of facts or a report is required, all the details should be taken from the logbook. Be sure all the facts are straight and in order, thus precluding any argument at a later date and also avoiding much correspondence.

Do not make any entry of an important nature without due consideration and discussion with the officers acquainted with the facts. Many masters make notes regarding important events or casualties on a pad so that the entry can be arranged in proper sequence and made as letter-perfect as possible before it is inserted in the logbook. Impress on all officers that a careless entry, not consistent with the facts, or an incomplete or untrue entry, may reflect against your company's interests.

Entries regarding the following are of particular importance for the proper handling of various claims:

1. Damage to the vessel, equipment, or cargo, and the cause;
2. Salvage or other assistance rendered or received;

3. Touching or striking submerged or floating objects;
4. Resting on the bottom either alongside or at anchor;
5. Touching bottom at any time.

Enter a description of the damage, if any, or a statement such as "Damage unknown at this time." Do not give an opinion or make a guess. Also enter the fact that bilge or tank soundings were taken, how often, and the results, as well as soundings around the vessel, if necessary, and the water found. Do not permit the officers to crowd too much on one page. If necessary use the next page and head it with the same date or attach a supplemental sheet.

No page should be torn or mutilated and no erasures or obliterations should be made. Correct errors in the logbook by drawing a single line through the incorrect entry and then initialing the correct entry. The incorrect entry should remain clearly visible; to render it illegible or to obliterate any part of it may lead to suspicion of falsification of the entry. Entries relating to checking mooring lines, bearings, decks, and tanks, and to other duties of the officer on watch should not be mere formalities. The watch officers must report what was actually done, not what should have been done.

All of this may seem elementary but it is surprising how often some officers forget to make the necessary entries.

Weather

At sea, pay particular attention to entries regarding heavy weather: efforts to avoid heavy weather damage such as changing course, slowing down, or heaving to; how the vessel is riding; and whether or not she is shipping any seas, especially if it is necessary to have the crew on deck to secure gear or to repair damage.

An entry sometimes forgotten on freighters is the time of starting and stopping cargo ventilation fans along with the reason for stopping the fans, such as heavy rain or spray. On older ships that are not equipped with blower systems, the time of trimming, covering, or unshipping ventilators should be entered and the reason for these acts. The weather entries in the log must substantiate those regarding the fans. When at sea, entries should be made at least daily regarding cargo ventilation.

Even in good weather when there is no question of damage to the vessel, weather entries must be made. Many lawsuits have been filed by seamen claiming to have slipped on rain-slick decks on days when the logbook showed that there wasn't a cloud in the sky.

Weather entries are equally important in port when many persons other than your crew may come aboard the vessel.

Many officers overlook entering precautions taken during periods of low visibility such as slowing down, sounding whistle signals, etc. A Coast Guard investigator examining the logbook will rightly question an entry reading "1030 thick fog set in" with no further details, nor will a vague entry such as "All precautions taken" suffice. Such an entry is of little value because it does not relate exactly what those precautions were. An investigating officer may have a different idea than you do of what constitutes "all precautions."

Diversion

Whenever you receive radio orders changing your destination, enter the time and position where the message is received. You may have to show this log entry, and perhaps also a copy of the radio telegram, to the government authorities at the new destination. This is especially important if the change of orders comes by radio-telephone; the log entry will be your only written proof of the diversion message.

Pratique

At each port of call where your vessel must pass pratique, enter the time pratique was granted along with the type of pratique granted.

Cargo, Ballast, and Stability

The log should contain full details regarding loading and discharging of cargo or ballast. Enter the number of longshore gangs and the times they board and leave the vessel. Enter stoppage of work at any time and the reason therefore: knocking off for meals or for the day, equipment breakdowns, weather, waiting for cargo or lighters, etc. Keep in mind that this information may be required months later, and the successful settlement of a claim may depend upon an entry in the logbook.

Many dry cargo companies require that the vessel's stability, stated as so many feet of metacentric height (GM), be entered in the log upon sailing from each port.

Damage to or by the Vessel

Damage of any kind to or by tugboats, barges, lighters, floating cranes, launches, or other craft alongside should be entered in the log, with the extent of damage, if known. Always include the name or number of the craft involved, the state of the weather, and whether another vessel was passing at excessive speed. If your ship is damaged by another craft it will be practically impossible to get an admission of fault or responsibility from the other person in charge. It is important, therefore, to note all facts in the logbook.

In the event of grounding or collision, enter the position along with full details of every maneuver made before and after the accident, every effort to avoid the accident, and an account of damage sustained, as far as can be ascertained. In case of grounding, describe the efforts made to refloat the vessel, and give the names of tugs or other vessels assisting or standing by. If it becomes necessary to abandon the vessel, every effort should be made, short of endangering lives, to save the current deck, engine, and official logbooks, and the current bell books.

End of Passage

At the end of each passage you and the chief engineer should inspect the hull, rudder, and propeller (while it is being turned over, if possible) for damage of any kind. Enter the results of this inspection in the log.

Idle Status

If your vessel is laid up or otherwise put on idle status with less than her normal complement of personnel, follow your company's instructions, if any, regarding the keeping of logbooks. Drafts should be taken daily and logged, and frequent inspections of the vessel should be made.

Repair Status

When a vessel goes into a shipyard or is laid up for repairs, the log of the previous voyage is usually continued unless you are instructed otherwise by your home office. Entries should include the time work commenced each day and the time of knocking off. If work is continued around the clock that fact should be noted in the log. Enter in the log in block letters the names and titles of all officials, such as Coast Guard inspectors, American Bureau of Shipping surveyors, etc., who board the vessel and who have any connection with the repair work. The draft should be taken and logged daily while the vessel is in the water. Do not neglect weather entries, particularly if any sandblasting, coating, or paintwork is being done.

OTHER LOGS

Although the deck logbook is the primary official record of the vessel's activities, there are various other documents that should receive similar care and attention. In the event of a casualty you may find many ship's records besides the logbook taken for use in an official investigation. If any occurrence on your vessel becomes the subject of a civil lawsuit, the plaintiff's attorney is sure to subpoena every paper that he can think of.

Bell Books

Whenever the vessel is maneuvering in harbor, an accurate record of engine orders must be kept in the bell book. The watch officers should also make notes in the bell book of the times of pilot boarding, passing navigational marks, first or last line, tugs alongside, etc. Every detail that might possibly be wanted later should go into the bell book; unnecessary data can always be omitted later from the deck logbook. The old adage, "Not everything in the bell book should go into the logbook, but everything in the logbook should be found in the bell book," is still a good rule to follow.

The bell book is used in making the deck logbook entry, and must be kept with the same care as the logbook itself. Errors in the bell book should be corrected in the same manner as for the logbook. Many officers have a bad habit of making bell book entries in pencil instead of pen. You should discourage this practice; the temptation to correct an error by erasing it and starting over is often irresistible.

When a vessel maneuvering in harbor reduces speed to avoid damage to other vessels or property, the reason for slowing down should be noted, such as "Passing pipeline dredge." Whenever you pass a vessel whose mooring lines are slack, note that fact. Vessels that suffer damage from passing ships because of the deficiency of their own moorings often claim excessive speed on the part of the passing vessel as the cause of the damage.

Medical Logs

Medical logbook entries are very important in proving the cause and extent of an injury or illness and the adequacy of treatment. Your company will undoubtedly have report forms for you to fill out in case of illness or injury to any of the crew. These should be treated as extensions of the medical log itself, and should be complete and accurate in every respect. Personal injury cases often surface years after the alleged incident and may not come to trial for several years more.

Oil Record Book

The oil record book is required by law and by international agreement and must be up-to-date whenever you enter a port. Officials are more conscious of water pollution now than in the past, and you can expect the oil record book to be scrutinized more often than was formerly the case, particularly on tankers.

Radio Messages

Keep copies of all radio messages that are sent or received. Any that pertain to vessel casualties must be retained for examination by government investigators and company attorneys. Any that relate to possible civil claims may have to be produced in court at a later date. Otherwise, normal messages regarding routine company business should be retained until the end of the voyage and then either filed or disposed of, in accordance with your company's instructions.

Course Recorder

If your vessel is involved in a collision you can be sure that the government investigators will take the course recorder chart, and when they are done with it the attorneys for the other vessel will want it. The second mate should check the course recorder daily, correct the time and course settings if necessary, and note the date on the paper at the same time. It will be easiest if the course recorder is kept on GMT rather than local time. As each roll of course recorder paper is used up, the starting and ending dates should be written on the outside of the roll, which should then be filed away with the completed logbooks and bell books.

ACCESS OF UNAUTHORIZED PERSONS TO LOGBOOKS

No unauthorized person should be permitted to read, examine, or take notes from the logbooks. All the officers should be instructed regarding this. If you have any doubt about whether a person should see the log or not, it is best to deny him access to it. Insurance companies or others handling various claims will often send an investigator on board to take notes from the logbook. These investigators frequently assume a cloak of authority as though they had a right to examine the logbooks, and very often they get away with it. Unless a person is known to you as a representative of your company, or has permission from your home office, you should not allow him to see the logbooks.

The above does not apply to representatives of the Coast Guard, American Bureau of Shipping, National Cargo Bureau, or government agencies. Such officials will have proper credentials. Anyone refused permission to see the logbook should be referred to the home office.

SIXTEEN

AGENTS

In most ports, and probably in all foreign ports, your company will appoint a local agent. The agent's job is to represent you, your vessel, and your company and to see that your vessel's stay in port goes as smoothly as possible. He will order tugs, pilot, and linehandlers; arrange transportation and medical treatment for your crew; coordinate repairs and stores deliveries; make any required reports to port authorities; advise you of special local laws or regulations; enter and clear at the customhouse for you; and generally assist you with your in-port business.

Many companies supply their masters with a book listing the agents that they use at each port where their vessels normally call. If you are ordered to a port where your company does not have an agent, they should appoint one without delay and send you a radio message giving the agent's name, cable address, and telex number.

If your vessel is chartered, the charterer may appoint his own agent. Many times the shipowner and charterer will use the same agent; if not, you must be sure to keep the charterer's agent informed of your ETA and of any particulars affecting the charterer's business.

At some small ports you may find that there is only one agency available and that it is associated with the cargo terminal. In such a case, where the agency is not truly independent, you must be especially careful to see that your company's interests are properly looked after, particularly in the event of a dispute between the vessel and the terminal.

Be sure to give your agent a daily update of your ETA beginning at least three or four days before arrival, or as soon as possible after departure on a short voyage. If you have any port requirements, such as men for the doctor, charts needed, etc., advise your agent by radio early enough that he will have time to make arrangements. Bear in mind that it may be difficult or impossible for him to obtain some services on weekends or holidays. Be sure to radio the agent to supply you with the local national flag on arrival, if you do not already have one; many governments are very sensitive about vessels displaying a courtesy flag.

The agent should meet the ship on arrival and should assist you with customs, immigration, quarantine, or other local authorities. Your agent is the best person to advise you on the delicate matter of gratuities to government officials.

Before the agent leaves the ship, be sure to get a telephone number from him so that you can call someone at the agency in case of emergency. Most large agencies maintain a twenty-four-hour answering service; if not, you should get the agent's home number. If you go ashore it would be wise to see that the chief officer has this number. If any emergency or serious difficulty arises, do not hesitate to call upon the agent for assistance.

In port, when your vessel's radio station is shut down, the agent will be your communications link with your company. He will use the telex machine in his office to relay messages from the home office to you, or vice versa. If you need to telephone your office from a foreign port where there is a language barrier, you may find it useful to go to the agent's office and have him make the telephone connections for you.

If you are asked to sign any document in a foreign language and you are not sure what you are signing, ask your agent to translate it for you.

In the event of a serious emergency, such as a badly injured crewman, you may have to put into a port where your company does not have an agent and when there is not time for them to appoint one. Be prepared to appoint your own agent if one is available and if the local authorities advise it. Often a ship without an agent is subject to delays that cost far more than the agency fee would.

If you do hire an agent yourself, he will probably want a letter of appointment from you. This is simply a signed and dated letter, addressed to the agent, stating that you appoint him as your local agent to represent you and your vessel. The appointment is binding upon your company and is the agent's assurance of being paid. Of course, you should radio full details to your company as soon as possible.

It is prudent to allow the agent to handle the order if you need fresh provisions in port and your company leaves the stores ordering to you, rather than to a company purchasing department. In many ports ship chandlers will board the vessel as soon as she is tied up, looking for business. Their prices are usually high and you may sometimes find that the prices shown on their bills are higher than those shown on the price lists. They are never at a loss to explain this. They may offer commissions, presents, kickbacks, or a percentage of the order.

Your agent probably knows most of the local ship chandlers and will give the order to the one he has found most reliable; or he may want to rotate orders amongst the various ship chandlers. This will prevent anyone on the vessel from using influence in placing the order. In some ports the agent may have a contract with a firm of ship chandlers. This might result in lower prices for an order placed through the agent than for an order placed directly with the chandler.

Most agents are very good, but some agents will do only the minimum work necessary to obtain their fee. Never hesitate to tell both the agent and your company if you are unhappy with the agency service. If you are especially dissatisfied, ask to have a different agent on your next call at the port. Most ports have several agencies and it is a simple matter for the company to change agents if they wish to do so. Also tell them if you are particularly pleased with the agency service; a good agent can be of tremendous assistance.

Your agent can offer much valuable advice but bear in mind that the responsibility for any decision made, as always, is yours.

APPENDIX A

SHIPPING ARTICLES AGREEMENT FOR FOREIGN OR INTERCOASTAL VOYAGE

Title 46, U.S. Code, Section 10304 provides that:

The form of the agreement required by section 10302 of this title shall be in substance as follows:

United States of America

(Date and place of first signature of agreement):

It is agreed between the master and seamen of the   , of which   is at present master, or whoever shall go for master, now bound from the port of   to   (here the voyage is to be described, and the places named at which the vessel is to touch, or if that cannot be done, the general nature and probable length of the voyage is to be stated).

The seamen agree to conduct themselves in an orderly, faithful, honest, and sober manner, and to be at all times diligent in their respective duties, and to be obedient to the lawful commands of the master, or of an individual who lawfully succeeds the master, and of their superior officers in everything related to the vessel, and the stores and cargo of the vessel, whether on board, in boats, or on shore. In consideration of this service by the seamen to be performed, the master agrees to pay the crew, as wages, the amounts beside their names respectively expressed, and to supply them with provisions according to the annexed scale.

It is agreed that any embezzlement, or willful or negligent destruction of any part of the vessel's cargo or stores, shall be made good to the owner out of the wages of the person guilty of the embezzlement or destruction.

If an individual holds himself or herself out as qualified for a duty which the individual proves incompetent to perform, the individual's wages shall be reduced in proportion to the incompetency.

It also is agreed that if a seaman considers himself or herself to be aggrieved by any breach of this agreement or otherwise, the seaman shall present the complaint to the master or officer in charge of the vessel, in a quiet and orderly manner, who shall take steps that the case requires.

It also is agreed that (here any other stipulations may be inserted to which the parties agree, and that are not contrary to law).

In witness whereof, the parties have subscribed their names to this agreement on the dates beside their respective signatures.

Signed by   , master, on the   day of   , nineteen hundred and

Signature of seaman	Time of service:
Birthplace	Months
Age	Days
Height:	Hospital money
Feet	Whole wages
Inches	Wages due
Description:	Place and time of entry
Complexion	Time at which seaman is to be
Hair	on board
Wages each month	In what capacity
Wages each voyage	Shipping commissioner's signature
Advance wages	or initials
Amount of monthly allotment	Allotment payable to
	Conduct qualifications

Note. In the place for signature and descriptions of individuals engaged after the first departure of the vessel, the entries are to be made as above, except that the signature of the consul or vice consul, customs officer, or witness before whom the individual is engaged, is to be entered.

APPENDIX B

FIGURES: FORMS

Listed in parentheses following the form title are its official form number and the figure number used in this text.

FIG. 1

NAVCG 718 E

Serial No. R. ____

U. S. Coast Guard

RECORD OF ENTRY

IN CONTINUOUS DISCHARGE BOOK

Name of seaman ____

Citizenship ____

Continuous Discharge Book No. ____

I acknowledge that the following entries have been made in my Continuous Discharge Book.

____
(Signature of seaman)

Date and place of engagement ____	Description of voyage ____ (Foreign, intercoastal, or coastwise)
Name of ship ____	Date and place of discharge ____
Rating ____	

Official No. ____

I HEREBY CERTIFY that I have made the above entries in the Continuous Discharge Book of the above-described seaman.

____ *Master.*

____ *Shipping Commissioner.*

HEADQUARTERS' COPY

NOTE.—Name of Master must appear if entry is certified by Shipping Commissioner. When Master performs duty of Shipping Commissioner he shall *sign* this form. Original of this record to be forwarded to the Commandant, Coast Guard. DO NOT GIVE THIS FORM TO THE SEAMAN.

16—1847r-2   U. S. GOVERNMENT PRINTING OFFICE

FIG. 2 201

DEPARTMENT OF TRANSPORTATION

C. G. 705 A
(Rev. 1-80)

UNITED STATES COAST GUARD

SHIPPING ARTICLES

(R. S. 4612, as amended--U. S. C., title 46, sec. 713)

Notice is hereby given that section 4519 of the U. S. Revised Statutes (U. S. C., title 46, sec. 577) makes it obligatory on the part of the master of a merchant vessel of the United States, at the commencement of every voyage or engagement, to cause a legible copy of the agreement (forecastle card), omitting signatures, to be placed or posted up in such part of the vessel as to be accessible to the crew, under penalty not exceeding ONE HUNDRED DOLLARS.

ARTICLES OF AGREEMENT BETWEEN MASTER AND SEAMEN IN THE MERCHANT SERVICE OF THE UNITED STATES

Required by act of Congress, title LIII, Revised Statutes of the United States (U. S. C., title 46, ch. 18)

NAME OF SHIP	OFFICIAL NO.	PORT OF REGISTRY	DATE OF REGISTER	REGISTERED TONNAGE		VOYAGE NO.
				Gross	Net	

OPERATING COMPANY ON THIS VOYAGE

Name		NUMBER OF SEAMEN AND APPRENTICES FOR WHICH ACCOMMODATION IS CERTIFIED	CLASS OF SHIP
Address (State number of house, street, and town)			

IT IS AGREED between the Master and seamen, or mariners, of the _____ PORT OF _____

_____ of which _____

is at present Master, or whoever shall go for Master, now bound from the Port of [1] _____

and such other ports and places in any part of the world as the Master may direct, and back to a final port of discharge in the United States, for a term of time not exceeding _____ calendar months. [2]

And the said crew agree to conduct themselves in an orderly, faithful, honest, and sober manner, and to be at all times diligent in their respective duties, and to be obedient to the lawful commands of the said Master, or of any person who shall lawfully succeed him, and of their superior officers, in everything relating to the vessel, and the stores and cargo thereof, whether on board, in boats, or on shore, and in consideration of which service to be duly performed the said Master hereby agrees to pay to the said crew, as wages, the sums against their names respectively expressed, and to supply them with provisions according to the annexed scale. And it is hereby agreed, that any embezzlement or willful or negligent destruction of any part of the vessel's cargo or stores shall be made good to the owner out of the wages of the person guilty of the same. And if any person enters himself as qualified for a duty which he proves himself incompetent to perform, his wages shall be reduced in proportion to his incompetency. And it is also agreed that if any member of the crew considers himself to be aggrieved by any breach of agreement or otherwise, he shall represent the same to the Master or officer in charge of the ship in a quiet and orderly manner, who shall thereupon take such steps as the case may require.

GOING ON SHORE IN FOREIGN PORTS IS PROHIBITED EXCEPT BY PERMISSION OF THE MASTER
NO DANGEROUS WEAPONS[3] OR GROG ALLOWED, AND NONE TO BE BROUGHT ON BOARD BY THE CREW

SCALE OF PROVISIONS to be allowed and served out to the Crew during the voyage in addition to the daily issue of time and lemon juice and sugar, or other antiscorbutics in any case required by law

		Sun. day	Mon. day	Tues. day	Wednes. day	Thurs. day	Fri. day	Satur. day
Water	quarts	5	5	5	5	5	5	5
Biscuit	pound	1/2	1/2	1/2	1/2	1/2	1/2	1/2
Beef, salt	pounds	1-1/4	1-1/4	1-1/4	1-1/4	1-1/4	1-1/4	1-1/4
Pork, salt	pound		1	1	1	1		
Flour	pound	1/2		1/2		1/2		1/2
Canned meat	pound		1/2		1/2		1/2	
Fresh bread	pounds	1-1/2	1-1/2	1-1/2	1-1/2	1-1/2	1-1/2	1-1/2
Fish, dry, preserved, or fresh	pound		1		1		1	
Potatoes or yams	pound	1/2						
Canned tomatoes	pint		1/3		1/3		1/3	
Peas	pint	1/3		1/3		1/3		1/3
Beans	pint	1/3		1/3		1/3		1/3
Rice	pint							1/3

		Sun. day	Mon. day	Tues. day	Wednes. day	Thurs. day	Fri. day	Satur. day
Coffee (green berry)	ounce	3/4	3/4	3/4	3/4	3/4	3/4	3/4
Tea	ounce	1/8	1/8	1/8	1/8	1/8	1/8	1/8
Sugar	ounces	3	3	3	3	3	3	3
Molasses	pint	3		1/2		1/2		
Dried fruit	ounces	3		3		3		
Pickles	pint		1/4	1/4	1/4	1/4	1/4	
Vinegar	pint			1/2				1/2
Corn meal	ounces	4	4	4	4	4		
Onions	ounces	4	1	1	1	1		
Lard	ounce	1	1	1	1	1	1	1
Butter	ounces	2	2	2	2	2	2	2
Mustard, pepper, and salt sufficient for seasoning.								

SUBSTITUTES

One pound of flour daily may be substituted for the daily ration of biscuit or fresh bread; two ounces of desiccated vegetables for one pound of potatoes or yams; six ounces of hominy, oatmeal, or cracked wheat, or two ounces of tapioca, for six ounces of rice; one-half pound of canned tomatoes for one-half pound of canned tomatoes; one-eighth of an ounce of coffee for one-eighth of an ounce of coffee; three-fourths of an ounce of tea for three-fourths of an ounce of tea; six ounces of canned fruit for three ounces of dried fruit; one-half ounce of lime juice for the daily ration of vinegar; four ounces of oatmeal or cracked wheat for one-half pint of corn meal; two ounces of pickled onions for four ounces of fresh onions.

When the vessel is in port and it is possible to obtain the same, one and one-half pounds of fresh meat shall be substituted for the daily rations of salt and canned meat; one-half pound of green cabbage for one ration of canned tomatoes; one-half pound of fresh fruit for one ration of dried fruit. Fresh fruit and vegetables shall be served while in port if obtainable. The seamen shall have the option of accepting the fare the Master may provide, but the right at any time to demand the foregoing scale of provisions.

The foregoing scale of provisions shall be inserted in every article of agreement, and shall not be reduced by any contract, except as above, and a copy of the same shall be posted in a conspicuous place in the galley and in the forecastle of each vessel.

It is also agreed that [4]

IN WITNESS WHEREOF the said parties have subscribed their names hereto on the days against their respective signatures mentioned.

_____ , Master, of _____ ,

on the _____ day of _____ , 19 ____

(Give address)

CITIZENSHIP REQUIREMENTS (crew exclusive of licensed officers)

	Subsidized Passenger Vessels	Subsidized Cargo Vessels	Nonsubsidized Vessels
	90 percent shall be citizens of United States, either native-born or naturalized. Legally admitted aliens may comprise other 10 percent but may be employed in Steward's Department only.	On and after Sept. 27, 1936, 100 percent citizens of United States, either native-born or naturalized.	On and after Dec. 25, 1936, 75 percent citizens of United States, either native-born or naturalized.
Native-born citizens	Number	Number	Number
Naturalized citizens			
First papers			
Admissible aliens			
Percentage (American citizens)			

I HEREBY CERTIFY that the above statement as to the citizenship of the crew signed on these articles is true and correct

_____
Master or Consular Officer

FIG. 2

ATTENTION OF MASTERS ESPECIALLY INVITED TO THE FOLLOWING REQUIREMENTS OF LAW

Authority of Master

(R. S. 4504 – 46 U. S. C. 546) Whenever the master of any vessel shall engage his crew, or any part of the same, in any collection district where no Coast Guard Official to perform the duties of shipping commissioner shall have been appointed, he may perform for himself the duties of such commissioner.

NOTE: Authority for the master to discharge seamen is contained in R. S. 4551 – 46 U. S. C. 643. In the following statutes, "master" may be substituted for "shipping commissioner" except in those statutes dealing with the shipment/discharge of seamen in foreign ports.

Agreement To Ship in Foreign Trade

(R. S. 4511 – 46 U. S. C. 564) The master of every vessel bound from a port in the United States to any foreign port other than vessels engaged in trade between the United States and the British North American possessions, or the West India Islands, or the Republic of Mexico, or of any vessel of the burden of seventy-five tons, or upward, bound from a port on the Atlantic to a port on the Pacific, or vice versa, shall, before he proceeds on such voyage, make an agreement, in writing, or in print, with every seaman whom he carries to sea as one of the crew, in the manner hereinafter mentioned:

(R. S. 4519 – 46 U. S. C. 577) The master shall, at the commencement of every voyage or engagement, cause a legible copy of the agreement, omitting signatures, to be placed or posted up in such part of the vessel as to be accessible to the crew; and on default shall be liable to a penalty of not more than $100.

Penalty for Shipment Without Agreement

(R. S. 4514 – 46 U. S. C. 567) If any person shall be carried to sea, as one of the crew on board of any vessel making a voyage as hereinbefore specified (R. S. 4511) without entering into an agreement with the master of such vessel, in the form and manner, and at the place and times in such cases required, the vessel shall be held liable for each such offense to a penalty of not more than $200. But the vessel shall not be held liable for any person carried to sea, who shall have secretly stowed away himself without the knowledge of the master, mate, or of any of the officers of the vessel, or who shall have falsely personated himself to the master, mate, or officers of the vessel, for the purpose of being carried to sea.

Shipment in Foreign Ports Before Consuls

(R. S. 4517 – 46 U. S. C. 570) Every master of a merchant vessel who engages any seaman at a place out of the United States, in which there is a consular officer, shall, before carrying such seaman to sea, procure the sanction of such officer and shall engage seamen in his presence; and the rules governing the engagement of seamen before a shipping commissioner in the United States shall apply to such engagements made before a consular officer, and upon every such engagement the consular officer shall endorse upon the agreement his sanction thereof, and an attestation to the effect that the same has been signed in his presence and otherwise duly made.

(R. S. 4518 – 46 U. S. C. 571) Every master who engages any seaman in any place in which there is a consular officer otherwise than as required by the preceding section shall incur a penalty of not more than $100, for which penalty the vessel shall be held liable.

Watches – Hours of Labor – Legal Holidays

(R. S. 4551 – Sec. 2 – 46 U. S. C., Supp. IV 673) In all merchant vessels of the United States of more than one hundred tons gross, excepting those navigating rivers, harbors, lakes (other than Great Lakes), bays, sounds, bayous, and canals, exclusively, the licensed officers and sailors, coal passers, firemen, oilers, and water tenders shall, while at sea, be divided into at least three watches, which shall be kept on duty successively for the performance of ordinary work incident to the sailing and management of the vessel. No licensed officer or seaman in the deck or engine department of any tug documented under the laws of the United States (except boats or vessels used exclusively for fishing purposes) navigating the Great Lakes, harbors of the Great Lakes, and connecting and tributary waters between Gary, Ind.; Duluth, Minn.; Niagara Falls, N. Y.; and Ogdensburg, N. Y., shall be required or permitted to work more than eight hours in one day except in case of extraordinary emergency affecting the safety of the vessel and/or life or property. The seaman shall not be shipped to work alternately in the fireroom and on deck, nor shall those shipped for deck duty be required to work in the fireroom, or vice versa; nor shall any licensed officer or seaman in the deck or engine department be required to work more than eight hours in one day; but these provisions shall not limit either the authority of the master or other officer or the obedience of the seamen when in the judgment of the master or other officer the whole or any part of the crew are needed for maneuvering, shifting berth, mooring, or unmooring, the vessel or the performance of work necessary for the safety of the vessel, her passengers, crew, and cargo, or for the saving of life aboard other vessels in jeopardy, or when in port or at sea, from requiring the whole or any part of the crew to participate in the performance of fire, lifeboat, or other drills. While such vessel is in a safe harbor no seaman shall be required to do any unnecessary work on Sundays or the following-named days: New Year's Day, the Fourth of July, Labor Day, Thanksgiving Day, and Christmas Day, but this shall not prevent the dispatch of a vessel on regular schedule or when ready to proceed on her voyage. And at all times while such vessel is in a safe harbor, eight hours, inclusive of the anchor watch, shall constitute a day's work. Whenever the master of any vessel shall fail to comply with this section and the regulation issued thereunder, the owner shall be liable to a penalty not to exceed $500, and the seamen shall be entitled to discharge from such vessel and to receive the wages earned. But this section shall not apply to vessels engaged in salvage operations: *Provided*, That in all tugs and barges subject to this section when engaged on a voyage of less than six hundred miles, the licensed officers and members of crews other than coal passers, firemen, oilers, and water tenders may, while at sea, be divided into not less than two watches, but nothing in this proviso shall be construed as repealing any part of section 222 of this title. This section shall take effect six months after June 25, 1936. (As amended June 25, 1936, c. 816, 2, 49 Stat. 1933; June 23, 1938, c. 597, 52 Stat. 944.)

Wages

(R. S. 4552 – 46 U. S. C. 644) The following rules shall be observed with respect to the settlement of wages:

First. Upon the completion, before a shipping commissioner, of any discharge and settlement, the master or owner and each seaman respectively, in the presence of the shipping commissioner, shall sign a mutual release of all claims for wages in respect of the past voyage or engagement, and the shipping commissioner shall also sign and attest it, and shall retain it in a book to be kept for that purpose, provided both the master and seaman assent to such settlement, or the settlement has been adjusted by the shipping commissioner.

(R. S. 4524 – 46 U. S. C. 591) A seaman's right to wages and provisions shall be taken to commence either at the time at which he commences work, or at the time specified in the agreement for his commencement of work or presence on board, whichever first happens.

(R. S. 4530 – 46 U. S. C. 597) Every seaman on a vessel of the United States shall be entitled to receive on demand from the master of the vessel to which he belongs one-half part of the balance of his wages earned and remaining unpaid at the time when such demand is made at every port where such vessel, after the voyage has been commenced, shall load or deliver cargo before the voyage is ended, and all stipulations in the contract to the contrary shall be void: *Provided*, Such a demand shall not be made before the expiration of, nor oftener than once in five days nor more than once in the same harbor on the same entry. Any failure on the part of the master to comply with this demand shall release the seaman from his contract and he shall be entitled to full payment of wages earned. And when the voyage is ended every such seaman shall be entitled to the remainder of the wages which shall be then due him, as provided in section 4529 of the Revised Statutes: *Provided further*, That notwithstanding any release signed by any seaman under section 4552 of the Revised Statutes, any court having jurisdiction may upon a good cause shown set aside such release and take such action as justice shall require.

Discharge of Seamen

(R. S. 4549 – 46 U. S. C. 641) All seamen discharged in the United States from merchant vessels engaged in voyages from a port in the United States to any foreign port, or, being of the burden of seventy-five tons or upward, from a port on the Atlantic to a port on the Pacific, or vice versa, shall be discharged and receive their wages in the presence of a duly authorized shipping commissioner under this Title (R. S. 4501 – 4612), except in cases where some competent court otherwise directs; and any master or owner of any such vessel who discharges any such seaman belonging thereto or pays his wages within the United States in any other manner, shall be liable to a penalty of not more than $50.

(R. S. 4551 – Subsec. (d) – 46 U. S. C., Supp. IV 643 (d)) Upon the discharge of any seaman and the payment of his wages, the shipping commissioner shall enter in the continuous discharge book of such seaman, if the seaman carries such a book, the name and official number of the vessel, the nature of the voyage (foreign, intercoastal, or coastwise), the class to which the vessel belongs (steam, motor, sail, or barge), the date and place of the shipment and of the discharge of such seaman, the rating (capacity in which employed) then held by such seaman, and the signature of the person making such entries and nothing more.

(R. S. 4551 – Subsec. (e) – 46 U. S. C., Supp. IV 643 (e)) For the purpose of furnishing evidence of sea service in the case of seamen preferring the certificate of identification instead of the continuous discharge book, the United States Coast Guard shall provide a certificate of discharge, printed on durable paper, in such form as to specify the name and citizenship of the seaman to whom it is issued, the serial number of his certificate of identification, the name and official number of the vessel, the nature of the voyage (foreign, intercoastal, or coastwise), the class to which the vessel belongs (steam, motor, sail, or barge), the date and place of the shipment and of the discharge of such seaman, and the rating (capacity in which employed) then held by such seaman. Records of service entered in either continuous discharge books or certificates of discharge shall contain no reference to the character or ability of the seaman. The shipping commissioner shall issue such certificate of discharge and make the proper entries therein, which certificate shall be signed by the seaman to whom it is issued and the master of the vessel and shall be witnessed by such shipping commissioner.

(R. S. 4551 – Subsec. (k) – 46 U. S. C., Supp. IV 643 (k)) Where vessels are required to sign on and discharge the crew before a shipping commissioner and no shipping commissioner is appointed or is available the functions and duties required by subsections (d) and (e) of this section to be performed by such shipping commissioner may be performed by a collector or deputy collector of customs; and where vessels are not required to sign on and discharge the crew before a shipping commissioner the duties and functions required by subsections (d) and (e) of this section to be performed by the shipping commissioner shall be performed by the master of such vessel. Any master who shall fail to perform such duties or functions shall be fined in the sum of $50 for each offense.

Discharge in Foreign Ports

(R. S. 4580 – 46 U. S. C. 682) Upon the application of the master of any vessel to a consular officer to discharge a seaman, or upon the application of any seaman for his own discharge, if it appears to such officer that said seaman has completed his shipping agreement or is entitled to his discharge under any act of Congress or according to the general principles or usages of maritime law as recognized in the United States, such officer shall discharge said seaman, and require from the master of said vessel, before such discharge shall be made, payment of the wages which may then be due said seaman; but no payment of extra wages shall be required by any consular officer upon such discharge of any seaman except as provided in this act.

PREVIOUS EDITIONS ARE OBSOLETE

C. G. 705 A
(Rev. l-80)

SHIPPING ARTICLES OF _____   **PAGE NO.** _____

PARTICULARS OF ENGAGEMENT

Line No.	SIGNATURE OF SEAMAN	CAPACITY	WAGES PER MONTH	NUMBER OF CONT. DIS. BOOK OR CERT. OF IDEN. OR MER-CHANT MARI-NER'S DOCU-MENT	SERIAL NUMBER OF LI-CENSE OR CERTIFI-CATE	BIRTHPLACE (If foreign-born, but naturalized, insert NAT. in parenthesis after country of birth)	DATE OF BIRTH	SOCIAL SECURITY No.	PLACE AND DATE OF SIGNING THIS AGREEMENT Place	Date	TIME AT WHICH TO BE ON BOARD	ADDRESS OF WIFE OR NEXT OF KIN	SIGNATURE OR INITIALS OF MASTER OR CONSUL	Line No.
1														1
2														2
3														3
4														4
48														48
49														49
50														50
51														51
52														52
53														53
54														54
55														55
56														56
57														57
58														58
59														59
60														60

State of _____, Port of _____

On this _____ day of _____, _____ personally appeared before me, the above-named seamen, severally known to me to be the same persons who executed the instruments above (shipping articles), who, each for himself, acknowledged to me that he had read or had heard read the same; that he was by me made acquainted with the conditions thereof, and understood the same; and that, while sober, and not in a state of intoxication, he signed it freely and voluntarily, for the uses and purposes therein mentioned.

FIG. 2   205

SHIPPING ARTICLES OF _____   PAGE No. _____

PARTICULARS OF DISCHARGE

RELEASE

Line No.	PLACE, DATE, AND CAUSE OF LEAVING SHIP OR OF DEATH				TIME OF SERVICE		WAGES EARNED		DEDUCTIONS	BALANCE OF WAGES PAID ON DISCHARGE	DATE WAGES PAID AND RELEASE SIGNED	RELEASE	ATTESTATION OF MASTER OR CONSUL	Line No.
	Place	Date	Cause		M	D	Regular Wage					We, the undersigned seamen, do hereby, each one for himself by our signatures herewith given in consideration of settlements made, release the Master and owners from all claims for wages in respect of this voyage or engagement, and I, the Master, do also release each of the undersigned seamen from all claims, in consideration of this release signed by them. _____ Master.		
1														1
2														2
3														3
4														4
47														47
48														48
49														49
50														50
51														51
52														52
53														53
54														54
55														55
56														56
57														57
58														58
59														59
60														60

I hereby certify that the entries in the Discharge Books of seamen included in these articles agree with the applicable entries herein, or Certificates of Discharge have been issued in accordance therewith.

_____
Master or Consular Officer

DEPT. OF TRANSPORTATION
U. S. COAST GUARD
CG—785(T) (Rev. 7-67)

MASTER'S REPORT OF SEAMEN SHIPPED OR DISCHARGED

BUDGET BUREAU APPROVAL
04#3032

IN THE CREW OF THE S.S.

OFFICIAL NUMBER OF SHIP

DESCRIPTION OF VOYAGE
☐ GREAT LAKES   ☐ COASTWISE   ☐ NEARBY FOREIGN
☐ OTHER

MASTER'S NAME

NAME AND ADDRESS OF OWNER OR OPERATOR

LINE NO	NAME AS APPEARING ON U.S. SEAMAN DOCUMENT (First, middle initial, last)	Z OR BK NUMBER	LICENSE OR CERTIFICATE OF REGISTRY NO.	ALIEN (Check X)	YEAR OF BIRTH	CAPACITY IN WHICH ENGAGED	DATE AND PLACE OF ENGAGEMENT	DATE AND PLACE OF DISCHARGE
1								
2								
3								
4								
5								
6								
7								
8								
9								
63								
64								
65								
66								
67								
68								
69								

FIG. 3   207

REPORTING INSTRUCTIONS

1. Every person employed on United States merchant vessels of 100 gross tons and over is required to possess a U. S. Merchant Mariner's Document bearing the stamp "Validated for Emergency Service."

2. The information contained in this report should be identical with the same information required on form CG–718A and CG–718E.

3. This report must be submitted by the master of every merchant vessel of the United States of 100 gross tons or upward, when the vessel's crew is not engaged under supervision of a shipping commissioner; except, vessels employed exclusively on the navigable rivers, fishing or whaling vessels, yachts and ferry or tug used in connection with the ferry operation on the Great Lakes, lakes, bays and sounds, bayous, canals and harbors.

4. ALIEN COLUMN ABOVE – Check (X) for aliens only. Blank space will indicate United States citizens.

MASTER'S STATEMENTS
(Strike out inapplicable items, if any)

1. I have entered into an agreement with the crew as required by law. (46 USC 574)
2. Not less than 65 per cent of the deck crew exclusive of licensed officers are of a rating not less than able seaman. (46 USC 672)
3. Not less than 75 per cent of the crew in each department are able to understand any order given by officers of the vessel. (46 USC 672)
4. Number of lifeboatmen is in accordance with certificate of inspection; every lifeboatman possesses a document endorsed for this rating. (46 USC 222)
5. Every member of the crew possesses a license, certificate of registry, or U. S. Merchant Mariner's Document for the rating in which he is employed. (46 USC 222, 224a, 229, 246, 643)

CERTIFICATION

I HEREBY CERTIFY that all the above entries and statements on this form are true to the best of my knowledge and belief.

DATE	LICENSE NUMBER	Z OR BK NUMBER

CITIZENSHIP REQUIREMENTS

Seamen claiming American Citizenship who have not presented documentary evidence of such citizenship and whose continuous discharge book of Merchant Mariner's Document shows a question mark with reference to citizenship shall not be employed except within the percentage of aliens authorized.

VESSEL CATEGORY (Check appropriate box)	CITIZENSHIP
☐ SUBSIDIZED PASSENGER VESSELS (90 percent Americans including licensed officers) (Aliens may be employed only in steward's department)	UNITED STATES CITIZENS
☐ SUBSIDIZED CARGO VESSELS (100 percent Americans)	ALIENS
☐ NON-SUBSIDIZED VESSELS (75 percent Americans excluding licensed officers)	TOTAL CREW
	PERCENTAGE OF UNITED STATES CITIZENS

SIGNATURE OF MASTER

70

Form **1078**

(Rev. December 1984)

Department of the Treasury—Internal Revenue Service

Certificate of Alien Claiming Residence in the United States

(This certificate has no effect on citizenship)

Your name

Your social security number

Address (Number and street or rural route)

Your occupation

City, town or post office, State, and ZIP code

Date of employment

Name and address (including ZIP code) of withholding agent

Employer identification number

Under penalties of perjury, I declare that I am a citizen or subject of _____, that I was admitted to the United States on or about _____, under a _____ visa or permit; that I have established residence in the United States; and I understand that my income derived from all sources, including sources outside the United States, will be subject to tax under the Internal Revenue laws applicable to residents of the United States until I abandon my residence in the United States.

Date _____, 19 ____

_____
Your signature

Instructions

Who May File.—A resident alien may file the original and one copy of this certificate with the withholding agent to claim the benefit of U.S. residence for income tax purposes. (A withholding agent is responsible for withholding tax from your income.)

The withholding agent keeps the original certificate and sends the copy to the Internal Revenue Service Center, Philadelphia, PA 19255.

Taxation of Aliens.—If you are a resident alien, you must report income on Form 1040, Form 1040A, or Form 1040EZ in the same manner as U.S. citizens.

If you are a nonresident alien, you must report income on Form 1040NR. Your income, regardless of source, that is effectively connected with the conduct of your U.S. trade or

Income that you derive from sources in the United States is taxed at a flat 30% or lower treaty rate if it is not effectively connected with the conduct of your U.S. trade or business.

Resident Aliens.—For tax years beginning after 1984, specific new rules apply for determining residency. For details, see Publication 519, U.S. Tax Guide for Aliens.

Social Security Number.—Enter the number from your social security card. If you do not have a social security number, you can apply for one by filling out **Form SS-5**, Application for a Social Security Number card. You can get Form SS-5 from a Social Security Administration office.

FIG. 5

The United States of America

TREASURY DEPARTMENT
BUREAU OF CUSTOMS

CLEARANCE OF VESSEL TO A FOREIGN PORT

District of ....

Port of ....

These are to certify all whom it doth concern:

That ....

Master or Commander of the ....

burden .... *Tons, or thereabouts, mounted with* ....

Guns, navigated with .... *Men,* ....

.... *built, and bound for* ....

....

....

....

....

with passengers and having on board ....

....

....

MERCHANDISE AND STORES,

hath here entered and cleared his said vessel, according to law.

Given under our hands and seals, at the Customhouse of ....

.............................., *this* .... *day of* ....

one thousand nine hundred ...., *and in the* ....

year of the Independence of the United States of America.

....
Deputy Collector of Customs.

210   FIG. 6

DEPARTMENT OF THE TREASURY
UNITED STATES CUSTOMS SERVICE

Form Approved
O.M.B. No. 1515-006

MASTER'S OATH OF VESSEL IN FOREIGN TRADE

19 CFR 4.7, 4 8, 4.9, 4.20, 4.61,
4.63, 4.75, 4.81, 4.85, 4.87

☐ ENTRANCE   ☐ CLEARANCE

1. NATIONALITY, NAME & TYPE OF VESSEL	2. VESSEL BUILT AT	3. MANIFEST NO.
		4. NAME OF DISTRICT AND PORT
5. NAME AND ADDRESS OF OWNER	6. NAME AND ADDRESS OF OPERATOR	7. TIME AND DATE OF ARRIVAL
		8. MAXIMUM DRAFT ON ARRIVAL/DEPARTURE

MASTER'S CERTIFICATE ON PRELIMINARY ENTRY

I certify that the within manifest contains a just, true, and full account of all the cargo, and other items, including passengers and their baggage, required by law to be manifested.

_____ Master's Signature

I certify this manifest was this day produced to me as the _____ manifest. If produced as copy, I certify I have examined and compared it with the original and find it agrees therewith.
(Original/Duplicate)

Date, Time, Preliminary Entry	Customs Officer's Signature

MASTER'S OATH OF FORMAL ENTRY/CLEARANCE

On Entry: (a) I swear that the statements contained in any manifest (including any passenger or stores list) presented on entry or on arrival at domestic ports in a coastwise movement (or, if a foreign vessel, in any declaration made on such arrival that the vessel is in ballast only) are true. (b) I do solemnly swear that I have to the best of my knowledge and belief delivered to the appropriate post office every letter and every bag, packet, or parcel of letters on board the said vessel during her last voyage, or in my possession or under my power or control, except where waybilled for discharge at other ports in the United States at which the said vessel is scheduled to call and which the Postmaster General has not determined will be unreasonably delayed by remaining on board the said vessel for delivery at such ports. (c) I solemnly swear that the ownership of this vessel, except as may be otherwise stated on this form, is as indicated in any register, or document in lieu thereof, produced on entry.[1] (d) I swear that no part of the vessel has been sold or transferred since the granting of the register, except as may be otherwise stated on this form, and that no foreign subject or citizen has, to the best of my knowledge and belief, any share, by way of trust, confidence, or otherwise, in the vessel.[1] (e) If the vessel is documented to engage in trade on the northern, northeastern, and northwestern frontiers of the United States, I swear that any articles purchased in a foreign country for the use of the vessel and designated "sea stores" are for the exclusive use of the vessel and are not intended for sale, transfer, or private use.

On Clearance: (a) If clearing for a foreign port, I do solemnly, sincerely, and truly swear that the manifest of the cargo on board the vessel, now delivered by me to the District Director of Customs, and subscribed with my name, contains, according to the best of my knowledge and belief, a full, just, and true account of all the goods, wares, or merchandise now actually laden on board the said vessel, and of the value thereof; and if any other goods, wares, or merchandise shall be laden or put on board the vessel previous to her sailing from this port, I will immediately report the same to the said District Director. I do also swear that I verily believe the duties on all foreign merchandise therein specified have been paid or secured, according to law, and that no part thereof is intended to be relanded within the United States, and that if by distress or other unavoidable accident it shall become necessary to reland the same, I will forthwith make a just and true report thereof to the District Director of the district wherein such distress or accident may happen. So help me God. (b) I swear that the statements contained in any manifest presented on departure from domestic ports in a coastwise movement (or, if a foreign vessel, in any declaration made in such a movement that there has been no lading on board the vessel) are true. (c) I swear that I do not have under my care or control and will not receive or transport any letter that has not been regularly received from a United States post office or does not relate to the cargo of the vessel. 18 U.S.C. 1699; 19 U.S.C. 282, 1431, 1434 & 1435; 39 U.S.C. 902(b); 46 U.S.C. 42, 91, 94, 313 & 314.

9. NAME OF MASTER OR AUTHORIZED OFFICER	10. SIGNATURE OF MASTER, LICENSED DECK OFFICER OR PURSER

CUSTOMS USE ONLY

11. LOAD LINE EXPIRES	12. TONNAGE MARK ☐ NONE ☐ SUBMERGED ☐ NOT SUBMERGED

13. SOLAS CERTIFICATES EXPIRES	14. PASSENGERS ALLOWED PER COAST GUARD CERTIFICATE	15. NO. PASSENGERS DISEMBARKING/EMBARKING
16. CERT. FIN. RESP. NO. (Oil Pollution)	17. CERT. FIN. RESP. (Passenger Death/Injury)	18. CERT. FIN. RESP. (Passenger Transportation Indemnification)

19. PURPOSE (Entrance)	20. PURPOSE (Clearance)
☐ D (Discharge foreign cargo) ☐ X (Export cargo aboard on arrival) ☐ L (Lade cargo for export) ☐ F (Foreign cargo to be retained on board) ☐ N (No cargo transactions) ☐ Y (Military cargo for discharge)	☐ D (Discharge foreign cargo) ☐ X (Export cargo aboard on arriva ☐ L (Lade cargo for export) ☐ F (Foreign cargo retained on bo ☐ N (No cargo transactions) ☐ Y (Military cargo laden)

21. TONNAGE YEAR BEGINS[2]	22. NO. AND RATE OF PAYMENTS[2]	23. AMOUNT[2]	24. CERTIFICATE NO.[2]
25. FIRST PAYMENT AT[3]	26. DATE[3]	27. LAST PAYMENT AT[3]	28. DATE[3]
29. FEE CERTIFICATE NO.	30. TOTAL FEES	31. TIME AND DATE ENTERED	32. TIME AND DATE CLEARED

33. SIGNATURE AND TITLE OF OFFICER RECEIVING ENTRY/CLEARANCE

FOOTNOTES: 1. Applicable to American vessel arriving direct from a foreign port.
2. Arrival only.
3. To be filled in only if no tonnage duty is collected because five payments have been made during the tonnage year at the rate applicable to the current entry of the vessel.

The Paperwork Reduction Act of 1980 says we must tell you why we are collecting information, how we will use it, and whether you have to give it to us. We ask for information to carry out the Customs Service laws of the United States. This form is by the master of a vessel to attest to the truthfulness of the forms, certificates, and r fest on board and which must be presented to Customs. This form is also used by Cus to verify the various certificates and numbers and expiration dates same. It is mande and to your benefit.

This form may be printed by private parties provided the supply printed conforms to the official form in size, wording, arrangement, and quality and color of paper. For sale by District Directors of Customs.

Customs Form 1300 (0820

FIG. 7   211

DEPARTMENT OF THE TREASURY UNITED STATES CUSTOMS SERVICE Part 4, C.R.	**GENERAL DECLARATION** ☐ Arrival ☐ Departure		Form Approved O.M.B. No. 48–RO459
1. Name and description of ship		2. Port of arrival/departure	3. Date-time of arrival/departure
4. Nationality of ship	5. Name of master	6. Port arrived from/Port of destination	
7. Certificate of registry (Port; date; number)		8. Name and address of ship's agent	
9. Gross register tons	10. Net register tons		
11. Position of the ship in the port (berth or station)			
12. Brief particulars of voyage (previous and subsequent ports of call; underline where remaining cargo will be discharged)			
13. Brief description of the cargo			
14. Number of crew (include master)	15. Number of passengers	16. Remarks	
Attached documents (indicate number of copies)			
17. Cargo Declaration	18. Ship's Stores Declaration		
19. Crew List	20. Passenger List	21. Date and signature by master, authorized agent or officer**	
22. Crew's Effects Declaration	23. Maritime Declaration of Health*		
space for U.S. Customs use only			

*Only on arrival.

**Only the Master, Licensed Deck Officer, or Purser may sign; documents attached as shown in items 17–22 need not be signed.

This form may be printed by private parties provided it conforms to the official form in size (except that it may be up to 14 inches in length), wording, arrangement, style, size of type, and quality and color of paper. (Section 4.99 C.R.) For sale by district directors of Customs.

964-543   (Previous editions may be used)   **Customs Form 1301 (3-9-78)**

Form Approved. OMB No. 48R0534

DEPARTMENT OF THE TREASURY
UNITED STATES CUSTOMS SERVICE

CARGO DECLARATION
(Oath to be taken on Customs Form 1300)
4.7(a), C.R.

CUSTOMS FORM 1302 (12-30-77)

FIG. 9   213

DEPARTMENT of the TREASURY ● UNITED STATES CUSTOMS SERVICE

CARGO DECLARATION
Outward With Commercial Forms
(Oath to be taken on Customs Form 1300)

Form Approved
OMB No. 48-RO534

Page Nr.

:), C.R.

1. Name of ship		2. Port where report is made (not required by United States)	
3. Nationality of ship	4. Name of master	5a. Port of loading	5b. Port of discharge

'L Nr.

6. Marks and Nrs. (MN) Container Nrs. (CN) Seal Nrs. (SN)	7. Number and kind of packages; Description of goods	(Answer Col. 8 OR Col. 9)	
		8. Gross Weight (lb. or kg.)	9. Measurement (per TSUS)

Customs Form 1302-A(1-14-77)

DEPARTMENT OF THE TREASURY UNITED STATES CUSTOMS SERVICE	SHIP'S STORES DECLARATION ☐ Arrival ☐ Departure	Form Approved O.M.B. No. 48– RO486

Page No.

1. Name of ship	2. Port of arrival/departure	3. Date of arrival/departure
4. Nationality of ship	5. Port arrived from/Port of destination	
6. Number of persons on board 7. Period of stay	8. Place of storage*	
9. Name of article	10. Quantity	11. For Official Use

DECK
Article	Quantity
Ammunition, 38 cal.	Rds.
Revolver, 38 cal.	Ea.
Rope, Fiber	Ft.
Rope, Wire	Ft.

ENGINE
Diesel Oil	Gals.
Fuel Oil	Bbls.
Fresh Water	Tons
Lube Oil	Gals.

STEWARD
Cereal & Paste	Lbs.
Coffee	Lbs.
Dairy	Lbs.
Eggs	Doz.
Fish *Frozen - Fresh & Salt*	Lbs.
Fruit *Fresh - Dried & Canned*	Lbs.
Meat *Fresh - Canned & Salt*	Lbs.
Poultry	Lbs.
Vegetables *Fresh - Frozen & Canned*	Lbs.
Sugar	Lbs.

GENERAL
Detergents & Soap	Lbs.
Grease	Lbs.
Kerosene & Solvent	Gals.
Paint	Gals.
Paint, Additives	Gals.

BONDED
Beer ,	Cases
Cigarettes	Ctns.
Cigars	Ea.
Gin	Btls.
Liquers	Btls.
Tobacco	Lbs.
Whiskey	Btls.
Wine	Btls.

NARCOTICS
Codeine Sulfate.....gr.	Tablet
Morphine Sulfate.....gr.	Tubex
Paragoric	Pints
Phenobarbital.....gr.	Tablet

Also such broken and sundry stores as linen, crockery, silver, spare parts, tools, instrument hospital supplies and slop chest stores as required by law and/or necessary for the safe and efficient navigation and operation of the vessel.

12. Date and signature by master, authorized agent or officer

Not required by the United States.

CUSTOMS FORM 1303 (3-20-75)

FIG. 11

215

FIG. 11   215

DEPARTMENT OF THE TREASURY
UNITED STATES CUSTOMS SERVICE

CREW'S EFFECTS DECLARATION

19 CFR 4.7a (b) (d)

Form Approved
O.M.B. No. 1515-0001

Page No

No.	5. Family name, given names	6. Rank or rating	2. Articles acquired abroad by officers and members of the crew (except those exclusively for use on voyage or cleared through Customs authorities)	7. No. of crewmember's declaration of articles intended to be landed (if none, show "None" opposite name)

Name of ship

Nationality of ship

Date and signature by master, authorized agent or officer

This form may be printed by private parties provided the supply printed conforms to the official form in size, wording, arrangement, and quality and color of paper. For sale by District Directors of Customs.

CUSTOMS FORM 1304 (10-26-81)

DEPARTMENT OF THE TREASURY
UNITED STATES CUSTOMS SERVICE

CREW MEMBER'S DECLARATION

Customs Form
5129 (9-22-76)

4.7, 4.7a, 4.81, 6.7, 6.9, 148.61-67, C.R.

Form Approved
O.M.B. No. 48-R049

1. CREWMEMBER'S ARTICLE NO.

Nr — 11456388

2. CARRIER (Vessel Flag, Name)		3. PORT OF ARRIVAL
4. CREWMEMBER'S NAME	5. RANK	6. DATE OF ARRIVAL
7. ADDRESS		

List all articles obtained abroad and prices paid, or fair value if not purchased. Include serial number with all articles subject to registration such as cameras, radios etc. List articles to remain on board separately from those articles to be landed in the United States. List separately articles intended for sale, barter, exchange, or carried by you as an accommodation for someone else. See additional instructions and information on reverse.

I. To be Filled in by Crewmember		II. For Customs Officer's Use			
QUANTITY AND DESCRIPTION OF GOODS	COST, OR VALUE OF GIFTS, ETC.	TARIFF DESCRIPTION	VALUE	RATE	DUTY

I certify that the above statement is a just, true and complete account of all articles of foreign origin for which written declaration and entry are required when landed in the United States (defined on reverse side) and I also certify that this statement is a just, true, and complete declaration of all such articles which I am landing in the United States.

TOTAL

8. CUSTOMS OFFICER ACCEPTING ENTRY	9. SIGNATURE OF CREWMEMBER	10. DATE

RECEIPT FOR DUTY AND RELEASE SLIP
To be filled in by Crewmember

PORT	CREWMEMBER'S ARTICLE NO.
	Nr — 11456388

NAME	CARRIER

REPEAT LIST OF ARTICLES TO BE LANDED (Include serial numbers when appropriate.)

For Customs Officer's Use

DATE	DUTY
	$

Articles listed at left have been examined and passe...

PIECES OF BAGGAGE
RELEASED:

of Custor...

The customs officer accepting the declaration and entry shall draw lines through unused spaces on receipt with ink or indelible pencil.
NOTICE: Liquidation of amount of duties and taxes, if any, due on this entry is effective on date of payment of this amount (Section 159.10, C.R.). For i... porter's right to protest or Government's right to redetermine this amount, see section 514 Tariff Act of 1930 as amended.

M-52

FIG. 13   217

WELCOME
TO THE
UNITED STATES

DEPARTMENT OF THE TREASURY
UNITED STATES CUSTOMS SERVICE

CUSTOMS DECLARATION

FORM APPROVED
OMB NO. 1515-0041

Each arriving traveler or family head must give the following information:

1. Name: _____
         Last   *First*   *Middle Initial*

2. Date of Birth: ____/____/____ 3. Airline/Flight: _____
        Month / Day / Year

4. U.S. Address: _____

_____

                                        YES   NO

5. I am a U.S. Citizen   ☐   ☐
   If No,
   Country: _____

                                          YES   NO

6. I reside permanently in the U.S.   ☐   ☐
   If No,
   Expected Length of Stay: _____

7. The purpose of my trip is or was
   ☐ BUSINESS   ☐ PLEASURE

8. I am/we are bringing fruits, plants, meats, food, soil,   YES   NO
   birds, snails, other live animals, farm products, or   ☐   ☐
   I/we have been on a farm or ranch outside the U.S.

9. I am/we are carrying currency or monetary   YES   NO
   instruments over $5000 U.S. or the foreign   ☐   ☐
   equivalent.

10. The total value of all goods I/we purchased
    or acquired abroad and am/are bringing to
    the U.S. is (visitors indicate value of gifts
    only): $ _____
                          U.S. Dollars

SIGN REVERSE OF DECLARATION AFTER YOU READ WARNING.
(Do not write below this line.)

INSPECTOR'S NAME	STAMP AREA
BADGE NO.	

Customs Form 6059B (051283)

WARNING

MERCHANDISE

U.S. residents must declare the total value of ALL articles acquired abroad (whether worn or used, whether dutiable or not, and whether obtained by purchase, as a gift, or otherwise) which are in their or their family's possession at the time of arrival. The value of repairs and alterations made abroad must also be included. Visitors to the U.S. must declare the total value of all gifts they are bringing with them.

CURRENCY AND MONETARY INSTRUMENTS

The transportation of currency or monetary instruments, regardless of the amount, is legal; however, if you take out of or bring into the United States more than $5000 (U.S. or foreign equivalent, or a combination of the two) in coin, currency, travelers checks or bearer instruments such as money orders, checks, stocks or bonds, you are required by law to file a report on a Form 4790 with the U.S. Customs Service. If you have someone else carry the currency or instruments for you, you must also file the report. FAILURE TO FILE THE REQUIRED REPORT OR FALSE STATEMENTS ON THE REPORT MAY LEAD TO SEIZURE OF THE CURRENCY OR INSTRUMENTS AND TO CIVIL PENALTIES AND/OR CRIMINAL PROSECUTION.

AGRICULTURAL PRODUCTS

To prevent the entry of dangerous agricultural pests the following are restricted: Fruits, vegetables, plants, plant products, soil, meats, meat products, birds, snails, and other live animals or animal products. Failure to declare all such items to a Customs/Agriculture Officer can result in fines or other penalties.

```
IF YOU HAVE ANY QUESTIONS ABOUT WHAT MUST BE
REPORTED OR DECLARED ASK A CUSTOMS OFFICER.
```

I have read the above statements and have made a truthful declaration.

SIGNATURE

If the value of articles and repairs acquired abroad is over $1400 per person then list the items below and show the price paid or fair retail value.

DESCRIPTION OF ARTICLES	PRICE	CUSTOMS USE
TOTAL		

Customs Form 6059B (Back)   U.S. GOVERNMENT PRINTING OFFICE: 1983-407-268

FIG. 14   219

CHECK APPLICABLE INFORMATION ONLY

CARRIERS & LINE NUMBER

ADDRESS

IMPORTING VESSEL, VEHICLE OR AIRCRAFT

NOTICE

DISCREPANCIES MUST BE PROPERLY ACCOUNTED FOR OR CARRIER MAY BE ASSESSED PENALTIES, DUTIES, TAXES OR LIQUIDATED DAMAGES.

RECD ON IN BOND MANIFEST NO. | DATE ISSUED | FROM PORT OF | ARR. DATE | MANIFEST NO. | DISTRICT & PORT CODE | FACILITY NO. | DATE | CUSTOMS ISSUING OFFICER

SEC. 1 - DISCREPANCY IDENTIFICATION (1) Report only shortage or overage. (2) Report full-case shortage and within-case shortage on different numbered lines.

CUSTOMS, IMPORTER/BROKER, OR CARRIER | CUSTOMS USE ONLY | IMPORTER/BROKER | CARRIER

Line No.	1 — a. NUMBER OF PIECES AND DESCRIPTION / b. T.S.U.S. NO. (NOT REQUIRED FOR CARRIER)	2 — ENTRY, I.D. OR G.O. NO. OR 'NONE'	3 — CUSTOMS DISCREPANCY CODE	4 — LIQUIDATED DAMAGES IF APPLICABLE	5 — PENALTIES IF APPLICABLE	6 — CONCEALED SHORTAGE ACTION / INITIALS CUSTOMS OFF.	7 — VALUE	8 — RATE a. DUTY b. TAX / NET REFUND a. DUTY b. TAX	9 — EXPLANATION CODE (SEE REVERSE)
1	a. b.							a. b.	
2	a. b.							a. b.	
3	a. b.							a. b.	
4	a. b.							a. b.	
5	a. b.							a. b.	

TOTAL:

SEC. II - DECLARATION

_____ (NAME OF IMPORTER/BROKER)

☐ Merchandise reported on Lines _____ above was not received. Any such merchandise later received will be entered properly.
(If importer checks this declaration the carrier must execute section III or V.)

☐ Shortage of merchandise on Lines _____ was concealed. To the best of my knowledge the merchandise was landed in that condition at the original port of landing. The merchandise and packing have been set aside, and request is hereby made for customs examination at importer's premises at expense of importer. (It is not necessary to obtain carrier's signature in section III for concealed shortage.)

_____
SIGNATURE OF IMPORTER OR HIS AGENT   DATE

SEC. IV - POST ENTRY

RECEIPT NO. _____

_____
SIGNATURE OF CUSTOMS OFFICER   DATE

SEC. III - DECLARATION OF IMPORTING CARRIER OR HIS AGENT.

Carrier certifies explanation code shown in column 9 regarding discrepancies is correct.

Unless explanation code indicates otherwise, carrier agrees to non-delivery and/or removal without customs release.

Manifest is amended and post entry requested if necessary.

I Certify that required evidence to support above code will be retained in my files for one year.

_____
SIGNATURE OF IMPORTING CARRIER OR HIS AGENT   DATE

SEC. V - DECLARATION OF BONDED CARRIER OR HIS AGENT

Merchandise reported above was not delivered to importer, or was improperly delivered for the reason shown in column 9 above.

_____
SIGNATURE OF BONDED CARRIER OR HIS AGENT   DATE

Customs Form 5931 (9-26-78)   ORIGINAL-CUSTOMS CONTROL COPY

Form Approved O M B No 048-R545

DEPARTMENT OF THE TREASURY
UNITED STATES CUSTOMS SERVICE

RECORD OF VESSEL/AIRCRAFT
FOREIGN REPAIR OR EQUIPMENT PURCHASE

47.4 14 67 CR 47 4 14 860 C M

1 FUNCTION OF THIS DOCUMENT

"X" ONE
☐ **DECLARATION** (COMPLETE ITEMS 1 THROUGH 16 ONLY)
☐ **ENTRY** (ITEMS 1-15 AND 19-25)

ITEMS BELOW FOR ENTRY ONLY DO NOT USE FOR DECLARATION

18 ENTRY NUMBER AND DATE

CUSTOMS USE ONLY

2 OWNER NAME AND ADDRESS

3 REPRESENTED LOCALLY BY

4 VESSEL NAME OR AIRCRAFT REGISTRY NUMBER

5 NAME OF MASTER/COMMANDER

19 NAME OF PRINCIPAL AND SURETY

6 PORT ARRIVED FROM | 7 VOYAGE/FLIGHT NO | 8 U S PORT OF ARRIVAL | 9 DIST./PORT CODE | 10 ARRIVAL DATE

20 BOND NUMBER | 21 BOND AMOUNT

12 DESCRIPTION OF WORK PERFORMED INCLUDING IDENTIFICATION OF MATERIALS/EQUIPMENT PURCHASED

11 LOCATION (CITY & COUNTRY) AND DATE OF REPAIRS ETC AND SAILING DATE FROM THAT COUNTRY

COST IN FOREIGN MONEY

13 Material, Parts or Equipment | 14 Labor

22 EXCHANGE RATE | 23 ENTERED U S COST | 24 DUTY - NOT ENTERED COST IN U S MONEY

15 TOTAL AMOUNT DECLARED ⌂

15a Material, Etc | 15b Labor

ITEMS BELOW FOR DECLARATION ONLY: DO NOT USE FOR ENTRY

16 CERTIFICATION OF MASTER-COMMANDER

AS MASTER-COMMANDER OF THE SAID VESSEL/AIRCRAFT, I HEREBY SUBSCRIBE TO THE DECLARATION STATEMENT ON THE BACK OF THIS DOCUMENT

17 CUSTOMS USE ONLY

I have examined the vessel's log, which indicates:
☐ The undeclared repairs or purchases which I have listed on the back of this declaration
☐ no undeclared repairs or purchases

A SIGNATURE

B TITLE | C DATE

A. SIGNATURE

B TITLE | C DATE

25 CERTIFICATION OF MASTER/COMMANDER, OR AUTHORIZED AGENT OF THE OWNER

I HEREBY SUBSCRIBE TO THE STATEMENT RELATIVE TO AN ENTRY ON THE BACK OF THIS DOCUMENT ("X" Box A or Box B)

A ☐ (full and complete) | B ☐ (Incomplete)

C SIGNATURE

D. TITLE | E. DATE

FIG. 16   221

WHSE. NO. 0861

| TREASURY DEPARTMENT
UNITED STATES CUSTOMS SERVICE

UNITED STATES DEPARTMENT OF JUSTICE
Immigration and Naturalization Service | PASSENGER LIST
CREW LIST
(Cross out one)

(Oath to be taken on Customs Form 1300) | Form Approved
OMB No. 43-R0516

Sheet No.

Class *(First, Cabin, Tourist, or Other)* |

CARRIER *(Nationality, name, and official number of carrier)*

| Date of arrival/departure *(Cross out one)* | Port of arrival/departure *(Cross out one)* |

| Last foreign port before arrival in United States *(Place and Country)* | *(Date departed)* |

| If departing, show first port at and date on which carrier arrived in United States on this trip. | If departing, show first foreign port after departure from United States. |

(1) NAME IN FULL		(2) Date of Birth Nationality and passport number	(3) CREW		(4) Crew *(departing U.S. Flag vessels only)* USCG Z or C.D.B. number and name and address of next of kin	(5) This column for use Government officials only *(except when carrying certain passengers. See Instructions)*
Family name	Given name and middle initial		Position	Where shipped or engaged		

Total Number   Agent _____
1-418 (Rev. 7-1-74) Y

INSTRUCTIONS

ALL NAMES AND OTHER DATA INSCRIBED ON THIS FORM MUST BE IN THE ENGLISH LANGUAGE

PASSENGERS

Incoming.—Complete columns (1) and (2), and (5) when required below. Deliver one complete alphabetical list, regardless of nationality, to United States Public Health Service, United States Immigration Service, and two such lists to United States Customs Bureau on arrival at first port in the United States. If insufficient space in column (2), information may extend into column (3).

In column (5) show opposite a passenger's name the compartment or space occupied if that passenger is not allotted space for his or her exclusive use in the proportion of at least 36 clear superficial feet (steerage); the sex and the married or single status of each passenger in such case; and the age of each passenger of 8 years or under. In addition, the age of each deceased passenger and the cause of death shall be shown, regardless of class.

Departing.—Complete columns (1) and (2). Deliver one complete list to the United States Immigration Service at the last port of departure—to which is attached the Arrival/Departure Card (Form I-94) given to each nonimmigrant alien when he last arrived in the United States; otherwise, prepare and attach a new Form I-94.

CREW

Incoming.—Complete columns (1), (2) and (3). Deliver one complete alphabetical list to United States Public Health Service, United States Immigration Service, and two such lists to United States Customs Bureau on arrival at the first port in the United States.

Where a crewman is a returning resident alien, show his alien registration receipt card number in column (2) in lieu of passport number.

Departing.—Submit a single copy of this form to the Immigration office at the port from which the vessel is to depart directly to a foreign port or place, executed in accordance with the following instructions. Complete all items in the heading of the form and place the following endorsement on the first line of the form: "Arrival Crewlist, Form I-418, filed at *(Show U.S. port of arrival)*." A Form I-418 which does not bear this endorsement will not be accepted.

Notification of Changes in Crew.—(1) Under a heading "Added Crewmen," list the names of nonresident alien crewmen who were not members of the crew and manifested on Form I-418 as such when the vessel last arrived in the United States, and attach for each added crewman his Form I-95 or Form I-94 given to him when he last arrived in the United States; otherwise, prepare and attach a new Form I-95. (2) Under a heading "Separated Crewmen," list the names of all alien crewmen who arrived in the United States on the vessel as members of the crew on the occasion of the vessel's last arrival in the United States but who for any reason are not departing with the vessel, and for each such separated crewman, show his nationality, passport number, specific port and date of separation, and the reasons for failure to depart. (3) If there are no added and/or separated alien crewmen upon departure, endorse the form "No changes in nonresident alien crew upon departure."

The list required under (1) and (2) may be incorporated in a single Form I-418, if space permits.

United States Flag Vessels Only.—Complete column (1), (2), (3) and (4). Deliver two complete crew lists to United States Customs Bureau at the last port of departure. The customs officer will certify one copy of this crew list in the space provided below and that copy shall be presented to the United States Customs Bureau at the first port of arrival in the United States and on the return voyage. Show birthplace in column (2) in lieu of passport number.

CREW LIST VISA APPLICATION

Submit form in duplicate to a United States consular officer. For each alien crewman not in possession of a valid individual visa or Immigration and Naturalization Service Form I-151, note columns (4) and (5) of the duplicate copy as follows: column (4) insert his date, city and country of birth, column (5) insert place of issuance and the authority issuing passport held by such crewman. Same information is required at port of entry when applying for waiver of visa.

Execute the following oath before a Customs Officer as to all arriving passengers on all vessels. The oath is to be executed before a Customs Officer as to all departing crew on United States Flag Vessels, and before an Immigration Officer or other officer authorized to administer oaths as to all departing passengers on all vessels.

FIG. 16   223

I certify that Customs baggage declaration requirements have been made known to incoming passengers; that any required Customs baggage declarations have been or will simultaneously herewith be filed as required by law and regulation with the proper Customs officer; and that the responsibilities devolving upon this vessel in connection therewith, if any, have been or will be discharged as required by law or regulation before the proper Customs officer. I further certify that there are no steerage passengers on board this vessel (46 U.S.C. 151-163).

_____
Signature of Master

Show in box below number of United States citizens and alien passengers embarked or to be debarked separately at each foreign port involved. If passenger list consists of more than one page, summarize on last page only. Separate summary should be prepared for each class when manifested separately.

Foreign Port of	Embarkation (Cross out one) Debarkation	Number of passengers	
		U.S.C.	Aliens
Total			

CERTIFICATION OF COPY OF CREW LIST OF UNITED STATES FLAG VESSEL

I certify that this is a true copy of the original crew list of the above-named American vessel, which original crew list is on file in this office.

Given under my hand and seal of office at the customhouse at _____ on _____

_____ Customs Officer.

FIG. 17

Family name	Given name	Initial	Soundex

Home address and name of relative or friend residing there

Address in the U.S.	Date and place of birth

Hair	Eyes	Height	Weight	Sex	
				☐ M ☐ F	'A' No.

Action by Immigration Officer	Passport (No. and Nationality)
	Arrived by

U. S. Immigration Officer
Form 1-95A (Rev. 9-1-64)

Form Approved
Budget Bureau No. 43R 350.3

CREWMAN'S LANDING PERMIT

ANY HANDWRITTEN ENTRIES MUST BE IN BLOCK CAPITAL LETTERS

FIG. 18   225

AIRCRAFT/VESSEL REPORT

Form Approved
O.M.B. No. 43.R0497

☐ ARRIVAL	☐ DEPARTURE
Last Foreign Port_____	First Foreign Port_____

Airline/Vessel (Name & Nationality)	Flight Number	Port of Arr/Dep	Date of Arr/Dep

TYPE OF TRANSPORT – CHECK ONE

1. ☐ U.S. military – including charters to military
2. ☐ Commercial – scheduled
3. ☐ Commercial – chartered
4. ☐ Foreign military

Total Passengers

Do Not Write in These Blocks – For INS Use Only

Passengers Inspected	Passengers Deferred	Deferred Port

Attach CF 7507, ICAO Declaration, or I-418, or List Crew Below.

CREW: **Name**   **Status**

FOREIGN PORT AND COUNTRY	PASSENGERS		
	USC	ALIEN	TOTAL
TOTAL			

FORM 1-92 (See instructions on reverse of form) United State Department of Justice
(REV. 6-1-73)N WHSE. #0360   Immigration and Naturalization Service

FIG. 19

FORM APPROVED
BUDGET BUREAU NO. 43-R044

APPLICATION TO PAY OFF OR DISCHARGE ALIEN CREWMAN
(To be filed in triplicate. See Instructions on reverse)

I

CARRIER	ARRIVAL MANIFEST FILED AT (PORT)	DATE OF ARRIVAL

I hereby request authorization to PAY OFF/DISCHARGE the alien crewmen listed below.

II

NAME IN FULL		NATIONALITY AND PASSPORT NUMBER	POSITION	ACTION BY INS
FAMILY NAME	GIVEN NAME AND MIDDLE INITIAL			

(If additional space is required, attach list in triplicate)

III

REASON FOR REQUEST:

IV

ARRANGEMENTS FOR DEPARTURE FROM THE U.S. OF THE LISTED CREWMEN ARE (SCHEDULED TIME, DATE AND PORT OF DEPARTURE, AIR CARRIER AND FLIGHT NUMBER OR VESSEL.)

SIGNATURE

MAILING ADDRESS →

TITLE

Application (Granted) (Denied)		
OFFICE	DATE	
SIGNATURE AND TITLE	COPY ☐ MAILED ☐ DELIVERED	DATE
	SIGNATURE AND TITLE	

FORM I-408
(9-1-68)

UNITED STATES DEPARTMENT OF JUSTICE
IMMIGRATION AND NATURALIZATION SERVICE

FIG. 19   227

NOTICE

SECTION 256 OF THE IMMIGRATION AND NATIONALITY ACT (8 U.S.C. 1286)

It shall be unlawful for any person, including the owner, agent, consignee, charterer, master, or commanding officer of any vessel or aircraft, to pay off or discharge any alien crewman, except an alien lawfully admitted for permanent residence, employed on board a vessel or aircraft arriving in the United States without first having obtained the consent of the Attorney General. If it shall appear to the satisfaction of the Attorney General that any alien crewman has been paid off or discharged in the United States in violation of the provisions of this section, such owner, agent, consignee, charterer, master, commanding officer, or other person, shall pay to the collector of customs of the customs district in which the violation occurred the sum of $1,000 for each such violation. No vessel or aircraft shall be granted clearance pending the determination of the question of the liability to the payment of such sums, or while such sums remain unpaid, except that clearance may be granted prior to the determination of such question upon the deposit of an amount sufficient to cover such sums, or of a bond approved by the collector of customs with sufficient surety to secure the payment thereof. Such fine may, in the discretion of the Attorney General, be mitigated to not less than $500 for each violation, upon such terms as he shall think proper.

INSTRUCTIONS

1. FILING: The application must be completed in triplicate and delivered or mailed to the nearest office of the Immigration and Naturalization Service.

2. EXECUTION: The signature and title of either the owner, agent, consignee, charterer, master or commanding officer of the vessel or aircraft seeking authorization to pay off or discharge crewmen must be included on the application.

3. GENERAL: Inadequate or incomplete data required in items III, Reason for request, and IV, Arrangements for departure, may result in denial of the application.

4. DISPOSITION: The original and triplicate of an application which is granted will be returned to the applicant. The triplicate must be submitted with the departure manifest. The duplicate application will be retained by the Immigration and Naturalization Service with the arrival manifest.

FIG. 20

CHANGE LIST

S.S. ___Seven Seas_____ Dept.____Deck_____ Voy. No.___90_____

Total Wages	BILLS						CHANGE					Total
	$100	$50	$20	$10	$5	$1	50¢	25¢	10¢	5¢	1¢	
1,255.60	12	1			1		1		1			1,255.60
1,125.80	11		1		1		1	1		1		1,125.80
1,015.75	10			1	1		1	1				1,015.75
1,010.00	10			1								1,010.00
1,145.58	11		2		1		1			1	3	1,145.58
800.50	8						1					800.50
702.45	7					2		1	2			702.45
715.56	7			1	1		1			1	1	715.56
695.98	6	1	2		1		1	1	2		3	695.98
685.90	6	1	1	1	1		1	1	1	1		685.90
555.20	5	1			1				2			555.20
595.43	5	1	2		1			1	1	1	3	595.43
430.90	4		1	1			1	1	1	1		430.90
455.65	4	1			1		1		1	1		455.65
480.23	4	1	1	1					2		3	480.23
476.31	4	1	1		1	1		1		1	1	476.31
12,146.84	114	8	11	6	11	3	10	8	13	8	14	12,146.84

```
                Hundreds   114 =   $11,400.00
                Fifties      8 =       400.00
                Twenties    11 =       220.00
                Tens         6 =        60.00
                Fives       11 =        55.00
                Ones         3 =         3.00
                Halves      10 =         5.00
                Quarters     8 =         2.00
                Dimes       13 =         1.30
                Nickels      8 =          .40
                Cents       14 =          .14
                Deck Depart. total   $12,146.84
```

Other departments are made up in a similar manner or the entire crew can be put on one change list.

FIG. 21   229

VESSEL DATA

S.S._____CALL LETTERS_____OFFICIAL NUMBER_____

HOME PORT _____   PANAMA CANAL TONNAGE:
NET TONNAGE _____   NET _____
GROSS TONNAGE _____   GROSS _____
DISPLACEMENT: SUMMER _____TONS SUEZ CANAL TONNAGE:
      "   WINTER _____TONS NET _____
                 TROPICAL _____TONS GROSS _____
DEADWEIGHT: SUMMER _____TONS   HORSEPOWER _____
      "   WINTER _____TONS SPEED, NORMAL _____
      "   TROPICAL _____TONS PROPELLER DIAM. _____
DRAFT: SUMMER _____   "   PITCH _____
DRAFT: WINTER _____   LENGTH O.A. _____
DRAFT: TROPICAL _____   LENGTH REG. _____
F.W. ALLOWANCE _____   LENGTH B.P. _____
FREEBOARD: SUMMER _____   BREADTH, MLD _____
FREEBOARD: WINTER _____   DEPTH   "   _____
FREEBOARD: TROPICAL _____   WHERE BUILT _____
CAPACITY: BALE _____CU.FT. DATE BUILT _____
CAPACITY: GRAIN _____CU.FT. LENGTH OF ANCHOR CHAIN
F.W. CAPACITY _____TONS   PORT _____ STBD._____ SIZE _____
CONSUMPTION PER DAY _____TONS   WEIGHT OF ANCHORS
FUEL CAPACITY: _____BBLS   PORT _____ STBD._____
CONSUMPTION: SPARE ANCHOR _____
PER DAY, STEAMING, LOADED _____BBLS   STREAM _____ KEDGE _____
PER DAY, STEAMING, LIGHT _____BBLS   BBLS PER MILE, LOADED
IN PORT, WORKING   _____BBLS   BBLS PER MILE, LIGHT
IN PORT, IDLE   _____BBLS

SEVEN SEAS STEAMSHIP CORPORATION
CHARTERING DIVISION
TIME SHEET

Name of vessel:_____Port_____

Cargo:_____Quantity_____ _____

Arrival: Day_____Date_____Time _____

Draft before commencing: F_____A_____M_____S.G._____

Notice of Readiness served: Day_____Date_____Time_____

Notice accepted; Day_____Date_____Time_____

Docked or anchored: Day_____Date_____Time_____

Commenced Loading/Discharging: Day_____Date_____Time_____

Completed Loading/Discharging: Day_____Date_____Time_____

Draft on completing Load./Disch.F_____A_____M_____S.G._____

Undocked: Day_____Date_____Time_____

Sailed: Day_____Date_____Time_____

TIME WORKED. LIST SUNDAYS AND   HOLIDAYS WHERE THEY OCCUR.

Day: _____Date:_____From:_____To:_____Hours_____Min._____

Day:_____Date:_____From:_____To:_____Hours_____Min._____

Day:_____Date:_____From:_____To:_____Hours_____Min._____

Day:_____Date:_____From:_____To:_____Hours_____Min._____

Day:_____Date:_____From:_____To:_____Hours_____Min._____

Day:_____Date:_____From:_____To:_____Hours_____Min._____

Day:_____Date:_____From:_____To:_____Hours_____Min._____

TIME NOT WORKED ACCOUNT OF WEATHER, HOLIDAYS, GEAR BREAKDOWN, ETC.

Day:_____Date:_____From:_____To:_____Reason_____

Day:_____Date:_____From:_____To:_____Reason_____

Day:_____Date:_____From:_____To:_____Reason_____

	DAYS	HOURS	MIN.

Total Time Used:

Time Allowed:_____Per Charter Party

Despatch/Demurrage:
Signed without prejudice to any of the terms, conditions and
exceptions of governing charter party.

Charterer's Agent   Master

FIG. 23   231

SEVEN SEAS STEAMSHIP CORPORATION

S.S. SEVEN SEAS   STATEMENT OF FACTS   Voy.90

<u>LOSS OF BLADE</u>

		1965	EST		
(1)	Lost blade in Lat.39-40N Long.70-00W	15 May	0415	Hrs	0945GMT
(2)	Returning to New York	15 May	0510	"	
(3)	Arrived Ambrose. Pilot on board	16 May	1310	"	
(4)	Made fast, Todds Drydock #10	16 May	1730	"	
(5)	Left Drydock	18 May	1300	"	
(6)	Discharged Pilot;Departure Ambrose	18 May	1545	"	2045GMT
(7)	Arrived Deviation point Lat.39-40 N	19 May	0450	"	0950GMT
	Long.70-00 W				

	Date	Time	Dist	Fuel
From Lat. 39-40 N. Long. 70-00 W.	15 May	0415		8355
To: Ambrose Pilot	16 May	1310	192	
Todd Drydock #10	16 May	1730	23	8249
Left drydock	18 May	1300		8225
Departure Ambrose	18 May	1545	23	
Arrived Deviation point Lat.39-40 N. Long.70-00 W.	19 May	0450	192	8050

From Deviation point Lat.39-40 N. Long.70-00 W

To New York (Todds) and return   4days 00 hrs   45 min.

Total distance   430 miles

Fuel consumed   305 bbls.

Chief Engineer   Master

D E V I A T I O N

1. _____Changed course from_____(t) to _____(t)
   a. Position_____

2. _____Arrival_____

3. _____Anchored (or docked)

4. _____Patient (   ) disembarked in launch or ambulance
   and sent to_____Hospital.

5. _____Left anchorage or dock.

6. _____Departure.

7. _____Vessel back on original track and original course resumed
   a. Position_____

8. Diversion position (la) to _____(2)

        a. Distance_____miles.

        b. St.Time_____hrs._____min.

        c. Av.Speed_____knots

        d. Fuel Consumed_____bbls.

        e. Water Consumed_____tons.

9. Arrival to anchorage or dock
        a. Distance_____miles.

        b. St.Time _____hrs._____min.
        c. Fuel Consumed_____bbls.
        d. Water Consumed_____tons.

10. Detention at anchorage or dock_____hrs._____min.

11. Anchorage or dock to departure

        a. Distance_____miles.
        b. St.Time_____hrs._____min.
        c. Fuel Consumed_____bbls.
        d. Water Consumed_____tons.

12. Departure to original track

        a. Distance_____miles.
        b. St.Time_____hrs._____min.
        c. Av.speed_____knots.
        d. Fuel Consumed_____bbls.
        e. Water consumed_____tons.

13. Recapitulation of 8, 9, 10, 11 & 12
        a. Total distance_____miles.
        b. Total time_____hrs._____min.
        c. Fuel Consumed_____bbls.
        d. Water Consumed_____tons.

14. With reference to original track
        a. Distance from la to 7a _____miles
        b. Time at_____knots to steam from la to 7a____hrs. __mi
        c. Estimate of fuel that would have been consumed from
          la to 7a if vessel had not been diverted_____bbls.
        d. Estimate of water that would have been consumed from
          la to 7a if vessel had not been diverted_____tons.

15. Final Recapitulation
        a. Actual distance run (13a)_____miles.
        b. Distance along Original Track (14a)_____miles.
        c. Net loss_____miles.
        d. Actual Time Consumed (13b)_____hrs._____min.
        e. Time to run from la to 7a (14b) _____hrs._____min.
        f. New Time Lost_____hrs._____min.
        g. Actual Fuel Consumed (13c)_____bbls.
        h. Estimated fuel Consumed (14c)_____bbls.
        i. New fuel loss_____bbls.
        j. Actual Water Consumed (13d)_____tons.
        k. Estimated Water Consumed (14d)_____tons.
        l. New Water Loss_____tons.

FIG. 25   233

SEVEN SEAS STEAMSHIP CORPORATION
DAMAGE REPORT

Report of damage to vessel, dock, pier or other property or to another
vessel other than by collision.

Vessel_____Voy.No._____ Port_____

Last Port_____Next Port_____

Draft Fwd_____Aft_____Mean_____

Date and actual time of accident_____19___GMT_____Local_____

Was another vessel at fault. Give name and details_____

Give date and time when Master or owner was notified of damage to your
vessel_____

Damage to dock, pier or other installation_____

Name of owner or occupant_____
Give details if accident caused other than by another vessel_____

Was damage to your vessel or other damaged property surveyed?_____
Name of person(s) surveying damage_____

Name and address of pilot_____
Damage sustained by your vessel_____

State weather: Wind & force_____Visability_____
Vessel's engine:
Was main engine being used?_____
How many boilers in use?_____
Was steering gear in good condition?_____
Names of tugs_____

Show on outline diagram of ship the position of the tugs around the ship
giving the names of tugs and how made fast. Use another sheet and attach
to this report.
Give names and home addresses of:
Master_____
Officer on watch_____
Seaman at wheel_____
Lookout_____
Engineer on watch_____
Extent of damage to your vessel_____

Extent of damage to other property_____

Explain how accident occurred.(Use another sheet of paper if necessary.)
_____
_____
_____

Date_____   _____
                                                      Master

FIG. 26

SEVEN SEAS STEAMSHIP CORPORATION

STEVEDORE DAMAGE REPORT
To
Ship, Cargo, Equipment
Or Gear.

S.S._____VOY. NO._____PORT_____

DATE OF THIS REPORT_____

DATE AND TIME OF DAMAGE_____

EXTENT OF DAMAGE_____

HOW DID DAMAGE OCCUR?_____

WAS SHIP'S GEAR AT FAULT? EXPLAIN_____

WAS DAMAGE SURVEYED?_____DATE_____PORT_____

NAMES OF THOSE ATTENDING SURVEY_____

WAS DAMAGE TO

VESSEL REPAIRED?_____TEMPORARILY_____PERMANENTLY_____

DATE OF REPAIRS_____PORT_____

WAS FULL COST OF REPAIRS PAID BY STEVEDORES?_____

_____CHIEF OFFICER_____   _____MASTER_____

RECEIVED COPY OF THE ABOVE REPORT: DATE_____TIME_____

            I/WE ADMIT
                  DENY LIABILITY_____

                                    STEVEDORE

                        ADDRESS_____

THIS REPORT TO BE MADE UP WHEN DAMAGE IS CAUSED BY STEVEDORE, BARGEE
LIGHTERMEN, REPAIRMEN, ETC.

Six copies of this report are to be made up and distributed as
follows: One copy to stevedore or other causing damage.
          Three copies to home office, attention Insurance Dept.
          One copy to Agent.
          One copy for vessel's file.

FIG. 27   235

Approved OMB No. 2115-0003

DEPARTMENT OF TRANSPORTATION U. S. COAST GUARD CG-2692 (Rev. 6-82)	REPORT OF MARINE ACCIDENT, INJURY OR DEATH	RCS No. G-MMI 2115-0003
		UNIT CASE NUMBER

SECTION I. GENERAL INFORMATION

1. Name of Vessel or Facility		2. Official No.	3. Nationality	4. Call Sign	5. USCG Certificate of Inspection Issued at:
6. Type ((Towing, Freight, Fish, Drill, etc.)	7. Length	8. Gross Tons	9. Year Built	10. Propulsion (Steam, diesel, gas, turbine...)	
11. Hull Material (Steel, Wood...)	12. Draft (ft. - in.) FWD. / AFT.	13. If Vessel Classed, By Whom: (ABS, LLOYDS, DNV, BV, etc.)	14. DATE(of occurrence)	15. TIME (Local)	

16. Location (See Instruction No. 10A)

17. Estimated Loss or Damage TO:

18. Name, Address & Telephone No. of Operating CO.

VESSEL $ _____

CARGO $ _____

OTHER $ _____

19. Name of Master or Person in Charge	USCG License ☐ YES ☐ NO	20. Name of Pilot	USCG License ☐ YES ☐ NO	State License ☐ YES ☐ NO
19a. Street Address (City, State, Zip Code)	19b. Telephone Number ( )	20a. Street Address (City, State, Zip Code)	20b. Telephone Number ( )	

21. Casualty Elements Check as many as needed and explain in Block 44.)

NO. OF PERSONS ON BOARD _____

☐ DEATH- HOW MANY? _____

☐ MISSING- HOW MANY? _____

☐ INJURED- HOW MANY? _____

☐ HAZARDOUS MATERIAL RELEASED OR INVOLVED

(Identify Substance and amount in Block 44.

☐ OIL SPILL-ESTIMATE AMOUNT:

☐ CARGO CONTAINER LOST/DAMAGED

☐ COLLISION (Identify other vessel or object in Block 44.)

☐ GROUNDING

☐ FLOODING; SWAMPING WITHOUT SINKING

☐ CAPSIZING (with or without sinking)

☐ FOUNDERING OR SINKING

☐ HEAVY WEATHER DAMAGE

☐ FIRE

☐ EXPLOSION

☐ COMMERCIAL DIVING CASUALTY

☐ ICE DAMAGE

☐ DAMAGE TO AIDS TO NAVIGATION

☐ STEERING FAILURE

☐ MACHINERY OR EQUIPMENT FAILURE

☐ ELECTRICAL FAILURE

☐ STRUCTURAL FAILURE

☐ WAKE DAMAGE

☐ FIREFIGHTING OR EMERGENCY EQUIPMENT FAILED OR INADEQUATE (Describe in Block 44.)

☐ LIFESAVING EQUIPMENT FAILED OR INADEQUATE (Describe in Block·44.)

☐ BLOW OUT (Petroleum exploration/production)

☐ OTHER (Specify)

_____

_____

22. Conditions

A. Sea or River Conditions (wave height, river stage, etc.)	B. WEATHER ☐ CLEAR ☐ RAIN ☐ SNOW ☐ FOG ☐ OTHER (Specify)	C. TIME ☐ DAYLIGHT ☐ TWILIGHT ☐ NIGHT	D. VISIBILITY ☐ GOOD ☐ FAIR ☐ POOR	E. DISTANCE (miles) (of visibility) _____ F. AIR TEMPERATURE (F) _____ G. WIND SPEED & DIRECTION _____ H. CURRENT SPEED & DIRECTION _____

23. Navigation Information ☐ MOORED, DOCKED OR FIXED ☐ ANCHORED ☐ UNDERWAY OR DRIFTING	SPEED _____ AND COURSE _____	24. Last Port _____ Where Bound	24a. Time and Date of Departure

25. FOR TOWING ONLY	25a. NUMBER OF VESSELS TOWED	Empty	Loaded	Total	25b. TOTAL H.P. OF TOWING UNITS	25c. MAXIMUM SIZE OF TOW WITH TOW-BOAT(S)	Length	Width	25d. (Describe in Block 44.) ☐ PUSHING AHEAD ☐ TOWING ASTERN ☐ TOWING ALONGSIDE ☐ MORE THAN ONE TOW-BOAT ON TOW

SECTION II. BARGE INFORMATION

26. Name	26a. Official Number	26b. Type	26c. Length	26d. Gross Tons	26e. USCG Certificate of Inspection issued at:
26f. Year Built	26g. ☐ SINGLE SKIN ☐ DOUBLE SKIN	26h. Draft FWD / AFT	26i. Operating Company		

26j. Damage Amount

BARGE $ _____

CARGO $ _____

OTHER $ _____

26k. Describe Damage to Barge

PREVIOUS EDITIONS MAY BE USED   SN 7530-00-FO1-1730

236   FIG. 27

REVERSE OF CG-2692 (REV. 6-82)

SECTION III. PERSONNEL ACCIDENT INFORMATION

27. Person Involved ☐ MALE or ☐ FEMALE ☐ DEAD ☐ INJURED ☐ MISSING	27a. Name *(Last, First, Middle Name)* 27b. Address *(City, State, Zip Code)*	27c. Status ☐ CREW ☐ PASSENGER ☐ OTHER *(Specify)*
28. Birth Date	29. Telephone No. ( )	30. Job Position	31. *(Check here if off duty)* ☐

32. Employer -*(If different from Block 18., fill in Name, Address, Telephone No.)*

33. Person's Time	YEAR(S)	MONTH(S)	34. Industry of Employer *(Towing, Fishing, Shipping, Crew Supply, Drilling, etc.)*
A. IN THIS INDUSTRY -			
B. WITH THIS COMPANY -			35. Was the Injured Person Incapacitated 72 Hours or More? ☐ YES ☐ NO
C. IN PRESENT JOB OR POSITION -			
D. ON PRESENT VESSEL/FACILITY -			36. Date of Death
E. HOURS ON DUTY WHEN ACCIDENT OCCURRED -			

37. Activity of Person at Time of Accident

38. Specific Location of Accident on Vessel/Facility

39. Type of Accident *(Fall, Caught between, etc.)*	40. Resulting Injury *(Cut, Bruise, Fracture, Burn, etc.)*
41. Part of Body Injured	42. Equipment Involved in Accident

43. Specific Object, Part of the Equipment in Block 42., or Substance *(Chemical, Solvent, etc.)* that directly produced the Injury.

SECTION IV. DESCRIPTION OF CASUALTY

44. Describe How Accident Occurred, Damage and Recommendations for Corrective Safety Measures. *(Attach Additional Sheets if necessary).*

45. Witness *(Name, Address, Telephone No.)*

46. Witness *(Name, Address, Telephone No.)*

SECTION V. PERSON MAKING THIS REPORT

47. Name (PRINT) *(Last, First, Middle)*	47b. Address *(City, State, Zip Code)*	47c. Title
47a. Signature		47d. Telephone No. ( ) 47e. Date

FOR COAST GUARD USE ONLY   REPORTING OFFICE:

APPARENT CAUSE

CASUALTY CODE **A B C**	INVESTIGATOR *(Name)*	DATE	APPROVED BY *(Name)*	DATE

FIG. 27   237

INSTRUCTIONS

FOR COMPLETION OF FORM CG-2692

REPORT OF MARINE ACCIDENT, INJURY OR DEATH

AND FORM CG-2692A, BARGE ADDENDUM

WHEN TO USE THIS FORM

1. This form satisfies the requirements for written reports of accidents found in the Code of Federal Regulations for vessels, Outer Continental Shelf (OCS) facilities, mobile offshore drilling units (MODUs), and diving. The kinds of accidents that must be reported are described in the following instructions.

VESSELS

2. A vessel accident must be reported if it occurs upon the navigable waters of the U.S., its territories or possessions; or whenever an accident involves a U.S. vessel wherever the accident may occur. (Public vessels and recreational vessels are excepted from these reporting requirements.) The accident must also involve one of the following (ref. 46 CFR 4.05-1):

A. All accidental groundings and any intentional grounding which also meets any of the other reporting criteria or creates a hazard to navigation, the environment, or the safety of the vessel;

B. Loss of main propulsion or primary steering, or an associated component or control system, the loss of which causes a reduction of the maneuvering capabilities of the vessel. Loss means that systems, component parts, subsystems, or control systems do not perform the specified or required function;

C. An occurrence materially and adversely affecting the vessel's seaworthiness or fitness for service or route including but not limited to fire, flooding, failure or damage to fixed fire extinguishing systems, lifesaving equipment or bilge pumping systems;

D. Loss of life;

E. Injury causing any person to be incapacitated for a period in excess of 72 hours.

F. An occurrence not meeting any of the above criteria but resulting in damage to property in excess of $25,000. Damage cost includes the cost of labor and material to restore the property to the condition which existed prior to the casualty, but it does not include the cost of salvage, cleaning, gas freeing, drydocking or demurrage.

MOBILE OFFSHORE DRILLING UNITS

3. MODUs are vessels and are required to report an accident that results in any of the events listed by Instruction 2-A through 2-F for vessels. (Ref. 46 CFR 4.05-1, 46 CFR 109.411)

OCS FACILITIES

4. All OCS facilities (except mobile offshore drilling units) engaged in mineral exploration, development or production activities on the Outer Continental Shelf of the U.S. are required by 33 CFR 146.30 to report accidents resulting in:

A. Death;

B. Injury to 5 or more persons in a single incident;

C. Injury causing any person to be incapacitated for more than 72 hours;

D. Damage affecting the usefulness of primary lifesaving or firefighting equipment;

E. Damage to the facility in excess of $25,000 resulting from a collision by a vessel;

F. Damage to a floating OCS facility in excess of $25,000.

5. Foreign vessels engaged in mineral exploration, development or production on the U. S. Outer Continental Shelf, other than vessels already required to report by Instructions 2 and 3 above, are required by 33 CFR 146.303 to report casualties that result in any of the following:

A. Death;

B. Injury to 5 or more persons in a single incident;

C. Injury causing any person to be incapacitated for more than 72 hours.

238   FIG. 27

DIVING

6. Diving casualties include injury or death that occurs while using underwater breathing apparatus while diving from a vessel or OCS facility.

    A. COMMERCIAL DIVING. A dive is considered commercial if it is for commercial purposes from a vessel required to have a Coast Guard certificate of inspection, from an OCS facility or in its related safety zone or in a related activity, at a deepwater port or in its safety zone. Casualties that occur during commercial dives are covered by 46 CFR 197.486 if they result in:

        1. Loss of life;
        2. Injury causing incapacitation over 72 hours;
        3. Injury requiring hospitalization over 24 hours.

In addition to the information requested on this form, also provide the name of the diving supervisor and, if applicable, a detailed report on gas embolism or decompression sickness as required by 46 CFR 197.410(a)(9).

Exempt from the commercial catagory are dives for:

        1. Marine science research by educational institutions;
        2. Research in diving equipment and technology;
        3. Search and Rescue controlled by a government agency.

    B. ALL OTHER DIVING. Diving accidents not covered by Instruction (6-A) but involving vessels subject to Instruction (2), VESSELS, must be reported if they result in death or injury causing incapacitation over 72 hours.
(Ref. 46 CFR 4.03-1(c)).

HAZARDOUS MATERIALS

7. When an accident involves hazardous materials, public and environmental health and safety require immediate action. As soon as any person in charge of a vessel or facility has knowledge of a release or discharge of oil or a hazardous substance, that person is required to immediately notify the U. S. Department of Transportation's National Response Center (telephone toll-free 800-424-8802 - in the Washington, D.C., area call 202-426-2675). Anyone else knowing of a pollution incident is encouraged to use the toll-free telephone number to report it. If etiologic (disease causing) agents are involved, call the U. S. Public Health Service's Center for Disease Control in Atlanta, Ga. (telephone 404-633-5313). (Ref. 42 USC 9603; 33 CFR 153; 49 CFR 171.15)

COMPLETION OF THIS FORM

8. This form should be filled out as completely and accurately as possible. Please type or print clearly. Fill in all blanks that apply to the kind of accident that has occurred. If a question is not applicable, the abbreviation "NA" should be entered in that space. If an answer is unknown and cannot be obtained, the abbreviation "UNK" should be entered in that space. If "NONE" is the correct response, then enter it in that space.

9. When this form has been completed, deliver or mail it as soon as possible to the Coast Guard Marine Safety or Marine Inspection Office nearest to the location of the casualty or, if at sea, nearest to the port of first arrival.

10. Amplifying information for completing the form:

    A. Block 16 - "LOCATION" - Latitude and longitude to the nearest tenth of a minute should always be entered except in those rivers and waterways where a mile marker system is commonly used. In these cases, the mile number to the nearest tenth of a mile should be entered. If the latitude and longitude, or mile number, are unknown, reference to a known landmark or object (buoy, light, etc.) with distance and bearing to the object is permissible. Always identify the body of water or waterway referred to.

    B. Tug or towboat with tow - Tugs or towboats with tows under their control should complete all applicable portions of the CG-2692. SECTION II should be completed if a barge causes or sustains damage or meets any other reporting criteria. If additional barges require reporting, the "Barge Addendum," CG-2692A, may be used to provide the information for the additional barges.

    C. Moored/Anchored Barge - If a barge suffers a casualty while moored or anchored, or breaks away from its moorage, and causes or sustains reportable damages or meets any other reporting criteria, enter the location of its moorage in Block (1) of the CG-2692 and complete the form except for Blocks (2) through (13). The details will be entered in SECTION II for one barge and on the "Barge Addendum," CG-2692A, for additional barges.

    D. SECTION III - Personnel Accident Information -SECTION III must be completed for a death or injury. In addition, applicable portions of SECTIONS I, II and IV must be completed. If more than one death or injury occurs in a single incident, complete one CG-2692 for one of the persons injured or killed, and attach additional CG-2692's, filling out Blocks (1) and (2) and SECTION III for each additional person.

NOTICE: The information collected on this form is routinely available for public inspection. It is needed by the Coast Guard to carry out its responsibility to investigate marine casualties, to identify hazardous conditions or situations and to conduct statistical analysis. The information is used to determine whether new or revised safety initiatives are necessary for the protection of life or property in the marine environment.

FIG. 28   239

FORM FS-281d
Rev. June 1950

DEPARTMENT OF STATE
FOREIGN SERVICE OF THE UNITED STATES OF AMERICA
MARINE NOTE OF PROTEST
(22 United States Code 1173)

Port of ....

On this .... day of ...., 19........., before me,

...., American .... for

...., and the dependencies thereof,

personally appeared ...., Master of the vessel called

the .... of the b.. tons or thereabout, and declared

that on the .... day of .... last past he sailed in and with the ship

from the port of ...., laden with ...., and arrived,

in the ship, at .... on ...., and
                                                                                    (Insert the date and hour)

having experienced ....
                                              (State facts which constitute the protest)

hereby enters this Note of Protest accordingly, to serve and avail him hereafter, if found necessary.

....
.... of the United
                                                                States of America.

Attested:

....
Master.

[SEAL]

.................................., ...
            (Date)   (Place)

I HEREBY CERTIFY that the within document is a true copy of a Marine Note of Protest, the
original of which is deposited as a part of the permanent archives of the American Consulate at

....

.... of the United
                                                    States of America.

240

FIG. 29

MARINE EXTENDED PROTEST
(22 U. S. Code 1173)

PORT OF ....

By this public instrument of declaration and protest be it known and made manifest to all whom these presents shall come or may concern, that on the .... day of ...., 19......, before ...., American .... for .... and dependencies thereof, personally came and appeared ...., Master of the vessel called the .... Official No. .... of the burden of .... tons or thereabout, then lying in this port of .... laden with .... cargo, who duly noted and entered with the said .... his protest, for the uses and purposes hereafter mentioned; and now, on this day, the .... day of ...., 19......, before me, ..., American .... at ...., comes the said ...., and requires me to extend this protest; and together with the said Master also come ...., and all crew members of said ship, all of whom, being by me duly sworn, do voluntarily asseverate as follows: That these appearers, on the .... day of ...., sailed in and with the said .... from the port of .... laden with .... and bound to the port of ....: That the said ship was then properly manned and equipped and in every respect seaworthy; that*

And these said appearers, upon their oaths aforesaid, do further declare and say: That during the said voyage they, together with the others of the said ship's company, used their utmost endeavors to preserve the said .... and cargo from all manner of loss, damage, or injury. Wherefore the said ...., Master, has protested in accordance with law and declares that all losses, damages, costs, charges, and expenses as stated herein that have happened to the said .... or cargo, or to either, are and ought to be borne by those to whom the same by right may appertain by way of average or otherwise, the same having occurred as before mentioned, and not by or through the insufficiency of the said ...., her tackle or apparel, or fault or neglect of this appearer, his officers, or any of his mariners, or fault or neglect in the proper loading, stowage, custody, and care of the cargo.

Thus done and protested in the port of .... this .... day of ...., 19......

IN TESTIMONY WHEREOF, these appearers have hereunto subscribed their names, and I, the said ...., have granted to the said Master this public instrument, under my hand and the seal of this .... to serve and avail him, and all others whom it does or may concern as need and occasion may require.

...................................., Master.   ...., of the United States of America.

...................................., First Officer.

....

(Position on crew)

....

* Here insert narrative of the facts of the voyage as they occurred, with full and minute particulars, with date, latitude, longitude, etc. If additional space is required, blank sheets may be used and securely attached to this document under the seal of the consular office.

FIG. 30   241

NOTE OF PROTEST
Notary Form

State of_____County of_____City of_____

On this, the_____day of_____19_____personally appeared

before me_____a Notary Public for and in the

State of_____at large in the city of_____

County of_____ _____ Master of
                            (Name of Master)

the S.S._____ of the burden of _____Tons
        (Name of vessel)   (Net tons)

or thereabouts, and declared that said vessel sailed on a voyage

from_____ on _____ bound for_____
     (Port of departure)   (Date)   (Name port)

with a cargo of_____Protests_____
                                       (Give state of weather,etc.)

_____

_____

_____

_____

and fearing damages from causes as above stated, the said Master

notes this, his Protest, before me, reserving the right to extend

the same at any time and place convenient.

                                    _____
                                              Master

Subscribed and sworn before me,

this_____day of_____

19_____.

_____
(Notary's signature and seal)

SEVEN SEAS STEAMSHIP CORPORATION

PORT INFORMATION DIRECTORY

TO ALL MASTERS: Copies of this information directory, completely filled in, should be posted at the following places on board your vessel on calling at any port, U. S. or foreign:

At the Gangway, protected from the weather.
In the Chartroom for the officer on duty.
In the Chief Officer's room.
In the Officer's Messroom.

Agent to fill in all spaces. If not applicable write 'None'.

Name of vessel:_____ Voy. No. _____

Port_____ Name of your dock is_____

Location of dock _____

Your Agent's office address is_____

Telephone number is_____

His home address is_____

His home telephone number is_____

IN CASE OF FIRE.

Port signal to be made by vessel in case
of fire on board_____

The nearest Fire Alarm signal on the
dock is located at_____

INFORM YOUR AGENT AS SOON AS POSSIBLE IF YOU HAVE A FIRE!

POLICE

Port signal, whistle or flag, if
police are required:_____

Telephone number to be used to call police:_____

DOCTOR

If you require a doctor advise agent unless other arrangements have been made. Advise him of the trouble so he can inform the doctor.

AMBULANCE

Advise Agent but if an emergency call this number _____
(Don't forget to give the name and location of the vessel.)

HOSPITAL

If in a U. S. port and time permits send the injured or ill seaman to a Marine Hospital if one is in the port.

U. S. MARINE HOSPITAL

Address:_____ Telephone_____
(Don't forget to give the seaman a Hospital Slip.)

IN FOREIGN PORTS

Nearest hospital: Address_____ Telephone_____
(Advise Agent as soon as possible if hospitalization is required.)

Be sure you inform whoever you call in any emergency the name and location of your vessel.

FIG. 32   243

4398 (MRNA)
Rev. 8-84

PANAMA CANAL COMMISSION   O.M.B. No. 3207-0001

SHIP'S INFORMATION AND QUARANTINE DECLARATION

Radio Call Letters	Arrived	Date	Hour of Arrival	Hour Boarded	Hour Cleared
	BALBOA/CRISTOBAL				

| Ship's Name (M.V.) (S.S.) | | Class (Passenger, Cargo, Tanker) | Port of Registry | Nationality | |

DATA FROM NATIONAL REGISTER

Gross	Net	Reg. length	Overall length	Reg. beam	FUEL ON BOARD

| | | | | | Tons or bbls. of oil |

DAILY CONSUMPTION OF FUEL

Tons or bbls.   Speed (knots)

MEAN AUTHORIZED TROPICAL DRAFT

Salt water	Fresh water			PRESENT DRAFT	DISPLACEMENT (at present draft)
		Fwd.			
		S.W.			
		F.W.		Aft	SUMMER DEADWEIGHT

Owners   ARMS AND MUNITIONS (description and quantity)

Agents	Operators	Charterers

From: (Original loading port)   Last port and date of departure   To: (Final port of discharge of cargo now aboard)   First port of call after leaving Canal ports

Via: (All ports in order and dates visited within past 90 days including original loading port and wayports to final port of discharge)

Expiration date of Certificates

SAFETY EQUIP. CERT.

MARPOL CERT.

CERT. OF FITNESS

VESSEL DOCKING AT: ☐ Cristobal   ☐ Balboa   ☐ Cargo operation   ☐ Bunkers .... tons   I.O.P.P. CERT.

SHIP DATA

CARGO (TONS) FOR DISCHARGE AT:		CARGO (TONS) FOR LOADING AT:			Cargo on board (tons)		Type of cargo		Deck load (Type and tonnage)
Balboa	Cristobal	Balboa	Cristobal						

TECHNICAL NAME	TRADE NAME	UN NUMBER	IMO CLASS	QUANTITY	LOCATION	CONTAINMENT

DANGEROUS CARGO DATA

CARGO DATA

TANKERS IN BALLAST	LAST CARGO CARRIED			GAS FREE?				HOW

Certified for passengers (number)	PASSENGERS ON BOARD (Total)	Transit	DISEMBARKING		SHIP'S PERSONNEL ON BOARD (Total)	Officers	Crew	Stowaways	H.O.B.'s
			Balboa	Cristobal				Yes	No

HEALTH QUESTIONS: (If more than 4 weeks have elapsed since the voyage began, it will suffice to give particulars for the last 4 weeks.)

1. Has there been on board during the voyage any case or suspected case of plague, cholera, yellow fever, smallpox, typhus or relapsing fever? (Give particulars in the schedule.)

2. Has plague occurred or been suspected among the rats or mice on board during the voyage, or has there been an abnormal mortality among them?

3. Has any person died on board during the voyage otherwise than as a result of accident? (Give particulars in schedule.)

4. Is there on board or has there been during the voyage any case of disease which you suspect to be of an infectious nature? (Give particulars in schedule.)

5. Is there any sick person on board now? (Give particulars in schedule.)

6. Are you aware of any other condition on board which may lead to infection or the spread of disease?

NOTE. In the absence of a surgeon, the master should regard the following symptoms as grounds for suspecting the existence of disease of an infectious nature. Fever accompanied by prostration or persisting for several days or attended with glandular swelling, or any acute skin rash or eruption with or without fever, severe diarrhea with symptoms of collapse, jaundice accompanied by fever.

QUARANTINE DATA

SCHEDULE TO THE DECLARATION

Particulars of every case of illness or death occurring on board, and dead bodies on board

• Recovered, still ill, died   ** On board; landed at (name of port); buried at sea

Name	Class Rating	Age	Sex	Nationality	Port of Embarkation	Date of Embarkation	Nature of Illness	Date of its onset	Results of Illness*	Disposal of case**

DERATING RECORD	Date last derated	Date of last exemption from derating	Where	Origin of meat in ship's stores

FIG. 32   245

VET.

| NUMBER, KIND AND ORIGIN OF ANIMALS ON BOARD | NUMBER AND KIND FOR LOCAL DISCHARGE |

I HEREBY CERTIFY THAT the foregoing statements and answers to all questions are true to the best of my knowledge and belief, that the list of all live animals now on board my vessel is complete, and that I acknowledge receipt of instructions regarding quarantine requirements. Sea Stores. Meats and Garbage, the landing of passengers and or members of the crew, and the discharge of cargo.

Signature of ship's surgeon

Signature of ship's master

Name typed or printed

Name typed or printed

□ NSQI   □ SQI   □ Veterinary inspection required   □ Hatches will remain closed, and cargo discharge operation delayed until authorized by Sanitation Inspector.

PRATIQUE GRANTED: Free   □ Provisional   Detained for quarantine: Reason

Reason for provisional pratique   □ Smallpox vaccination held on board   □ Restricted meat   □ Animals held on board   □ Invalid derat   □ Illness or death on board

□ Floats required   □ Applied   □ Ship's sanitation   REMARKS:

□ Spraying required   □ Certificate   □ By B.O. in bay

□ Advised re garbage   □ Discharge RA RH cargo   Subscribed and sworn to in my presence on boarded vessel; vessel cleared

□ Sanitation inspection   □ Derat inspection   □ Balboa   □ Cristobal

□ M.I.C. notified by radio   □ Sanitation notified   □ M.O.I.C. (n)   Balboa Cristobal, Panama   Boarding Officer   Delay Code

ADMEASURERS   ATTENTION: **Before signing this form be sure the set includes a total of six.**

PANAMA CANAL COMMISSION
WARNING TO SHIPMASTERS

You are hereby warned that WHILE YOUR VESSEL IS IN WATER OF THE PANAMA CANAL, regulations prohibit the introduction and, except as specifically authorized by the Republic of Panama, the unloading FOR ANY PURPOSE of cattle, sheep, other ruminants, or swine, or of fresh, chilled, or frozen meats on board your vessel which originated or were loaded aboard in a country where foot-and-mouth disease or rinderpest exists. The introduction or unloading of undrawn poultry carcasses from any such countries is restricted.

You are also informed that under regulations that garbage (see Item IV) containing scraps, parts, or other waste of these meats: (1) Shall not be thrown overboard in the waters of the Panama Canal Commission; (2) Must be kept in leakproof covered receptacles inside the guard rail while on board your vessel; (3) May be unloaded only in tight receptacles for incineration or other proper disposal under official supervision of the Departamento de Salud or by the office of Health and Safety if berthed at Panama Canal Commission controlled piers.

NAVIGATION REGULATIONS OF THE PANAMA CANAL COMMISSION

Item I. Prohibits the introduction into the Republic of Panama of cattle, sheep, other ruminants, or swine, which originated in a country in which foot-and-mouth disease or rinderpest exists and further prohibits any vessel having such live animals on board from transiting the Canal until such animals have been examined by the proper veterinarian authority.

Item II. Prohibits, generally, introduction into the Republic of Panama of any fresh, chilled, or frozen beef, veal, mutton, lamb, or pork from any country in which foot-and-mouth disease or rinderpest exists.

Item III. Prohibits the unloading of cattle, sheep, other ruminants, swine, or generally, of fresh, chilled, or frozen beef, veal, mutton, lamb, or pork from a country in which foot-and-mouth disease or rinderpest exist as specifically authorized by the Republic of Panama.

Item IV. Provides that no garbage derived from fresh, chilled, or frozen meat which has originated in any country in which foot-and-mouth disease or rinderpest exists shall be unloaded from any vessel in the Republic of Panama, including Panama Canal waters, except in tight receptacles for destruction under the direction of the Departamento de Salud or by the Office of Health and Safety if berthed at Panama Canal Commission controlled piers.

Item V. During the entire time this vessel is moored to any pier or wharf, all connecting lines should be properly fitted with Rat Guards placed 3 to 5 feet from side of vessel.

Item VI. Papers required by boarding party—On arrival, there shall be ready for immediate delivery to the boarding party for inspection or delivery, as the case may be, such papers, and numbers of copies of each, concerning tonnage of vessel, cargo, persons on board, health conditions, pratique, and such other matters upon which information is necessary, as may be prescribed by the Administrator. The required manifests, lists, and statements shall be sworn to by the master or agent of the vessel. Failure to have the prescribed papers upon arrival will subject the vessel to delay, but not to fine.

ALL PAPERS REQUIRED BY BOARDING PARTY AS HEREIN LISTED
SHOULD BE READY FOR IMMEDIATE INSPECTION

		All vessels arriving in Canal waters	Additional forms for transiting vessels
(a)	Ship's Information and Quarantine Declaration (Panama Canal form) (set of six)	1	0
(b)	Cargo declaration (Panama Canal form)	1	0
(c)	Crew list (Panama Canal form)	1	0
(d)	Passenger list: Passengers transiting/landing (Panama Canal form)	2	0
(e)	Dangerous cargo manifest and/or loading plan	4	1

FIG. 33   247

(g) Ship's plans (general arrangement, engine room, capacity, midship section, etc.) .... 0 [1] [3]

(h) Panama Canal Tonnage Certificate .... 0 [1]

(i) Ship's documents for inspection. See 35 CFR 101.10 .... 1 0

[1] For examination and possible retention.

[2] Not required unless such persons or cargo are carried.

[3] For taking up and subsequent return through agent or otherwise.

[4] Not required unless vessel is carrying packaged, dangerous goods.

[5] Not required of vessels of war or auxiliary vessels, as those terms are defined in the treaty concerning the permanent neutrality and operation of the Panama Canal (Sept. 7, 1977).

INSTRUCTIONS FOR DANGEROUS CARGOES SECTION

TYPE	TECHNICAL NAME	TRADE NAME	UN NUMBER	IMO CLASS	QUANTITY	LOCATION	CONTAINMENT
DANGEROUS CARGOES IN BULK	Give the correct technical or scientific name of each dangerous cargo. DO NOT USE ABBREVIATIONS.	Give the common or trade name of each dangerous cargo, if known.	Give the United Nations ID number of each dangerous cargo.	Give the International Maritime Organization's classification and division number of each dangerous cargo	Give the total amount (in tons) of each dangerous cargo.	Give the location of each dangerous cargo according to the area, as shown in the diagram below.	State how each dangerous cargo is contained (Cargo tank or hold.)
EXPLOSIVES	Same as above	Same as above	Same as above	Same as above	Same as above	Same as above	(Container, etc.)
RADIOACTIVE SUBSTANCES	Same as above	Same as above	Not applicable	Same as above	Same as above	Same as above	(Container, cask, etc.)
PACKAGED DANGEROUS GOODS (other than explosives or radioactive substance)	Not required	Not required	Not required	Same as above, except, group all dangerous cargoes within the same IMO class and division and show as one.	Give the total amount (in tons) of all the dangerous cargoes within the same IMO class and division.	Same as above	(Container, portable tank, drum, vehicle, boxed, etc.)

BELOW DECK

AREA 6	AREA 3
AREA 5	AREA 2
AREA 4	AREA 1

ABOVE DECK

AREA 12	AREA 9
AREA 11	AREA 8
AREA 10	AREA 7

LOCATION

NOTE: Vessels carrying flammable liquids in bulk, state name of liquid and flashpoint, or if vessel is in ballast condition and not gas free, state the name of the flammable liquid last carried and the flashpoint. No other information is required. (A liquid is considered flammable when the flashpoint is 61°C or 141°F or less.)

Paperwork Reduction Act Statement: The information requested on the shipping and navigation forms will be used by the Panama Canal Commission for economic analyses of traffic, for development of traffic forecasts, and for budget and planning formulations. Further, the information will be used for identification, billing, safety, sanitation, evaluation and statistical purposes. Customs, quarantine, and immigration information is for use by both the Commission and the Government of the Republic of Panama. Some of the information is used by vessel agents to assist in expediting vessel transits through the Canal. As required, the information provided may be made available to other U.S. Government agencies. The information requested on the shipping and navigation forms is required in order to transit the Panama Canal (35 CFR Part 101).

FIG. 34

4363
Rev. 11-79

PANAMA CANAL COMMISSION

CARGO DECLARATION
OF VESSELS PASSING THROUGH THE CANAL

O.M.B. No. 3207-0001

Instructions.—A declaration of cargo carried through the Panama Canal is required from each vessel making transit. The declarations are the basis of important statistics which are published for the benefit of shippers and ship's operators generally, but no information is disclosed concerning shipments by individual ships or lines.

Accurate information is desired concerning cargo, but it is not expected that small and unimportant items of cargo will be listed separately. Fractional parts of tons need not be shown. Cargo listed under the classification of general cargo should not exceed 500 long tons, if possible.

Please state cargo in tons of 2,240 pounds (long tons), if possible, but if another unit of measurement is used, state clearly what it is. The numbers in parenthesis following the names of commodities are code indexes for use in making tabulations and should be ignored.

Origin and destination may be indicated by either country or port. However, if port is not stated, shipments to or from the Atlantic Coast of the United States should be shown as Great Lakes, North Atlantic, South Atlantic, or Gulf. Great Lakes includes all U.S. Great Lakes ports, North and South Atlantic divide at Hampton Roads with Hampton Roads being included in North Atlantic. Gulf includes all U.S. Gulf of Mexico ports. Canadian Great Lakes includes all ports West of Montreal.

If cargo has been laden at more than one country, the tons from each country must be shown separately. For each of these separate countries the corresponding quantities and countries of discharge for cargo must be shown.

VOYAGE TYPE
(CHECK APPROPRIATE BOX)

- [ ] Scheduled common carrier
- [ ] Voyage charter
- [ ] Time charter.
- [ ] Other (specify).................

CONTAINERS

Number of containers carried (Total)....................

Number of empty containers............................

DESCRIPTION OF CARGO

Name of vessel .... Ship's No. ....

Total long tons of cargo..

Number of passengers transiting................................ Date of arrival......................

	TOTAL TONNAGE BY COMMODITY	COUNTRY OR PORT OF ORIGIN			COUNTRY OR PORT OF DESTINATION		
Asbestos (4)							
Asphalt (6)							
Beans, edible (8)							
Bricks & tile (14)							
Canned foods: (specify) Fish (16)							
Fruit (18)							
Milk (22)							
Vegetables (26)							
Other (specify)							
Cement (32)							
Chemicals: (specify) Ammonium compounds (34)							
Borax (sodium borate) (36)							
Carbon black (38)							
Caustic soda (sodium hydroxide) (40)							
Other (specify)							
Chemicals, petroleum: (specify) Benzene (48)							
Toluene (54)							
Other (specify)							
Clay, fire & china (58)							
Coal (60)							
Cocoa & cocoa beans (processed & unprocessed) (62)							
Coffee (processed & unprocessed) (64)							
Coke (coal type) (66)							
Cold storage cargo: (specify) Bananas (68)							

FIG. 34   249

Dairy products (70									
Fish (72)									
Fruit (excluding bananas) (74)									
Meat (76)									
Other (80)									
Copra & coconuts (84)									
Cotton, raw (86)									
Fertilizers (specify)									
Fibers, natural (specify)									
Fishmeal (96)									
Flour, wheat (98)									
Glass & glassware (102)									
Grains: (specify) Barley (104)									
Corn (106)									
Oats (108)									
Rice (110)									
Sorghum (112)									
Soybeans (296)									
Wheat (114)									
Other (specify)									
Groceries (118)									
Infusorial earth (124)									
Iron & steel mfg.:(specify) Angles, shapes & sec's. (126)									
Nails, tacks, spikes, bolts, screws, etc. (128)									
Plates, sheets & coils (130)									
Tubes, pipes & fittings (132)									
Wire, bars & rods (134)									
Other (specify)									
Liquors (142)									
Lumber: (specify) Boards & planks (144)									
Plywood, veneers, composition board (148)									
Other (specify)									
Machinery: (specify) Agricultural machinery & implements (152)									
Autos & trucks (unboxed) (154)									
Autos & trucks (boxed), accessories & parts (155)									
Construction machinery & equipment (156)									
Electrical machinery & apparatus (158)									
Motorcycles, bicycles & parts (160)									
Other (specify)									

FIG. 34

DESCRIPTION OF CARGO	TOTAL TONNAGE BY COMMOD- ITY	COUNTRY OR PORT OF ORIGIN				COUNTRY OR PORT OF DESTINATION			
Metals: (specify)									
Aluminum (166)									
Copper (170)									
Iron (172)									
Lead (174)									
Scrap (176)									
Tin & tinplate (178)									
Zinc (180)									
Other (specify)									
Molasses (190)									
Nitrate of soda (44)									
Oil, fish (194)									
Oil, vegetable (specify)									
Oil seeds (excluding soybeans) (196)									
Ores: (specify)									
Alumina & bauxite (206)									
Chrome (210)									
Copper (212)									
Iron (214)									
Lead (216)									
Manganese (218)									
Tin (220)									
Zinc (224)									
Other (specify)									
Paper & paper products (232)									
Peas, dried (234)									
Petroleum & products: (specify)									
Crude petroleum (238)									
Diesel oil (240)									
Gasoline (242)									
Jet fuel (244)									
Kerosene (246)									
Liquefied gas (247)									
Lubricating oils (248)									
Residual fuel oils (250)									
Petroleum coke (252)									
Other (specify)									
Phosphates (258)									

FIG. 34

251

Porcelainware (260)

Potash (262)

Pulpwood (264)

Resin (270)
Rubber (specify raw, manufactured, scrap)

Salt (282)

Seeds (excluding oil seeds)(286)

Skins & hides (288)

Sugar, raw (300)

Sulfur (302)

Tallow (304)

Textiles (308)
Tobacco & tobacco manufac-
tures (310)

Wax, paraffin (314)

Wines (316)

Wool, raw (320)

Other cargo (specify below)

Received by:

CERTIFIED CORRECT to the best of my knowledge and belief:

Panama Canal Commission

Signature of Master

FIG. 35

1509
Rev. 11-70

PANAMA CANAL COMMISSION
CREW LIST FOR INCOMING VESSELS

O.M.B. No. 3207-0001

INSTRUCTIONS—Two copies are required from each incoming vessel on this form. Copies are not required from vessels of the United States Navy or other vessels manned with regular United States Navy crews.

Persons composing the crew of the_____
(Insert nationality, rig, and name)

From_____ to_____

Balboa
Cristobal, Panama,_____, 19____
(Date)

	NAME (Last)	NAME (First)	NAME (Middle Initial)	CAPACITY OR DUTY	BIRTHPLACE (CITY & COUNTRY)	BIRTHDAY (DAY/MO./YR.)	CITIZEN OR SUBJECT OF	IDENTIFICATION OR Z. NO.
1								
2								
3								
4								
5								
6								
7								
8								
9								
10								
11								
12								
13								
14								
15								
16								
17								
18								
19								
20								
21								
22								
23								
24								
25								
26								
27								

The undersigned solemnly swears that the within list contains the names of all the crew of said vessel, including stowaways and workaways, so far as I can ascertain.

Subscribed and sworn to this_____day of

_____, 19____

_____
Master

_____
Boarding Officer

(See Reverse Side)

APPENDIX C

CONVERSION FACTORS

To Convert From:	To:	Multiply by:
Barrels, oil (US)	Cubic feet	5.61458
	Cubic meters	0.15889
	Gallons (Imp)	35.
	Gallons (US)	42.
	Hectoliters	1.5898
	Liters	158.984
	Long tons	0.1515 (or divide by 6.6)
	Metric tons	0.153931 (or divide by 6.49583)
	Pounds	339.4
	Short tons	0.1697 (or divide by 5.892)
Board feet (BM)	Cubic feet	0.08333
	Cubic inches	144.
	Cubic meters	0.00235975
Bushels (Imp)	Bags (Imp)	0.3333
	Bushels (US)	1.03205
	Cubic feet	1.28435
	Cubic inches	2,219.36
	Cubic meters	0.0363677
	Dekaliters	3.63677
	Gallons (Imp)	8.
	Liters	36.3677
	Quarts (Imp)	0.125
Bushels (US)	Bushels(Imp)	0.968946
	Cubic feet	1.24446
	Cubic inches	2,150.42

To Convert From:	To:	Multiply by:
Bushels (US)	Cubic meters	0.035239
	Dekaliters	3.523808
	Liters	35.2383
	Quarts, dry	32.
Cables (British)	Cables (US)	0.83333
	Feet	600.
	Kilometers	182.88
	Miles, nautical	0.098684
	Yards	200.
Cables (US)	Cables (British)	1.2
	Feet	720.
	Kilometers	0.219456
	Meters	219.456
	Miles, nautical	0.118421
	Yards	240.
Centimeters	Decimeters	0.1
	Feet	0.0328083
	Inches	0.3937
	Meters	0.01
	Millimeters	10.
	Yards	0.010936
Cubic centimeters (cc)	Board feet (BM)	0.00042377
	Cubic inches	0.06102338
	Ounces, liquid (US)	0.033814
Cubic feet	Barrels, oil (42 gal)	0.1782
	Board feet	12.
	Bushels (US)	0.80356
	Bushels (Imp)	0.778630
	Cubic centimeters	28,317.016
	Cubic decimeters	28.317016
	Cubic inches	1,728.
	Cubic meters	0.028317016
	Cubic yards	0.037037
	Gallons (Imp)	6.2289
	Gallons (US)	7.48052
	Hectoliters	0.2831625
	Liters	28.31625
Cubic inches	Board feet (BM)	0.0069444
	Bushels (US)	0.000465025
	Cubic centimeters	16.387162

To Convert From:	To:	Multiply by:
Cubic inches	Cubic feet	0.000578704
	Gallons (Imp)	0.0036046
	Gallons (US)	0.004329
	Gills	0.138528
	Liters	0.01638673
	Ounces, liquid (US)	0.55411
	Pints, liquid (US)	0.034632
	Quarts, liquid (US)	0.017316
Cubic meters	Barrels, liquid (31½ gal)	8.3865
	Barrels, oil (42 gal)	6.2898
	Board feet (BM)	423.77334
	Bushels (Imp)	27.496
	Bushels (US)	28.3776
	Cubic decimeters	1,000.
	Cubic feet	35.314456
	Cubic inches	61,023.38
	Cubic yards	1.3079428
	Gallons (Imp)	219.9675
	Gallons (US)	264.1703
	Liters	999.973 (1,000.)
Cubic yards	Cubic feet	27.
	Cubic inches	46,656.
	Cubic meters	0.7645594
	Liters	764.54
Decimeters	Centimeters	10.
	Feet	0.3281
	Inches	3.937
	Meters	0.1
	Yards	0.1094
Feet	Centimeters	30.48006096
	Decimeters	3.048006096
	Inches	12.
	Kilometers	0.0003
	Meters	0.3048006096
	Miles, nautical	0.00016447
	Miles, statute	0.00018939
	Yards	0.3333
Gallons (Imp)	Barrels, oil (US)	0.0286
	Cubic centimeters	4,546.0859
	Cubic feet	0.160544

To Convert From:	To:	Multiply by:
Gallons (Imp)	Cubic inches	277.42
	Gallons (US)	1.200952
	Liters	4.546
	Ounces (Imp)	160.
	Ounces, liquid (US)	153.72156
	Quarts (Imp)	4.
	Quarts, liquid (US)	4.8038
Gallons (US)	Barrels, oil (42 gal)	0.02381
	Cubic centimeters	3,785.434
	Cubic feet	0.133681
	Cubic inches	231.
	Cubic meters	0.00378543
	Gallons (Imp)	0.83268
	Gills (US)	32.
	Liters	3.785332
	Ounces, liquid (US)	128.
	Pints, liquid (US)	8.
	Quarts, liquid (US)	4.
Hectoliters	Bushels (Imp)	2.749688
	Bushels (US)	2.83774
	Cubic feet	3.53145
	Cubic inches	6,102.34
	Cubic meters	0.1
	Cubic yards	0.130798
	Dekaliters	10.
	Gallons (Imp)	21.9975
	Gallons, dry (US)	22.7026
	Gallons, liquid (US)	26.417
	Liters	100.
Hogsheads	Cubic feet	8.421875
	Cubic inches	14,553.
	Cubic meters	0.3384824
	Gallons (US)	63.
	Liters	238.476
Hundredweights, long (US)	Kilograms	50.80255
	Pounds	112.
	Tons, long	0.05
	Tons, metric	0.05082
	Tons, short	0.056

To Convert From:	To:	Multiply by:
Hundredweights, short (US)	Kilograms	45.359243
	Pounds	100.
	Tons, long	0.04464286
	Tons, metric	0.04535924
	Tons, short	0.05
Inches	Centimeters	2.54
	Decimeters	0.254
	Feet	0.08333
	Meters	0.0254
	Millimeters	25.4
	Yards	0.27777
Kilograms	Grams	1,000.
	Ounces (avdp)	35.27396
	Pounds	2.204622341
	Tons, long	0.0009842064
	Tons, metric	0.001
	Tons, short	0.0011023112
Kilometers	Feet	3,280.8333
	Meters	1,000.
	Miles, nautical	0.5396
	Miles, statute	0.6213699
	Yards	1,093.6111
Liters	Barrels, oil	0.0063
	Bushels (Imp)	0.02749688
	Bushels (US)	0.0283774
	Cubic centimeters	1,000.028
	Cubic feet	0.03531539
	Cubic inches	61.025
	Gallons (Imp)	0.219975
	Gallons (US)	0.264178
	Ounces, liquid (US)	33.8147
	Pints, liquid (US)	2.11336
	Quarts, dry (US)	0.908102
	Quarts, liquid (Imp)	0.879902
	Quarts, liquid (US)	1.05668
Meters	Centimeters	100.
	Decimeters	10.
	Fathoms	0.54686
	Feet	3.280833

To Convert From:	*To:*	*Multiply by:*
Meters	Inches	39.37
	Kilometers	0.001
	Miles, nautical	0.00054
	Miles, statute	0.000621
	Yards	1.093611
Miles, nautical	Cables (British)	10.
	Cables (US)	8.44444
	Feet	6,080.
	Kilometers	1.853187
	Meters	1,853.187
	Miles, statute	1.1515
	Yards	2,026.66667
Miles, statute	Feet	5,280.
	Kilometers	1.6093472
	Meters	1,609.3472
	Miles, nautical	0.86839
	Yards	1,760.
Millimeters	Centimeters	0.1
	Feet	0.003280833
	Inches	0.03937
	Meters	0.001
Pounds (avdp)	Grams	453.5924277
	Kilograms	0.4535924277
	Ounces (avdp)	16.
Square feet	Square centimeters	929.0341
	Square inches	144.
	Square meters	0.09290341
	Square yards	0.11111
Square inches	Square centimeters	6.4516258
	Square decimeters	0.064516258
	Square feet	0.0069444
	Square meters	0.0006451626
	Square millimeters	645.1626
Square meters	Square centimeters	10,000.
	Square feet	10.76387
	Square inches	1,549.9969
	Square yards	1.195985
Square yards	Square centimeters	8,361.307
	Square feet	9.

To Convert From:	To:	Multiply by:
Square yards	Square inches	1,296.
	Square meters	0.8361307
Tons, long	Hundredweights, long (US)	20.
	Hundredweights, short (US)	22.4
	Kilograms	1,016.04704
	Tons, metric	1.01604704
	Tons, short	1.12
Tons, metric	Hundredweights, long (US)	19.684212
	Hundredweights, short (US)	22.046223
	Kilograms	1,000.
	Pounds	2,204.62234
	Tons, long	0.9842064
	Tons, short	1.1023112
Tons, short	Hundredweights, long (US)	17.8571
	Hundredweights, short (US)	20.
	Kilograms	907.18486
	Pounds	2,000.
	Tons, long	0.8928571
	Tons, metric	0.90718486
Yards	Centimeters	91.44018
	Decimeters	9.144
	Feet	3.
	Inches	36.
	Kilometers	0.0009
	Meters	0.9144018
	Miles, nautical	0.0004934
	Miles, statute	0.0005681

INDEX

ABOUT THE AUTHOR

A graduate of the California Maritime Academy with a B.S. degree in nautical science, Captain Aragon has been going to sea for fifteen years aboard U.S. and foreign flag carriers. He began his shipboard career on an Army Corps of Engineers seagoing dredge, has worked aboard a tug, OBOs, containerships, and tankers, and has served as master on a variety of vessels, coastwise and foreign. This is his first book.